Timber technicalities : being definitions of terms used in the home and foreign timber, mahogany and hardwood industries, the sawmill and woodworking trades, as well as those employed in connection with architecture and building construction

Edwin Haynes

Timber Technicalities

BEING DEFINITIONS OF TERMS USED IN THE
HOME AND FOREIGN TIMBER, MAHOGANY AND HARDWOOD INDUSTRIES,

THE

SAWMILL AND WOOD-WORKING TRADES,

AS WELL AS THOSE EMPLOYED IN CONNECTION WITH

ARCHITECTURE AND BUILDING CONSTRUCTION

Compiled and Edited by
E D W I N   H A Y N E S

Editor of
"The Timber Trades Journal"

LONDON
WILLIAM RIDER AND SON, LIMITED
8 PATERNOSTER ROW, E.C. 4
NEW YORK: 19 WARREN STREET

PREFACE

THE principal title of this work does not fully convey the scope of its contents. At first it was intended to confine the definitions to terms in use in the timber trade, but the multifarious forms in which converted timber is applied in the arts and crafts opened up a wider field, and as the subject was pursued an ever-widening circle of interest was presented The present compilation includes terms applied to wood in the growing tree, in its manufactured forms as used in the chief consuming industries, and especially in architecture and building construction. The ordinary commercial and shipping terms in use in the timber trade and in general business transactions are also included.

Throughout the work the definitions have been carefully considered, but the meaning of any word in any circumstances must always be interpreted by reference to the context and to the particular trade or port, and to the nature of the goods or subject matter, and the physical circumstances, and in addition. to the terms and purpose of the contract between the individual parties. It cannot be too strongly emphasized that, generally speaking, the meaning of every word is variable and fluctuating, and the greatest care is required properly to interpret in any particular case the exact signification of the expression employed.

The Editor desires to acknowledge the kind assistance he has received from many friends in the timber trade, and especially for the collaboration of Mr. William Stevenson, the author of *Wood ; its Use as a Constructive Material* and *The Trees of Commerce*, who, although in his eighty-ninth year, still takes a keen interest in scientific subjects connected with the wood trade.

Great care has been taken to avoid errors and omissions, but should any be noticed by the reader, a communication on the subject will be welcomed by the publishers, with a view to future editions.   E. H.

LONDON,
     April, 1921.

vii

CONTENTS

Timber Technicalities.

A

@ A symbol meaning "at" or "from."

Abacus.—(1) A counting device; an office instrument for making calculations, much used in Russia and on the Continent. It consists of several wires stretched in a frame, each wire being strung with ten perforated balls. (2) In architecture, a table constituting the upper member or crowning of a column and its capital.

Abbreviations and Contractions in writing.—*See* Appendix I.

Abele.—The white poplar (*Populus alba*). The name is descriptive of the whiteness of the bark.

Aboard.—As "aboard of a man-of-war," or a ship, meaning to step on or enter within a ship, vessel or boat—a term derived from the deck or floor of a ship being originally of wood. *See* "Board."

Acacia (*Robinia pseudacacia*).—The common acacia is known in Europe as the false-acacia. Its wood is very tough and durable, hard and heavy, but it does not grow to large size. In America it is known as "locust wood."

Acceptance.—A draft or bill of exchange which a party has agreed to pay when due, by signifying his willingness to do so in writing across the draft.

Acceptor.—A person who accepts the obligation to pay a bill of exchange by writing his name transversely across the face of it.

Accommodation Bill.—A bill voluntarily accepted or endorsed by one person, without value received, for the accommodation of the drawer.

Accommodation Party.—A person who, without receiving value, voluntarily signs a bill for another as drawer, acceptor or endorser.

Account Sales.—A statement rendered by a broker or agent of goods sold, showing also charges incurred, commission, special discounts, the net proceeds of such sales, and due date of same.

Acorn.—The oval nut or fruit of oak trees In the species Q. *Pedunculata* the acorns are on long stalks, but with Q. *Sessiliflora* they are almost without stalks. Some species

B

are edible, and all more or less food for swine ; also used in preference to oak-bark for tanning purposes.

Actual Measure.—The measure in full, according to the system of measurement employed. It is often the opposite of "customary measure" (*which see*). In the flooring trade the term is used to distinguish between the nominal measure before manufacture and the actual width and thickness of the boards after planing.

Ad valorem.—A term meaning in proportion to value. An "ad valorem" duty is a duty at a certain percentage on the value of the goods.

Address Commission.—A customary charge paid by shipowners for services rendered in connection with the ship at loading port.

Adze.—A tool used for paring and smoothing the surface of a log of wood. The head is swung in a circular path, at right angles to the handle, and it is used as a paring tool for smoothing work and squaring up round logs.

Adzing and Boring Machines for Sleepers.—These machines adze the seatings for the chairs or rails across a railway sleeper, and bore the spike or bolt holes for holding them securely in place. There are a number of designs, some quite automatic in action and others only semi-automatic.

Adzing Machines for Sleepers.—These machines plane the seatings for the chairs or rails of railway sleepers. The work is done by means of revolving cutter blocks, and the sleepers are carried either over or under these blocks by an endless feed chain. *See also* " Adzing and Boring Machines for Sleepers."

Affidavit.—A written statement in legal proceedings, signed by the person making the same, and sworn by him to be true before a Commissioner for Oaths. A declaration to a statement not in legal proceedings, declared to be true before a Commissioner.

Afforest.—To turn ground into forest.

African Oak.—*See* " Oak."

After Growth.—Young trees that have sprung up through reproduction, clearances and cuttings. Sometimes called "second growth" or "stooled," as "stooled ash." Considered as young wood stronger than wood of mature trees, although experiments made by forest authorities in America with Ash and Hickory have proved the fallacy of this idea.

Agenda.—The order of business to be gone through at a meeting.

Agent.—An agent is one who acts as agent on behalf of a principal.

Ailanthus (*Ailanthus glandulosa*), known as the " Tree of Heaven."

—An ornamental tree indigenous in Japan and China, mostly grown for shade. Its wood is used by cabinet makers.

Air Seasoning.—Drying of wood in the open air.

Alburnum.—The sapwood of exogenous trees, termed "immature wood" compared with heartwood. In many hard woods—ebony, etc.—the sapwood is dressed off before land transport and shipment, as being of no value. In most cases it is of little value, being liable to decay. In a few others, however, it is esteemed in an equal degree to the heartwood, or in a greater measure.

Alder (*Alnus glutinosa*).—A soft, light, tough and (if not exposed to alternate wet and dry) very durable wood. Not liable to split or ignite. Used by engineers (for foundation piles and all kinds of water work), artificial limb makers and cabinet makers. The bark was formerly used by tanners and the cordwood for charcoal in the manufacture of gunpowder. *See also* "Clog" or "Clog-sole."

Alder Buckthorn (*Rhamnus frangula*) —A native of the South of England, but growing freely anywhere. It is a shrub rather than a tree, usually reaching 8 to 10 ft. in height. Chiefly valued for charcoal making.

All Over.—A term used to embrace several items. Same as "All round" (*which see*), also "Over all," "Overhead."

All Round.—A term used to express a number of items taken as a group. Same as "Over all" and "All over," *which see.*

Alligator.—A boat used in America in handling floating logs. It can be moved overland from one body of water to another by its own power, usually applied through drum or cable.

Allround Price.—*See* "Overhead Price."

Almond (*Amygdalus communis*).—A hard, compact wood, light, and owing to its beautiful colour, used for making fancy ware, but mainly in request in England as an ornamental flowering tree.

Alongside Delivery.—The custom of the particular port in a great measure governs the meaning of this phrase. Delivery from the vessel as customary at the port is variously understood to mean landed on the quay or into craft.

Amboyna Wood (*Pterocarpus indicus*) —A valuable ornamental wood used in the form of veneers. It is also used in inlaying and for snuff-boxes. It ranks very high as a "Burr-wood" —*see* "Burr-woods."

American Oaks.—These are numerous, but the only examples common on the European markets are "White Oak" or "Quebec Oak" (*Quercus alba*), and "Red Oak" (*Quercus* *rubra*), from the States and Canada. The former, from colour and texture, is the best. The shipments have undergone a change from the crude log form to that of planks and boards, the latter being artificially dried and ready for consumption in furniture, fittings, flooring, etc. These oaks do not rank so high as wainscots of European or Japanese origin. American oak finds a great outlet in the frames of railway wagons. *See* " Oaks."

American Yellow Poplar.—*See* " Whitewood."

Ammeter.—A meter for measuring the number of ampères of electricity being used at any particular moment.

Ampère.—Represents the quantity of electric current used irrespective of its strength (or voltage). When ampères are multiplied by the number of volts (representing the strength of the current) the results are termed watts.

Angle Bar.—The upright bar of wood which stands at the extremity of each angle of a polygonal window or canopy, and reaching from the bottom to the top of the window ; also the angular timbers of a spire, or anything built in a pyramidal or prismatic form.

Angle Bead.—A bead fixed vertically upon the exterior or salient angle of an apartment, to preserve it from injury, and to serve as a guide to float the plaster. A variant term for the above is " Staff-bead."

Angle Braces or Angle Ties.—Pieces of wood fastened across the angles of square and other angular frames in order to strengthen the joints of those parts and to keep the frames in proper shape.

Angle Rafter.—A rafter placed in the line of meeting of the inclined planes of a hip-roof, sometimes called a Hip Rafter.

Angle Rib.—A curved piece of wood placed at the angles of groined ceilings.

Angle Staffs.—Staffs, 1 to $1\frac{1}{2}$ in. square, grooved or flattened at one corner and fixed vertically at external angles of windows, doors, etc., where two surfaces of plaster meet, in order to render this part stronger, and avoid the liability of the plaster in such circumstances being broken or damaged. *See* " Angle Bead," which serves a like purpose but involves two quirks in the plaster.

Annual or Annular Layers.—The yearly growth of the tree, defined by concentric circles in exogens.

Anti-Sap Stain.—A process of dipping timber in a chemical solution, usually carbonate of soda, to prevent the sapwood becoming discoloured on exposure to the air.

Apple Tree (*Pyrus malus*).—A heavy, compact and fine-grown wood, not liable to ignition when exposed to friction. Used by toolmakers and turners.

Apron Piece.—A piece of timber fixed into the walls of a staircase and projecting horizontally, to support the carriage pieces and joisting in the half spaces or landings. It is sometimes called the Pitching Piece.

Araucaria (*Araucaria imbricata*).—A coniferous tree indigenous in South America and Australia. Grown in England for ornament on lawns and known as Monkey Puzzle.

Arbor.—*See* " Saw Arbor."

Arbor Vitæ, or White Cedar (*Thuya occidentalis*).—A native of the Northern States of America and Canada. Used largely for shingles in the States and for telegraph poles in Canada.

Arboretum.—A place in a park in which trees and shrubs are cultivated ; extended to a pleasure-park or municipal place of recreation, as at Derby, Nottingham, etc. This is the root-word of " Arboriculture," " Arborist," and allied forms or terms.

Arboriculture.—A term literally meaning the cultivation of trees but is generally used with regard to the planting and management of timber trees.

Arbutus (*Arbutus unedo*).—A hard, nicely veined, durable wood much used by cabinet makers and turners. Found in Great Britain and the South of Ireland.

Architrave.—The group of mouldings above and on both sides of a door or other opening, especially if square in form.

Area.—A term meaning extent of surface.

Arms.—The wooden cross-pieces at the top of telegraph poles upon which the insulators are placed

Arris (French *Aréte*) —The edge of a roof, or a stone, or a piece of wood. " A sharp arris " is a cutting edge.

Arris Fillet.—A triangular piece of wood used to raise the slates of a roof when they abut against the shaft of a chimney or wall, so as to throw off more effectually the rain from the joining, but more generally to raise the eave course of slated or tiled roofs. It is called also the Tilting Fillet.

Arris Gutter.—A wooden gutter in the form of a V in section, fixed to the eaves of a building, usually called " a V gutter."

Arris Rail.—A rail of triangular section used for fences.

As per advice.—In accordance with a previous or subsequent letter or wire giving instructions or information.

As they fall from the mill.—Another term for "Unassorted" (*which see*). This means all grades down to a certain line. One may be to exclude wane in any part, i.e., all sawn "die square" (*which see*); another also to admit wane to a limited extent. *See* "Wane, or Scant, or Cant," both excluding rot, taint, or dote.

Ash.—A well-known type of the temperate zone of the Northern Hemisphere. In that of Britain (*Fraxinus excelsior*) the wood ranks extremely high for lightness and elasticity, and is in great demand for exceptional and general purposes, especially since the introduction of flying machines. It is the old "wood of war" that furnished the "shield" and "spear."

Ash Trees Leafing.—The tradition is if the ash precedes the oak in foliage, we may anticipate a cold summer and unproductive autumn.

Ashlar.—(1) Freestone roughly squared in the quarry. (2) Hewn stones used in the facing of walls presenting a surface varied according to the tooling they receive. Hence dressed ashlar-facework may be plain or flat, grooved, chiselled, axe-dressed or rusticated.

Aspen (*Populus tremula*).—A tree of the poplar family, whose leaves tremble with the slightest impulse of the air. Aspen wood is plentiful in Russia, where it is used in the manufacture of 3-ply veneer, and is also imported into Sweden for making matches.

Aspen Leaf.—A favourite subject for poets, arising out of the long, thin stalk of the leaf—metaphorically never quiet.

> "And tremble like a leaf of aspen green ;"

or, as Sir Walter Scott says—

> "And variable as the shade
> By the light quivering aspen made."

Asphalte, or Asphaltum.—A smooth, hard, brittle, black or brown substance. Durable in the air. Used for road paving or as a damp-proof material for walls, cellars, pavements, roofs, etc. It is odourless except when heated.

Assorted.—All the merchantable pieces defined in their various qualities. Known also as "Graded" or "Bracked." Swedish sawn goods formerly were in three qualities— "1sts," "2nds," and "3rds." Later the "1sts" and "2nds" were merged into "mixed," and further numbers were added, which read "mixed," "3rds," "4ths," and even "5ths." A few years back the classification was again revised, and mixed are now styled "1sts" and the other qualities were raised a step.   Under " inferiors " and like denomin-ations, other grades as low as " 7ths " have come on the market.   This means that goods are now shipped in lower qualities than hitherto known.   *See* " Grade and Graded." The opposite is " Unassorted " (*which see*).

Astragal.—A convex moulding of rounded surface, generally from half to three-quarters of an inch.

At Sight.—These words written on bills of exchange or promissory notes signify that they are payable on demand and without allowance of days of grace.

Auger.—A carpenter's tool for boring holes larger than those made by a gimlet.

Automatic Dovetailing Machine.—Machine in which the dovetails in one board and the pins in another are cut at one operation by a single cutter.   The boards are placed on a table, one vertically and the other horizontally, and automatically traversed past the cutter a distance equal to the pitch re-quired.   The cutter then moves forward on to the work, the dovetail and pin are cut simultaneously, the cutter recedes and the movements are repeated.

Autumn Shipment.—Usually understood to commence 23rd September and end 22nd December.   For goods shipped from ports closed during the winter, it is usually taken to mean from 23rd September to close of season.

Average is of two kinds, Particular and General.   Particular average is partial loss caused by a peril insured against (whether damage or special charges), attaching particularly to the commodity insured, e.g., damage by saturation of wool, dissolving of sugar, etc.   Partial average and partial loss are the same thing, e.g., the position is the same whether ten bags of sugar be washed out 10 per cent. or whether nine bags are sound and one empty.   Whether an insurance shall cover partial loss or not, that is, whether an insurance shall be " with average " or " free of particular average," is merely a matter of arrangement and premium.   General average is an extraordinary sacrifice made in grave emergency for the collective benefit of the owners of ship, freight and cargo, e.g., the cutting away of a mast, the jettison of the cargo, water poured down the hold to extinguish a fire.   In each case the monetary loss has to be ascertained and dis-tributed over all the property saved according to the value of each of these interests.   The apportionment of the loss over all the interests involved is the work of an " average stater " (*which see*).

Average Measurement.—The mean between several dimensions. Thus, for example, average length, average thickness, cubic average.

Average Stater.—A professional expert whose office is to investigate, adjust and award in cases, especially of "General Average," that is, where a number of persons are affected in cases of loss, damage, etc., and to issue "Average statements." *See* "Average" *and* "Depreciation." Also known as "Average Adjuster."

Award.—The decision of an arbitrator, umpire, or referee in cases of disputes.

Axe, or **Hatchet,** the latter term representing the smallest type.— A tool for hewing and splitting wood having bevelled cutting edge acting like a wedge ; when provided with bevel on one side only, it is called a side hatchet. To "take up the hatchet" or to "bury the hatchet" are terms used by the American-Indians for "making war" and "declaring peace."

B

Back.—The upper or convex part of a saw tooth.

Backboards.—Thin boards used in picture framing for the back of the frame.

Backed, Bellied, and Jointed.—A prepared turned stave manufactured ready to put up with other similar staves to make a barrel. Fifty years ago the "lags" were not "turned," every part was done or carried out by hand.

Back Fillet.—The return of the projection beyond the face of a wall or jambs of a door.

Back Lining.—The piece of a sash frame parallel to the pulley stile, and next to the jamb.

Backs.—In carpentry, the principal rafters of a *roof*. The upper side of any piece of timber is also termed the *back*, the lower side being called the *breast* or *heart* side.

Bagac is a heavy construction lumber from the Philippines, weighing slightly heavier than American oak. It is of very close texture and great tensile strength. It is very similar in appearance to teak, but it has not the oily nature of that wood. It has been used in the East for making the coverdecks of ships and handrails, and it makes an exceptionally fine hardwood floor.

Baguette (Fr.).—A small moulding.

Bale Boards.—A term used for boards swinging from the ceiling of stables by means of chains, and used instead of stall divisions; also the boards used in bales of cloth.

Balk.—A beam, or piece of sawn or hewn timber, 4 to 8 in. square.

Ball Bearings.—Bearings in which steel balls are used to eliminate friction. The best type for journal bearings consists of a row, or rows, of balls held in a cage and revolving between two rings of hardened steel.

Baltic.—Of or appertaining to the sea which separates Norway and Sweden from Jutland, Denmark and Germany; situated on the Baltic Sea.

Baluster or **Balustrading.**—Small columns or pilasters protecting the outer ends of stairs and supporting the handrail. Corrupted in common language to "banisters" or "bannisters." In Tudor and Jacobean work the size or diameter of the balusters, usually 3 in. to 4 in., gave the widths of the clear spaces between, hence the screens were half solid. In late seventeenth-century staircases balusters were often replaced with solid boarding perforated to flowing designs, and carved on one or both sides. *See* "Handrail."

Band Resaw.—Band-saws used for resawing planks or flitches into boards are known by this name; they are provided with roller feed.

Band Saw.—A saw in the form of an endless steel belt, with teeth on roller edge, running over wheels.

> *Economy of the band saw.*—Not the least important point is the question of the waste of wood, and here the band saw gives by far the best results. The amount of wood lost in sawdust by a circular saw. 6 ft. diameter, per cut is $\frac{1}{8}$ in.; therefore when producing boards 1 in thick, the waste is 24 per cent. A band saw wastes at the most $\frac{1}{8}$ in. per cut, or, when cutting 1 in., 11 per cent. Again, to make a board cut by a circular saw, when planed on both sides, hold up to $\frac{7}{8}$ in., it must be cut 1 in. thick, i.e., $\frac{1}{8}$ in. must be allowed on each side for planing, while, on the other hand, owing to the superior cutting of the band saw, it is only necessary to allow $\frac{1}{32}$ in. on each side for planing, showing an additional saving of $\frac{1}{32}$ in. per cent. This gives a total saving of $\frac{1}{4}$ in. per cut by the use of the band saw.

Band-Saw Machine, with Self-acting Canting Table.—The tables of these machines have a self-acting canting motion for conveniently cutting sweeps of varying bevel.

Banister or **Bannister.**—A corruption of "baluster" (*which see*).

Barge Boards.—The raking-boards at the gable of a building to cover the ends of the roof timbers when they project beyond the walls. A variant of this is " verge-board."

Bark.—The exterior covering of the trunk and branches of a tree ; the rind.

Bark Peeling.—Sometimes called " barking," " stripping," or " flaying." The operation of removing the bark of a tree when the sap is flowing, usually from the middle of April to the commencement of June.

Barrel.—A round vessel or cask of greater length than breadth, bulging in the middle, made of staves bound with hoops and having flat ends or heads.

Barrel Saw.—*See* " Cylinder Saw."

Base.—In architecture, the base of a pillar is properly that part which is between the top of a pedestal and the bottom of the shaft ; when there is no pedestal, it is the part between the bottom of the column and the plinth.

Base Mouldings.—In architecture, projecting mouldings immediately above the plinth of a wall, pillar, or pedestal. *See* " Base."

Basswood (*Tilia Americana*) is a native of North America, where the various varieties are largely used for box making. In the United States it is known under different names in different regions. Among these names are linn, lynn, linden, lime, lime tree, whitewood, bee tree, wahoo, and silverleaf poplar. The name basswood is a corruption of the word bastwood, and bast is a reference to the strong inner bark which was formerly used in making ropes. This inner bark may be separated in strands at any season of the year.

Bast Matting.—Strips of the inner bark of the lime tree which have been separated into layers by steeping in water, woven together, thus forming the matting. Used to protect plants from frost and for packing furniture.

Bat.—A term allied to " beat." (1) A heavy stick or club ; (2) a piece of wood, usually willow, with a round handle and the blade about 3½ ft. long and 4¼ in. wide in the widest part, used in the game of cricket ; the making of bats has developed into a fine art ; (3) a portion of or half a brick, i.e., a " brick-bat."

Bataan is a species of Philippine mahogany of regular colour and texture, and takes a high polish. A large percentage of it comes forward with a fine figure, and it is sold for purposes for which only high-class mahogany can be used.

Batten and Batten Sizes.—2 in. thick and up sawn goods, formerly confined to 7 in., but now ranging from 5 in. to 8 in. It is used to distinguish them from the broader sizes, 9 in. and up, of "deals" or "planks" (*which see*). For freight, however, 2 in., 3 in., 4 in., 4½ in. and 5 in. are reckoned as battens.

Battledore.—A wooden instrument or toy used by hand in playing shuttlecock ; properly a baton or beetle for washing linen by striking it to knock out the dirt.

Bavins or **Kids** are the names given in different parts of the country to brushwood, fagots, chips of cut wood or wood refuse.

Bead.—A small moulding semicircular in section, generally used with a quirk or sinking. When flush with the face of the work it is called a " quirk-bead " ; when it is raised, a " cock-bead " ; and when round, or nearly so, a " staff-bead."

Beam.—Originally implied a " tree "; it has long served to describe the stem of a tree straight in its character. This straightness is reflected in " sunbeam " and " beam of light." Usually the term is applied to a hewn log or balk of timber. A variant form is seen in the Dutch and Danish " boom," German " baum."

Beamfillings.—Short lengths of logs or deals used for filling up spaces between the beams of a vessel ; they are necessary for the close stowing of a ship, and are usually carried at two-thirds the chartered rate of freight. *See* " Stowage Planks."

Beaver Boards.—Boards made of compressed wood fibre.

Bed-Laths or **" Slats."**—The cross-laths of a bed which support the mattress.

Bed Moulding.—Properly those members of a cornice which lie below the corona.

Beech (*Fagus Sylvatica*).—A tree indigenous in this country, and found throughout the western, the central, and most of the southern portions of Europe, also in the Caucasus The wood is light brown in colour, hard, moderately heavy, close, even in texture, with a fine silky grain. It grows to perfection on chalky soils ; in Buckinghamshire, for instance, where large quantities are used at High Wycombe in the manufacture of chairs.

Beetle.—A heavy wooden hammer or mallet (*see* " Mall," " Maul," and " Mallet "). Used to drive wedges, stakes and piles ;

beat or ram the ground, i.e., the original of the " ram," or weight in a pile-driving machine. In the Records of Boston, Lincolnshire, the corporation had a large cast bell-metal object, used in pile-driving, which they termed a " welkin " or " welking "—a term still used for a big ungainly man—a " welkin-fellow."

Bevel.—A term used to describe a sloped or canted surface.

Bevel Siding.—Lap siding ; siding weather board.

Bill of Entry.—A document handed to the Customs authorities by importers, declaring and describing goods before landing same.

Bill of Exchange.—A written order for payment of money drawn by one person on another. If drawn on a bank it is called a cheque.

Bill of Lading is a *formal receipt* subscribed by the master of a ship in his capacity of carrier, acknowledging that he has received the goods specified in it on board his ship, and binding himself (under certain exceptions) to deliver them, in the like good order as received, at the place, and to the individual named in the bill, or his assigns, on his or their paying him the stipulated freight, etc. When goods are sent by a ship under a charterparty, the bills of lading are delivered by the master to the merchant by whom the goods are shipped ; but when they are sent by a *general ship*—that is, by a ship not hired by charterparty, but employed as a general carrier —each individual who sends goods on board receives a bill of lading for the same. By the joint effect of custom and statute the bill of lading is a document of title to the goods and the ownership of the goods on sale may pass by endorsement of the bill of lading. A " through bill of lading " is a document made for the conveyance of goods from one place to another by several shipowners or railway companies. A " clean " bill of lading is a bill of lading which has nothing in the margin qualifying the terms in the bill of lading itself.

Bill of Sale.—A document of mortgage or transfer of movable property, the possession of which is retained by the transferrer or borrower, such as furniture, ships, etc. To be valid in England is subject to stringent conditions as to registration and form.

Billet.—A short round section of a log.

Billian or **Borneo Ironwood** (*Eusideroxylon Zwageri*).—A heavy, hard, strong and durable wood from North Borneo. Used for piles beam or planks.

Binders.—Long pliant shoots of hazel, ash, willow and similar trees, which have length and elasticity enough to allow them to be used for binding up bundles of fagots, making hurdles, etc.

Binding Joists.—Beams in framed floors which support the bridging joists above and ceiling joists below.

Birch (*Betula alba* or Common Birch).—Found in almost every country. The wood is of a light brown colour, moderately hard, plain and even in grain, and is easily worked; it is, however, unfitted for building purposes. Birch squares are imported from Finland for bobbin making and other uses.

Bit.—A tooth used in an inserted tooth saw.

Blackbutt (*Eucalyptus pilularis*).—An Australian timber, moderately heavy and very strong. Used for sleepers, paving, telegraph poles and carpentry.

Blackheart.—A serious defect in timber, found especially in ash.

Black Spruce (*Picea Nigra*).—A North American timber, tough and strong and only slightly resinous. Imported for making packing cases, etc.

Blackthorn (*Prunus spinosa*), " Sloe."—A hard, tough wood used for walking sticks.

Blanket Rate.—A rate to cover various specified services.

Blanks.—The rough sawed pieces from which spokes, handles, chair rounds, lasts and other turned goods are made.

Blaze.—(1) To mark, by cutting into trees the course of a boundary, road, trail, etc.; or trees cut and numbered for sale by auction or privately; (2) The chips made by a mortising chisel when at work; they are also called " cores."

Bled Timber.—Pine trees which have been turpentined.

Blind Lath.—Thin planed laths used in Venetian blinds.

Blind Slat Planing Machine.—Small four-cutter planing machines specially suitable for planing blind slats or blind laths.

Blind Slat Tenoning Machine.—A machine for forming the round ends on blind slats. The material is placed in the machine and caused to revolve slowly while a series of saws cut the tenon.

Blind Stile Mortising and Boring Machines.—Automatic machines in which blind stiles are mortised or bored in pairs; the distance between the mortises being accurately spaced by a notched bar, called a spacing bar, to which the stiles are attached.

Block.—The stem or stump of a tree; a mass of wood or stone; the piece of wood upon which criminals were beheaded.

Blockhead.—A dullard; a stupid person; one without brains. Originally a wig-maker's wooden dummy, upon which he worked and exhibited his wigs.

> "Strongly wedged up in a block-head."
> —Shakespeare, *Coriolanus*, ii. 3.

Block-house.—A place of defence made of logs.

" Blue Goods," or Blue Timbers.—Sawn goods which have become discoloured on the sapwood through stains by fungi. These are laid aside and occasionally shipped as blue goods, without warranty.

Blue Gum (*E. Saligna*).—A heavy, strong Australian timber.

Bluing.—Discoloration of the sapwood by low forms of vegetation acting as ferments.

Board or Boards.—(1) Thin layers of wood, from $\frac{1}{2}$ in. to 2 in. in thickness, when " plank " comes in. In the hardwood trade boards are classed as of any thickness up to $1\frac{1}{4}$ in. and any width; over that thickness they are termed planks. In the softwood trade it is customary to include as boards any thickness under 2 in. (2) A table, from having a flat or broad surface made of boards. This word and *broad* seems to be allied in origin, as "on board a ship" suggests—going over the broadside. *See* " Table."

Board of Trade Unit.—Generally represented by the initials " B.T.U." Is the unit by which the amount of electric current used is measured. It is equal to 1,000 watts for one hour. One B.T.U. is equal to 1·34 h.p. for one hour.

Board Foot.—The contents of a board 1 ft. square and 1 in. thick. The common unit of measure for logs and lumber in the United States and Canada. *See* " Board Measure."

Board Measure.—The board foot, the unit of measurement in the United States and Canada, is an invariable standard 12 in. square and 1 in. thick, or its equivalent of volume in any other shape. One thousand feet board measure of $\frac{1}{2}$-in. lumber is, therefore, equivalent to 2,000 ft. face of superficial measure. Lumber 1 in. or thicker is usually sold by board measure, and lumber under 1 in. is by the custom of the trade usually sold by face measure, not by board measure. When applied to inch lumber, this unit may be considered a measurement of surface, but with lumber of other dimensions it is a unit of volume containing 144 cubic in. A few examples will explain this more clearly. A board 12 ft. in length, 1 ft. in width and 1 in. in thickness contains 12 board ft. and its surface measurement is 12 sq. ft. A board 12 ft. long, 12 in. wide and 2 in. thick contains 24 board ft., while its surface measurement is still only 12 sq. ft. In Holland, in the days of Dutch wainscot, the standard board was 12 ft. × 11½ in. × 1 in. This "12 ft." became the standard of dimensions generally.

Board Rule.—An implement universally used in America for readily ascertaining the superficial area of boards. It has been adopted in this country for the measurement of American boards or lumber. It is 3 ft. in length, and consists of a flat flexible metal-tipped rod usually made of hickory, on the flat surface and edges of which are marked the figures by which the superficial area of the boards is ascertained.

Boathook Shafts.—Called also "Quants." Tapered handles, 14 to 24 ft. in length, according to length of boat-hook. This term is often shortened to "boathook"; for instance, "poles, rickers and boathooks, graded according to size."

Boat Skin.—Thin boarding used for boat-building.

Bobbin or Bobbins.—A small flange or head-ended piece of wood on which thread or silk is wound, usually bored through to receive a pivot or spindle. A variant term for this useful instrument is "spool." *See* "Bobbin Wood."

Bobbin Sandpapering Machine.—This tool is useful for smoothing curved and irregular work. The sandpaper is strained round a small cylinder of wood, or, if very small, the wood is coated with abrasive material. The cylinder is fitted to a revolving spindle provided with a reciprocating motion to prevent scratchy marks on the wood.

Bobbin Squares.—*See* "Bobbin Wood."

Bobbin Wood.—A close-grown class of soft or semi-hard wood, non-resinous in character, suitable for making what is popularly called "cotton-bobbins." Although small articles given away with the thread, they form in the aggregate an important factor in the home and foreign timber trades. The most popular woods are birch, alder and ash, of small or medium diameter, cut into lengths called "props." The first form of conversion is into "bobbin squares."

Bois d'arc.—*See* "Osage Orange."

Bois-Durci.—A French invention for utilizing the sawdust of hard woods, such as rosewood, ebony, etc. After the sawdust is reduced to fine powder, it is mixed with blood into a paste; other materials are added, and when pressed into moulds it receives the most beautiful impression. Used for medallions, etc.

Bole.—The trunk or stem of a tree, after it has attained the diameter of 8 in., which constitutes timber.

Bolection or Bilection.—That portion of a group of mouldings which projects beyond the general surface of a panel, or, more strictly speaking, before the framing round a panel or panels.

Bolection Doors.—Doors with bolection mouldings.

" Bolinder " or " Swedish " Cutters.—A circular cutter having six or eight cutting teeth, backed off in such a manner that, as they are reduced in size by sharpening, they still cut the same profile. Used for beading, tonguing, grooving, etc.

Bolt.—A segment sawed or split from a short log.

Bond Timber.—Timbers placed in horizontal tiers at certain intervals in the walls of buildings for attaching battens, laths, and other finishings of wood, and for raising the " grade " or " seats " for beam and joist ends.

Bone Dry.—Absolutely dry, or brought to the utmost dryness the atmosphere will admit. Also expressed as " dry stock."

Boom.—Logs or timbers fastened together end to end and used to hold floating logs. The term sometimes includes the logs enclosed, as a boom of logs.

Boost.—To lift ; to raise by pushing up ; to push up. A common word in New England, as in the lumber trade : e.g., " movements are on foot to *boost* the price of hemlock."

Borer. —*See* " Boring Machines."

Boring and Mortising Apparatus.—Usually referring to an apparatus similar to the boring apparatus, but provided with a longitudinal slide, so that the material can be given a reciprocating motion by means of a hand lever. By using a rotary mortise tool slot mortises with round ends are readily made in the timber.

Boring Apparatus.—Usually referring to a table for supporting the wood while under the action of an auger fixed in a saw bench spindle. The table has a vertical adjustment and also a cross slide, by means of which the wood is fed into the tool.

Boring Machines.—Consist of one or more rapidly revolving spindles carrying augers with means of either bringing the augers to the work or the work to the augers.

Boss.—*See* " Centre-piece."

Bottom Rail.—Horizontal piece of the frame of a door nearest the floor, or in post and rail fencing.

Bought and Sold Notes are notes of sale drawn up by the agent employed to sell goods and by which the bargain through him is completed. The bought note goes to the buyer and the sold note to the seller, and are signed by each party. Brokers sign their contract notes as agents for both seller and buyer.

Box.—*See* " Packing Case."

Box, or " Armstrong " Dovetailing Machine.—A machine used for cutting dovetails on the edge of boards by means of saws. The saws are fixed to discs set at an angle with the board, one cutting one taper of the dovetail and part of the end, and the second saw completing the work. The work is rapid and automatic. The dovetails are accurate. Armstrong was the original inventor and patentee. The patent has run out some years, and the machine is made by most woodworking engineering firms.

Boxboards, Caseboards or Shooks.—Thin boards cut to sizes for parts of boxes, imported in bundles.

Box Board Printing Machines.—Used for printing names, trade marks, etc., on box boards by means of large rollers driven by gearing. The type or design is fixed to one of the rollers. One or more coloured printing inks can be used simultaneously.

Box Board Branding Machines.—In which box boards, cask ends and other goods are branded by heated plates. The brand may consist of special designs, trade marks, names, etc.

Box Board Trimming Machines.—Consist of two revolving cutter-blocks adjusted so as to trim box boards exactly to one length or width, as the boards are passed between the cutters.

Box the Heart.—To cut boards from all sides of the heart, leaving the latter as a piece of timber.

Box Wood.—(1) Deal, batten or board-ends, largely used for cutting up for making boxes ; a variant term is " Case wood " at some of the ports. *See* " Firewood." (2) A valuable and well-known tree, the *Buxus sempervirens*, of Linnæus, that produces one of the hardest and most compact woods known to man. Used by the instrument-maker for pipes, flutes, wheels, parts of violins ; for combs, knife-handles, shuttles, etc. ; also used by turners and engravers.

Boxing.—A system of tapping pine trees in order to obtain the resin or crude turpentine. (2) The hollow part of the " stiles " or " jambs " or " sides " of a " sash-frame " (*which see*). (3) The recess into which " folding " or " boxing shutters " (*which see*) are placed.

Boxing Shutters.—A descriptive term for inside folding window shutters; when not in use turned into " wall " are kindred " boxes." *See* " Shutter." " Boxing shutters " may variantly be termed " folding shutters," and consist of many parts hinged together ; those least seen are " back-folds " or " back-flaps." The latter a common term to such hinges. Shutters are for other purposes, as cupboards and shops, the latter often working on the revolving system.

Brack.—Wood goods below the regular classifications; otherwise Culls (*which see; also* "Wrack").

Bracked.—*See* "Assorted."

Brake or Actual Horse-power.—The power available for actual work after deducting the power required to drive the engine or motor itself. One horse-power is equal to the work of raising 33,000 foot-pounds per minute. One electric horse-power is equal to 746 watts.

Brake-block.—A block that is, or may be, used to stop the motion of a body. Instance, for retarding or arresting the motion of wheels, as in railway engines, tenders, carriages, wagons, carts, etc.

Brand and Branded.—As applied to timber and sawn goods, are terms loosely used in the trade, or whose original meaning has undergone extension from "brant" or "brent" = burnt, or branded with a hot iron. A variant term for "branded" is "marked." *See* "Quality and Shipping Marks." Instance, "marked goods" and "branded goods" are one and the same thing.

Brands or Shipping Marks on Timber.—The distinguishing marks used by the shippers for the various grades or qualities of sawn and planed wood from America, Norway and the Baltic countries, which are stencilled on the ends, generally in red. White Sea and other Russian goods are more or less dry hammer stamped on their ends. *See* "List of Shipping Marks on Timber," published by William Rider & Son, Ltd., London.

Bratticing.—Sawn boarding for ventilating passages in mines.

Brazil-wood or Braziletto (*Cæsalpinia brasiliensis*).—A hard, heavy cabinet or dye wood from tropical America.

Brazing Apparatus for Band Saws.—An apparatus by means of which the two ends of a band saw are held in position during the process of joining them together by brazing or hard soldering.

Brazing Forge for Various Band Saws.—A small forge with bellows worked by foot, the top of the forge being provided with separate receptacles for holding water, charcoal, etc. By means of the bellows the heat is concentrated upon the joint to be brazed, until the brass brazing wire wrapped round it is melted and runs between the lapped joint.

Breaking down, in sawing, is dividing the balks or logs into boards or planks (American = cants) which can be sawed on the main saw. The operation is called "the falling cut," and as it involves getting on and off a pit or saw-frame, it is charged as two cuts.

Breast.—The lower side of any piece of timber.

Breast High.—At or having a height of 4½ ft. above the ground. A less height is known as "knee deep," and is applied to railway wagons to distinguish them from "deep-sided."

Breastsummer (written also "brestsummer" and "bressummer." —A stout beam or lintel spanning an opening in a wall; used principally above shop windows. See "Summer."

Bridging.—Pieces of wood placed between two beams or other pieces to prevent their approaching each other More generally called "strutting" or "straining pieces." See "Struts."

Bright.—Not discoloured; fresh from the saw; wood that has not been exposed to the weather. "Viewly" is an equivalent term on the North-East Coast.

Bright Deals.—A term applied to Canadian yellow pine deals passed direct from the saw-mills to craft for shipment, in contradistinction to others termed "floated," or carried on rafts, which get a little discoloured in transit.

Bright Floated.—Deals floated in clear water, but remaining over the water level, and in consequence not discoloured.

Broads.—A term used in the Canadian trade for deals of a width of 12 in. or upwards.

Broken Specification."—An original one as imported, with certain special lengths sold out, otherwise a depreciated specification of hewn or sawn timber, or sawn deals, battens or boards A variant term is "bad specification."

Broken Stowage.—See "Stowage."

Broker.—"An agent employed to make bargains in matters of trade or navigation for other people in return for a compensation called brokerage" He is in short a mercantile agent. A broker is not in possession of the goods which are the subject of the contract. He cannot as a rule buy or sell in his own name when acting for other people, and is not liable to be sued on the contract which he enters into on behalf of others, unless he appears on the contract to be a principal. When a broker makes a contract for others he enters the terms of the contract in his own book, and then sends a copy of the entry to both parties. The bought note is sent to the buyer and the sold note to the seller. These notes should be identical in terms, otherwise there may be no contract at all, especially, as often happens, when the broker has not entered the terms in his book

(From *Pannell's Reference Book*.)

Browsewood or Brushwood. (1) Twig and small branches of

trees ; (2) small trees and shrubs of a wood, or a thicket of small trees ; (3) small round wood for " brush backs " or " heads."

Buck.—To saw felled trees into logs. An American term.

Buckled.—(1) A term used for a saw blade that is bent ; (2) in joinery or cabinet making, a panel or veneer which is not flat.

Buckling.—A term applied to saws when they are twisted or distorted out of truth.

Buckthorn (*Hippophea Rhamnoides*).—A small growing tree usually found on sandy soil in an exposed maritime situation, A hard, lasting wood, which does not split or shrink in seasoning, is light yellow in colour, with greyish veining.

Buffing Machine.—Another name for a belt sanding machine, in which a belt, dressed with abrasive material, runs round two pulleys. Used for smoothing different articles, more especially those turned in a copying lathe.

Bühl Work.—A style of cabinet decoration common in France in the seventeenth century, so called from André Charles Boale ; work being embellished with metal marquetry. Also written as Baule or Baulle.

Built-up Boards or Stock.—*See* " Plywood, or Built-up Boards," " Three-ply," *and* " Multiply Boards."

Bunk, Dog Teeth, Log Shoes, Spurs, Chain Bracket.—These are names meaning one and the same thing, consisting of a dog attached to the chain of a log jack, provided with spikes or spurs. These latter dig into the log and so drag it up an incline.

Burls.—Local defects appearing in the grain of timber, produced by healing of wounds in the tree, or by knots. Abnormal growths or excrescences in the tree, known as " sap-burrs " or " twig-burrs." The latter, which are found at the roots of the tree, are valuable, but " sap-burrs " are worthless. *See* " Burrs."

Burr.—A protuberance common to certain trees, mainly those which have power to reproduce by " stooling " (*see* " Stool "), and those whose trunks or arms are exposed to the action of the sun, i.e., open-grown or unshaded ; of these there are two kinds—the " sap-burr," a worthless type, and the " twig-burr," on the whole a valuable one. *See* " Walnut Burrs " *and* " Burr Woods." When on the ground-level they are termed " Root-burrs." *See* " Excrescence."

Burr Woods.—Varied species which produce or yield merchantable or ornamental woods in the form of burrs. Of these an Indian yellow wood, known as " Amboyna Wood," ranks very high. It was introduced into Europe by the Dutch when they were lords of that island. *See* " Amboyna Wood," " Walnut Burrs." Poplars and several other woods are found with burrs, they are of no value. Yew when so found is an exception.

Bush or **Shrub** is the name applied to perennial ligneous plants which do not in their normal state of growth attain a girth of more than six inches ; otherwise known as " Underwood " or " Undergrowth."

Butt.—The base of a tree or the big end of a log.

Butt Cut.—The butt log or the log first cut above the stump. In oak, etc., " butts," it is difficult before cutting open to tell whether they are 1st, 2nd or 3rd cuts.

C

Californian Redwood (*Sequoia sempervirens*).—The most valuable of Californian timber trees, used for building, telegraph poles, etc. Soft, light, close grained and easily split.

Calling for Orders.—An arrangement made with a vessel to call at a certain port to receive orders for and to proceed to a port of discharge.

Callipers or Calipers.—An instrument for measuring the cubical contents of round and square logs. The kind now in general use are known as " Hull Calipers," which consist of a graduated beam to which is attached one fixed and one sliding arm Bow calipers are now seldom used.

Camber.—A piece of timber cut archwise or forming a segment of a circle. A natural curve in oak or other timber.

Cambium. –A term applied to the layer of mucilaginous viscid matter, particularly plentiful in spring, interposed between the woody layers and the bark in exogenous trees.

Camp Sheeting.—A lining of planks or boards for protecting an embankment.

Canary Whitewood, or American Whitewood or Poplar.— The product of the Tulip tree, *Liriodendron tulipifera.* A common and much used wood imported from the United States. Very variable in colour, the most esteemed being that wood possessing a clear deep yellow shade. The sap wood is perfectly white. or, at times, slightly grey, and is generally shipped separately under the term of clear saps.

Cant.—Another term for " wane " on a log of timber, implying that it is not die-square at the corners, or towards the top end of the tree : it presents itself as a shortened form of " scant " (*which see, and* " Wane "). " Cant " has some reference to the side of a log meaning " turn," as : " Give that log a cant with the ' cant-dog ' " (*which see*). It is also an American term for a log that has been slabbed on one or more sides.

Cant-dog or **Hook.**—A hand-spike with a hinged iron hook at the lower or heavy end, hooped and pronged ; a necessary tool or instrument where logs of timber are handled or turned over on land, or floated or rafted on water. It is allied to the act of turning—instance, " cant over " for " turn over."

Cant Moulding.—Any moulding with a bevelled face.

Cantilever.—A wooden or iron block framed into the side of a house under the eaves, to carry a cornice or other moulding.

Capping.—*See* " Coping."

Capping Rail.—The rail at the top of a fence. Sometimes called " saddleback."

Capstan.—Machine used for hauling timber into a saw mill. Consisting of a revolving capstan head round which a rope is twisted two or three turns, sufficient purchase being thus obtained for hauling in the log.

Carcase.—The structure of a building before finishing is added.

Cargo.—The general name for all the merchandise carried on board a trading ship. It means the entire cargo of the ship usually, but the meaning may vary, according to the contract and circumstances.

Carriage.—(1) The timbering hidden or supporting part of a staircase ; (2) the timber or iron-work of a gun ; (3) a two- or four-wheeled vehicle with many parts ; (4) the price or expense of carrying goods.

Case.—*See* " Packing Case."

Case Harden.—In seasoning timber a piece is said to be case hardened when the exterior becomes dry while the interior remains moist. This is generally due to the application of a high degree of heat in a short time, i.e., by drying in an overheated kiln.

Caseboards.—*See* " Boxboards," *also* " Shooks."

Casement.—A compartment between the mullions of a window, but more generally a glazed sash or frame hinged to open like a door or to slide up and down in a sash window.

Cask.—A barrel-shaped vessel made in varying sizes, of staves, headings and hoops fitted close together, to hold liquid.

Catalpa (*Catalpa lignonioides*).—A native of India, but introduced here as an ornamental tree ; especially in towns. Not much in use here commercially, though valued in India.

Catamaran.—A small raft used in America, carrying a windlass and grapple, used to recover sunken logs.

Caul.—A piece of wood or zinc, the reverse of any curved surface that is to be veneered, which is heated and pressed on the face of the veneer after it is laid, to keep it in position until dry.

Cedar.—A name no longer confined to the Lebanon cedar (*which see*) but applied to other species of the genus as well as to junipers and other coniferous trees. Various " cedars " are known to commerce, but that associated with the English trade is West Indian or Mexican cedar (*Cedrela odorata*), which is a light wood beautifully marked, resembling the allied mahogany but much softer and easily split. Used for furniture, but mainly for cigar boxes. Various so-called cedars are common in the hardwood market, the principal being several varieties derived from the West Indies and Central America, while other minor supplies are obtained from the northern districts of South America, Southern States of North America, East Africa, India, Australia and other parts of the world. The principal uses for this mahogany-like wood are for cigar-box making, pencil manufacture, boat building and a few other minor purposes.

Cedar (of Lebanon) (*Cedrus Lebani*).—The choicest of all ornamental trees, though the British variety is inferior to the Eastern. Of little value commercially, the wood, which is light and reddish white in colour, being by no means durable. Used by builders of small boats, and to a limited extent by cabinet makers and embalmers. The American variety is imported for lead pencil casings.

Ceiling.—Timber finished on one side only, used for wainscotting, ceiling rooms, etc. Literally a " covering "—usually restricted to something overhead—as " a plaster ceiling," " a boarded ceiling," or a " ceiling made of ceiling boards," in some cases " vaulted," " arched " or " groined," i.e., not flat or horizontal. *See* " Vaulted Ceiling."

Ceiling Boards.—Wrought boards, usually narrow and tongued and grooved, used for making ceilings. They differ in no degree from " wall boards," but simply derive their name from the purpose to which they are applied.

Ceiling Joists.—Joists to which the ceiling of a room is attached —a term derived from the purpose to which the "joists" are applied.

Centre-piece.—Usually an imposing ornament of plaster or composition fixed (in some cases hung by copper cords) in the centre of a plaster ceiling. In a "groined ceiling," or the roof of a "vaulted ceiling," it becomes a "boss."

Centring.—Temporary wooden supports placed under vaults and arches to sustain them whilst they are in building; they usually remain in position until the material they support is properly set. The act of removal is termed "Striking the centres."

Certificate of Origin.—A Government certificate stating the country of origin to enable the re-entry of the wood into the country of production free of duty.

Chamber.—A room or apartment distinguished from a hall, chapel, etc. A *great chamber* usually adjoined or was contiguous to a hall, and answered to the modern *drawing* room (properly *withdrawing* room).

Chamfer, Plain or Moulded.—An angle slightly pared off is said to be "chamfered": where not continuous the original angle remains, in which case the work is termed "Stop chamfered," and the "stops" may be moulded, shaped or carved. *See* "Stop-chamfer."

Charcoal and Charcoal Burners.—A class of coal distinguished from coal won from the earth by mining, the latter known in the Middle Ages as "sea-coal," from that coal being largely conveyed from the Tyne district by water to London. Charcoal is the residue of wood slowly burned or smothered in piles under coverings of stone, earth, turf, etc., the men employed being known as "charcoal burners." It is a superior form of fuel for smelting ores, feeding forges or warming houses, and an ingredient in the manufacture of gunpowder. It takes 10 tons of wood to make 2¼ tons of charcoal.

Charterparty.—The name given to a contract in writing, between the owner or master of a ship and the freighter, by which the former hires or lets the ship, or a principal part of the ship, under certain specified conditions, for the conveyance of the goods of the freighter to some particular place or places. Generally, however, a charterparty is a contract for the use of the whole ship.

Check.—A longitudinal crack in timber caused by too rapid seasoning. To prevent wide boards from season checks they should be "cleated." Before seasoning the ends should be whitewashed, as it does not attract or retain the heat from the sun's rays. The formula of the United States Government for whitewash is: To 10 parts of best freshly slaked lime add one part of hydraulic cement. Mix well with salt water and apply quite thin.

Checked Sarking.—Sawn boarding for covering roofs under the slates, usually ⅝ in in thickness and cut for overlapping.

Cherry (Common = *Cerasus vulgaris*; Wild, Black-fruited = *Cerasus sylvestris*).—A home-grown fancy wood. Very firm and close grained when seasoned. Mainly used by cabinet makers, but also for wooden shoe pegs and the small branches for pipes.

Chestnut.—*See* "Horse Chestnut" *and* "Sweet Chestnut."

Chimney.—A French term which shows the source from which we obtained those useful constructional features. The term embraces the "fire-place," and yields as its accessories "chimney-piece," "chimney-shaft," "chimney-pot," etc. They were not known in England before the twelfth century, and then only sparingly in castle building. Instances survived into the last century of rural chimneys wrought in wood or clay passages for smoke.

Chip Breaker.—A pressure bar in front of the cutter knives in a planing machine, which is designed to prevent splinters from being torn from the face of a board as it passes through the machine.

Chipped Grain.—A defect in timber caused by the grain of the wood being torn out in patches by the action of the planer knives.

Chipping Machines and Chips.—The original form of the "planing machine" with top, bottom and side chippers, but no fixed knives, hence not producing shavings in dressing or preparing boards or flooring—a mode that survives in "moulding machines," where the work is done on the principle of "chipping." The Americans favour the "chipping process" to a more pronounced extent than is practised in Europe.

Chocks.—Pieces of hardwood employed on shipboard to aid in the support of various articles such as anchor chocks, rudder chocks, boat chocks, etc.

Christiania Standard.—A measure for timber now seldom used consisting of 120 pieces 11 ft. 9 in. × 1¼ in. = 103½ cub. ft.

C.i.f.—A commercial term, "cost, insurance, and freight," meaning that the seller delivers the goods to the carrier and agrees to pay all charges to bill-of-lading destination. On delivery to buyer of bill of lading with insurance policy attached the seller's responsibility usually ceases. *See also* " Cost, freight and insurance."

Cill.—*See* " Sill."

Circular Cross-cut Saws with Self-acting Motion.—A machine for cross-cutting planks or logs in which a circular saw is used, having a reciprocating motion imparted to it by power, the plank or log being stationary while under the action of the saw.

Circular Saw.—A disc of steel with saw teeth on its periphery revolved on an arbor.

Circular Saw Benches (Plain).—In which the material is fed past the saw by hand, a fence being used to guide the material.

Circumference or Periphery.—The curve which encloses a plane figure, as the periphery or circumference of a saw.

City Cut.—A term applied to spruce deals cut in the mills at the city of St. John, New Brunswick, in contradistinction to the goods manufactured at the country mills of the province by circular saws.

City-wood.—A term long applied to the finest growth or quality of West Indian or true mahogany, now scarce, small and dear, shipped from the city of San Domingo.

Clamping Machine for Sashes and Doors.—A clamp which secures doors and sashes in place after they have been glued.

Clap-board.—A quarter-sawed board, 4 to 6 in. wide and 4 to 20 ft. long, tapering to a thin edge on one side, used for covering the sides of buildings. In England, according to Bailey, a " clap-board " is also a stave or staff for casks. For roof covering they appear to have originally been cleft-boards with a feather edge, similar to those used in close-boarded riven oak fences, now often sawn and creosoted.

Cleading.—A term used in Scotland for a jacket or outer covering of wood, to prevent radiation of heat, as from the boiler, cylinder, etc. Also used to describe the boards of the lining of carts.

Clear Lumber.—Lumber without specific defects, such as knots, splits, shakes, etc.

Clearance.—A mercantile marine term denoting permission from the Customs-house officers for the departure of a ship from port, denoting that all formalities have been observed, and all dues, etc., paid.

Clearing Goods Shipped.—Lodging particulars of the goods at the Customs-house on special forms. Goods shipped must always be cleared either by shipper or his agents.

Cleat.—Pieces of wood or iron hooping fastened to the end of a board or plank to prevent splitting whilst seasoning.

Cleft.—Made by splitting.

Clog or Clog-sole.—The wooden sole of a shoe; an old form of footwear common in Lancashire and worn by both sexes. It is a special branch of the timber trade, nearly wholly conducted in " alder-wood " and " birch " (*which see*). With " clog-soles " are allied " patten-soles." Clog-soles are of two kinds, one mounted to resemble a boot, the other a shoe.

Cloth Boards.—Thin boards used in the textile trades in the centre of a bale of material. Also known as "lapping boards."

Clump of Trees or Shrubs.—A cluster, formerly written *plump*. It is our word *lump*, with the initial *c* added.

Coarse Grain.—Applied to the grain of timber which has wide annual rings.

Cocobolo.—A turnery wood from Central America.

Cocus Wood (*Brya ebenus*) —A hard, heavy wood from the West Indies.

Coffer.—A variant term for a " chest," " hutch " or " arke." It implies a fitment or object larger than a " box " or " casket," usually of wood.

Coffin.—A case for enclosing a dead body, a term allied to " *sarcophagus* " and " coffer." In the eleventh and twelfth centuries they were wrought in stone, but only for persons of distinction. It has been customary, during the last three or more centuries, to make them of wood, and use them for all classes of persons.

Collar Beam.—A beam extending between the two opposite main rafters of a framed principal above the tie beam. In the instance of a " queen-post " roof it may be termed " wind-beam." In a " hammer-beam " roof it becomes in practice, but not in name, a " tie-beam " in an elevated position. *See* " Hammer-beam."

Collars.—A term when applied to timber, refers to the limbs, arms or topwood.

Combined Log and Deal Frame.—A machine with reciprocating saw frame, with feed rollers which can be used for feeding forward logs or deals and flitches as required.

Combined Rip and Cross-cut Bench.—In which two saws are mounted on separate spindles, one with teeth suitable for cross-cutting, the other for ripping. Either saw is brought into position for work as required.

Comb-grain, quarter sawed, edge grain, rift sawn, vertical grain, are all synonymous terms and refer to wood sawn parallel, or approximately so, to the medullary rays. Practically, however, the angle of the annual rings should not exceed 45 degrees from vertical. This method of cutting pitch pine is especially desirable for flooring, inasmuch as edge grain is more durable under the wear to which flooring is subjected.

Common Pitch.—A term applied when the length of the rafters is equal.

Common Rafter (otherwise "roof-spar").—The upper part and sometimes the only timbering of a roof ; the light or scantling part, placed at intervals as supports for the laths, tiles, slates, etc., which form the covering. *See* "Roof Timbers."

Compass Roof.—One in which the tie from the foot of one rafter is attached to the opposite rafter at a considerable height above its foot. "Compass window" is a term for a window circular in plan.

Compo Boards.—Boards of wood fibre and other substances, used in the interior of houses in place of lath and plaster. *See* "Beaver Boards" and "S.X." Boards.

Compression.—(1) One of the technical tests applied to wood to arrive at its power of resisting thrust or pressure longitudinally ; (2) a wood column whose office it is to support beams and floors overhead, as corn chambers, illustrate wood as a substance in compression. The like may be said of the strut, head or upper beam of a queen-post roof, or a block of wood carrying a smith's anvil : compression is the opposite of "tension" (*which see*). Struts, wherever they occur, as in gates, are considered to be in compression, but exceptions occur in practice.

Concave Saw.—A circular saw, concave in form.

Concentric Rings.—Woody layers which define the yearly growth of a tree.

Conifers.—Trees of the order of Coniferæ or cone-bearing trees. *See* "Coniferæ."

Coniferæ (*Lat.* cone-bearers).—An important natural order of exogenous trees, embracing pines, firs, juniper, cypress, yews, etc., the fruit of which is a cone. Many kinds of coniferæ are productive of turpentine and resins. As the name suggests, they are cone-bearing trees.

Coniferous.—Belonging to the order of Coniferæ.

Conk.—An American term for the decay in the wood of trees caused by fungus.

Consignment.—The despatch of goods to a broker or agent for the purpose of sale.

Consignee.—A person to whom goods are delivered.

Consignor.—The person who sends the goods.

Constantine Measure.—A system of log measurement in the New York market used in measuring square hewed foreign woods, chiefly mahogany and cedar logs. From first-class hewed timber there is deducted 2 in. width from one face and 1 in. from the other face at right angles to it, this deduction being made to straighten the log and to remove axe marks. The face measurements are then used to compute the cubical contents of the log. If the log is defective the contents are reduced one-half.

Contorted.—Twisted together.

Contractions and Abbreviations in writing.—*See* Appendix I.

Conveyor for Sleepers.—A travelling chain or chains provided with dogs for conveying sleepers either to or from the various machines for sawing, adzing or boring them.

Coolibah (*Euc. microtheca*).—A tree growing in the northern portion of West Australia, the wood of which is claimed to be harder than lignum vitæ.

Cooperage.—The art of making bulging vessels of pieces of wood bound together by hoops. *See* "Wet or Tight Cooperage," "Dry Cooperage," *also* "White Cooperage."

Cooper-ware.—The lower end of ash poles, cut in lengths from 16 to 18 ft. for wagon tilts and cooper work.

Coping (in architecture).—The top of a building, or the brow of a wall made sloping; its equivalent in wood appears to be "capping."

Coppice or Copse.—A natural wood or plantation, of which the trees are cut over from time to time, without being allowed to attain the size of timber trees, sending up new shoots from their roots or stools. Fir trees are incapable of being treated in this manner, refusing to send up new shoots; but many other trees readily do so. Oak has been much planted as coppice in consequence of the great demand which existed at one time for its bark. Chestnut copses are planted for hop-poles; ash with a view to its employment for handles, implements, hoops, etc.; hazel, for crate making, etc.; willow or osier, for basket making.

Copse. *See* "Coppice."

Copying Lathes.—Sometimes called "Spoke lathes." These lathes have two or more mandrels geared together so as to revolve in unison.   Between one set of centres is fixed the " dummy " or copy, the work being fixed between the others; a roller bears against the copy and causes a cutter head to act on the work, forming it into the shape of the model as the saddle carrying the tools is automatically traversed along the bed.

Cord.—A cord of wood measures 8 ft. × 4 ft. × 4 ft. and contains 128 cubic feet.

Corduroy Road.—A term applied to roads in the backwoods and swampy districts of the United States of America, formed of the halves of trees sawn in two longitudinally and laid transversely across the track.   A road thus laid presents a ribbed appearance like the cloth called corduroy (French *cordduroy*).

Cordwood.—Wood for firing purposes, or for charcoal burning.

Core.—The waste cut out of a mortise, also the base or interior part of veneered work or the internal core of a billet of wood in riving lathwood billets, which are used for fuel.

Corner Post.—In " timber " or " half-timber " buildings the corner posts of the archways or the fabrics were usually great up-ended oak timbers moulded, carved and panelled, supporting brackets worked on the same lines.

Cornice.—A horizontal moulding at the top of a pedestal, door, window or house.

Coromandel or Calamander Wood (*Diospyros quæsita*).—One of the most valuable ornamental woods of Ceylon, used for turnery and veneers.

Cortex.—The rind or bark of a tree.

Cost, Freight and Insurance.—The price charged for goods when it covers not only the cost but the expense of insuring and carrying them.   Usually abbreviated " C.i.f."   In French " C.a.f.," Coût, assurance, frêt. *See also* "C.i.f."

Cotchel.—A term applied to a small lot or parcel of timber or other merchandise.   Often used to describe timber or other goods brought in by the captain of a vessel on his own account.

Cotoneaster frigida.—A tree introduced into England from Nepaul in 1824.   Its wood is in request for ornamental purposes, but little used commercially except for making golf clubs, though it is extremely hard, close grained and difficult to splinter.

Cottonwood (*Populus deltoides*).—A tree found in North America, where in the Western States it reaches a height of 100 ft., with a trunk 6 or 8 ft. in diameter. The wood is light and soft, and when absolutely dry a cubic foot weighs 24·24 lb. Used for paper pulp, packing cases and fuel, but owing to a tendency to warp and difficulty in seasoning, of little use for timber.

Counter (French, *contour*).—A table or board, on which money is counted and goods are laid ; an essential piece of office or shop furniture. Lighter in construction than that implied by the term " bench," but not extending to a " seat."

Counter Tops.—Wood suitable for or used for the tops of tables or counters in offices or shops.

Cove.—Any kind of concave moulding. The concavity of a vault ; commonly applied to the curve which is sometimes used to connect the ceiling with the walls of a room.

Crab.—Sometimes termed a " Log turner." A simple form of overhead crane which moves in one direction only, usually across the bed of a large sawing machine. Used for loading or turning over heavy logs which cannot be dealt with by hand labour.

Crabark.—*See* " Krabark "

Cradle.—A term used on the Pacific Coast for the framework of timbers in which ocean-going rafts are built.

Cramp.—A joiner's appliance for drawing the parts of a frame together.

Crane.—An apparatus for lifting heavy weights and transporting them to different positions. Made in many forms and patterns *See* " Jib Cranes," " Overhead Travelling Cranes," " Portable Jib Cranes."

Cratewood.—Small strips of timber used for framing or making an open casing to contain manufactured articles.

Creosoting.—*See* " Timber, Preservation of."

Crib.—A term used in the Canadian trade for a raft or boom of logs, also for a small raft which, with others, makes up a full raft. A little bedstead.

Crooks.—Sections of crooked timber much prized in wooden shipbuilding, for ships' bends and knees, and for large and boat construction.

Cross-cut Benches.—Working with circular saws and used for cross-cutting all descriptions of work. Usually the wood is placed on a table which slides past the saw.

Cross-cut Saws.—Saws arranged for cutting across the fibres of the wood ; these require sharp teeth bevelled off to a cutting point, and have a scribing action.

Cross-cutting.—To cut a board or timber at right angles to the general direction of the fibres.

Cross Grain.—As applied to the grain of timber, a piece in which the wood elements or fibres interweave and are not constant in any one direction, but are spiral or twisted.

Crotch.—*See* " Curl."

Crowntrees.—Wood used in coal mines as sleepers or as substructure for pit-props.

Croze.—The cross groove in the staves of cooperage in which the edge of the head is inserted.

Cruise.—To estimate the amount and value of standing timber.

Cruiser.—One who cruises or surveys a timber limit.

Cube.—A regular solid body, with six equal square sides.

Cull, Culls and Culler.—Loose terms in the wood-trade (a trade favourable to distortions or extensions) ; properly a beautiful flower plucked in its prime is a " cull," and a lady thus culling is " a culler." (1) The timber merchant, whose immediate ancestor was a " woodmonger," dubs a piece of wood he views inferior " a cull," as he " culled " it from something superior, hence " culls " become a distinct class. The " culler " himself is not a man connected with low or poor quality goods, he " culls " all qualities to the very highest. *See* " Lathwood Culls." (2) An American term for logs which are rejected or parts of logs deducted in measurement on account of defects.

Cupshake.—Curved splits in timber which sometimes separate the annual rings, rendering the timber useless for constructive purposes. Spanish chestnut may be mentioned as a timber liable to this defect, also Oak, Elm, Lignum Vitæ and other woods.

Curb.—Circular wood frames used in well-sinking.

Curb Rafters.—The upper rafters of a Mansard roof.

Curb Roof.—Another name for a mansard roof (*which see*).

Curl.—A curl is that part of the stem of a tree where the heart of the branches meet. They may occur, in a more or less degree, in all trees, but are notable and much sought after when produced from the mahogany tree. At times, in the mahogany trade, they are described as " fans," " crutches " or " crotches," the latter being an American term.

ırly Grain.—As applied to the grain of timber, pieces in which the fibres undulate, but do not cross each other. When the undulations are large, wood is said to be wavy grained.

ırve.—A crooked line that departs gradually from the straight direction.

ıstom.—Long established practice existing from time immemorial. If a general practice in the realm it is part of the common law. If a local practice its existence must be proved in Court according to law. For a custom, immemorial existence is essential, otherwise it may be only Usage (*which see*)

ıstom of Port.—A usage prevailing at a port in question. *See* "Custom of Port of London."

ıstom of the Port of London.—As far as overside goods are concerned the decision in a legal case explains the position. "The following custom of the Port of London is a reasonable, certain, and valid one—namely, that in the case of cargoes of goods (including both Baltic and pitch pine timber) the receiver, instead of being liable to receive the goods from the ship's tackle alongside into craft, is liable only to provide sufficient craft alongside ready to receive the goods, and is under no obligation to have any men thereon to receive the goods from the ship's tackle or to stow the goods therein, and the shipowner is bound to do the whole work of delivering the goods into barges whether dock company's barges or outside barges, and of stowing the goods therein in the reasonable and ordinary manner, so that the goods may not be damaged or imperilled, and so that the barges may be loaded to the usual and reasonable extent and may be safely and properly navigable" (*Glasgow Navigation Co.* v. *W. W. Howard Bros. & Co.*, 1920, 26 T.L.R. 247.)

The same custom also applies to goods landed on the quay.

ıstom Sawing.—An American expression for the sawing of timber under contract prices per 1,000 board feet.

ıstomary Measure.—A form of measure established by custom or common usage ; it is the opposite of " actual measure " (*which see*). It has little application in the woodtrade beyond log or balk timber, in which latter field—as in the instance of waney or octagonal logs, measured by callipers—it is a measure short of actual. The reverse is the case with round logs measured by string, quarter girth, 144 divisor. *See* " Hoppus's Measure." In the mahogany trade " Brokers' measure "—difficult to define—is considered fully actual.

D

Customary Square.—*See* " Square."

Customs Measure.—Refers to goods measured by Customs Fund officials who issue " Blue-Books " of contents. It is the old working machinery that obtained in the days of duties on imported wood, kept active for the benefit of the public and supported by the merchants requiring their services. When called upon they require instructions, what form of measure is required—" actual " or " customary," " string " or " calliper," and what divisor they are to use in or on square, waney or round timbers. *See* " Customary," " Actual " *and* " Hoppus's Measure."

Cut.—In timber sawing a longitudinal cut through the width of the deal is termed a " deep cut " ; through the thickness, a " flat cut " ; across the grain, a " cross cut " ; sawn into a triangular section, is said to be cut " arris wise." Also an American term for a season's output of logs or sawn wood from a sawmill.

Cut Over.—A district or forest from which all the merchantable timber has been taken.

Cutter-block.—The revolving portion of a planing or moulding machine that carries the knives or shaped tools which work the tongues, grooves and mouldings.

Cutter Grinding Machine.—A machine for sharpening long plane irons used on wood-planing machines. The cutter is fixed to a canting plate, which is set to give the required bevel. The plate is attached to a reciprocating slide, to which motion is imparted either by hand or power. The cutter is brought up to a emery wheel or cup which grinds the cutter to the required bevel.

Cutter Head.—The shaft of a planing machine on which is mounted one or more cutting knives.

Cutting.—The act of sawing, understood to imply to the deep way of the wood, or cutting the faces of boards and planks, not the edges, in which case the operation is termed " ripping " (*which see*). A slip of a tree for grafting.

Cyclone.—A cylindrical receptacle for receiving dust or refuse from machinery. *See* " Cyclone Dust Collector."

Cyclone Dust Collector.—A cylindrical drum of galvanized iron terminating in a long cone. A metal worm extends round the inner surface. Air laden with dust or shavings is blown into an opening at the top and passes round the cone with a spiral motion. The air escapes from an opening in the top, while the wood refuse falls out at the bottom.

Cylinder Saw.—A steel shaft and a cast-iron head to which is fastened a steel drum or cylinder, the walls of which are parallel with the mandrel for the entire length. The cutting edge consists of a toothed steel band attached to the free end of the drum. Known also as "Barrel Saw."

na Recta.—A moulding formed of a curve of a contrary flexure, deriving its name from its resembling a wave—hollow above, and swelling below.

na Reversa.—A similar moulding to above, but more commonly called an Ogee.

ress (*Cupressus*).—An evergreen conifer, the best known species in Europe being the Common Cypress (*C. Sempervirens*). It is a very hard, compact and durable wood; the ancients considered it indestructible. It is not liable to the attacks of insects and was formerly much used in cabinet making. It is supposed to be the ancient Gopher Wood, and specimens in museums are supposed to be several thousand years old. The doors of St. Peter's at Rome made in the time of Constantine are known to have lasted 1,100 years. In recent years the Red or Louisiana Cypress (*Taxodium distichum*) has been sold in this country.

D

lo.—A framing round a room about breast high.

lo-head Saw.—A grooving saw which can be adjusted to cut any size groove by the insertion of one or more cutter heads between two outside saws of special pattern.

ople Figure.—*See* "Figure in Wood" *and* "Fleck and Flecked."

ys of Grace.—Bills payable in England (other than bills payable on demand) are due for payment three days after the time specified on the face of the bill, which three days are known as "days of grace." For method and time of presentment the Bills of Exchange Act should be consulted.

ıd-eye, Dead Men's Eyes.—In ships, little blocks usually bored with three holes, giving them the appearance of human skulls, hence the name. This is undoubtedly an older form of block than that fitted with "pulleys" or "shivers." W. S. Gilbert, in the comic opera of "H.M.S. Pinafore," makes one of his characters on the ship respond to the name of "Dick Deadeye."

ıd Freight.—The compensation paid by the merchant who freights a whole ship to the shipmaster for the space which he fails to fill with cargo.

Dead Rollers.—Rollers used for the handling of timber, which are not power driven.

Deadwood.—The product from dead standing trees, the bark and the sapwood of which have rotted away.

Deal, Batten and Board Ends.—Merchantable in the trade, commence at 6 ft., and usually end at 8 ft. They are bought at a lower rate than the full lengths and carried on the ships at two-thirds the full chartered rates, but only to the extent required by the captain in stowing his cargo, in which phase they are termed " deal ends, etc., for stowage." At some ports " lathwood billets " are used instead and at the reduced rates.

Deal (coniferous wood).—A piece of sawn-wood timber, 2 in. to 4 in. in thickness, by 9 in. and over in width. In London and the South an old custom has been to rate all above 9 in. as " planks " ; but in the pitch-pine trade this has become obsolete. Deals, sawn into twelve or more thin boards, are termed " leads " ; in the " picture-frame " trade " backboards." In the pitch-pine export trade the term is applied to pieces 9 in. and up in width, and 3, 4 or 5 in. in thickness. A Quebec deal is a piece of any width and 3 in. and up in thickness.

Deal Frames.—These are similar in principle to a log frame, but usually have vertical feed rollers instead of horizontal ones which keep the deal up to a fence and thus obtains straight cutting.

Deal or Plank Sizes.—Imply sawn goods of 9 in. and upwards ; but when exceeding 11 in. in width they are further usually defined as " broad deals " or " broad planks."

Deal-carrier.—Usually a member of a gang of men whose business or calling is to carry deals from his mate, the " hicker " (see " Hick and Hicking "), to his mate, the " stower " (which see). This work at some ports and towns is done on the shoulder—protected by a leather pad—sometimes transferring a part of the load to the other shoulder by the aid of a " hand-stick " placed across and tailing under the piece carried ; which, by pulling down the head-end, brings weight upon the otherwise unworking shoulder. In the instance of London, and some other ports, the goods are carried in a slanting position on the backs of the men.

Debenture is a deed of acknowledgment of debt by a company and usually contains a charge on the company's property as security for the debt.

Debenture Timber.—A term used for imported timber used for mining and similar purposes, and which is more nearly round than square.

ciduous.—A term applied to trees which annually lose and renew their leaves.

cimal and Duodecimal (Latin *decimus*, tenth—from *decum* = "ten"—and Latin *duodecim* = "twelve").—They form the bases of the two systems of numerical computation, the latter termed "the Teutonic long hundred" of ten dozen to the hundred, or twelve hundred to the thousand, as still used in "slates" and "staves" (*which see*). This "long hundred" was in use at the time of the Norman Conquest, and the Latin scribes recorded it in "the Domesday Survey Book" as "the English mode of computation." It survives in our "shilling," being of *twelve* pence.

ck Cargo.—The part of the cargo of a trading ship which is carried on the deck of the vessel ; prohibited or restricted in the winter season.

ck Planks.—Wood in long lengths ready prepared in narrow widths for use for ships' decks, which go to prove that "plank," as implying widths of over 9 in., has trade exceptions.

eping.—Sawing through the deep way of timber or boards, usually called "deep-cutting," of which the above is possibly an abbreviation.

game (*Calycophyllum candidissimum*)—A wood often confused with lancewood and difficult to distinguish from this latter. It is received from the same localities, in the same form—but in rather better dimensions—and is used for the same purposes.

Crederé Commission.—A term used to express the additional premium charged by an agent or broker, in return for which he warrants the solvency of the purchaser, and renders himself personally liable for the payment of the price of the goods he may sell according to the terms of the contract.

murrage.—Primarily an allowance to the owners or a master of a ship for staying in a loading or discharging port longer than the time first agreed. *See* "Charterparty," "Shipping Days," "Shipping Documents," *and* "Shipping Season."

sity Rule.—An authorized and approved set of specifications of the Southern Pine Association under which pitch pine timbers are graded.

it and Indent.—Used in the sense of a bruise caused by a blow forming a cavity, as in damage done to a fine wood or veneered surface, and is interchangeable with "dint." Indent, properly, relates to something like a saw, from its root being a tooth ; but its sharpness becomes a waved line in parting a dead or indenture from its counterpart.

Dentels (Lat. *denticulus* = a little tooth).—Ornaments resembling teeth, used in the bed-moulding of Ionic, Corinthian and composite cornices, with which elevated constructional features they are always associated.

Depreciation.—Diminution in value, as applied to wood-goods in transit or in stock, may be a serious business matter to be guarded against by insurance, especially on sea, and may become subject of "general" or "particular average," and adjustment by "average staters," "surveyors" or "arbitrators." *See* "Average" *and* "Average Stater."

Desiccating.—The artificial drying of wood by means of heated air.

Desiccation.—Of wood-goods—the act of making dry ; the state of being dried. It is an important factor in the wood trade of the United States, where "artificially dried stock" is largely used and shipped for builders' and cabinet makers' consumption. Its use is extending, especially in the instance of drying "three-ply" and, or, "built-up boards or stock."

Desk.—(1) An inclining table for the use of writers and readers ; an important piece of office furniture, usually constructed with some under and occasionally over fitment. (2) A part of a pulpit, a clerk or precentor's "desk," extending as church furniture to a "rostrum."

Die-square.—A term used as a guarantee in a contract, implying the goods are hewn or sawn square, or square on the edges. It is the opposite of "waney." *See* "Wane" *and* "As they fall from the mill."

Dimension Timber.—Usually taken to mean logs of from 6 in. × 6 in. and up, 10 ft. in length and up. In America the word "dimension" is used for larger pieces of lumber than inch boards and includes smaller sizes of timbers, from 2 × 4 up. The general term "timbers and dimension" includes, of course, both light and heavy timbers. The exact boundary line between timbers and dimension is not closely defined, but the word "dimension" is most commonly applied to sizes from 2 × 4 to 2 × 12 and to 3-in. thickness in the same range of widths.

Discount.—The interest allowed for settlement of accounts when due or before due. The due date is usually regulated according to the custom of the trade. In the wholesale timber trade the revised terms of credit are—to builders and other consumers of wood for spot goods, four month's bill nett, from the first of the month following delivery, or monthly account less 2½ per cent. discount at end of month following delivery. *Ex* ship terms four months' acceptance from date of ship's arrival, or cash less 2½ per cent. discount at one month from same date.

Disforest or Disafforest.—To turn into common land. To return from the privilege of a forest to the state of common ground, or to remove the forest laws from the bounds and view of certain lands. By charter of Henry III many forest areas were disafforested.

Dishonour of a Bill.—When the person on whom a bill is drawn fails to accept it or pay it when due, he is said to dishonour it. The act of drawing or of indorsing a bill implies an obligation to pay it, and the person in whose favour it is drawn has thus recourse against the drawer and indorsers should the drawee fail to accept or pay. In order to preserve this recourse it is indispensable that notice of dishonour shall at once be given to the drawer and indorsers as prescribed by the Bills of Exchange Act.

Dispatch Money.—The amount called for under a charterparty (where so agreed) when a vessel is loaded in less time than the charterparty allows. It is a payment for saving the ship's time.

Divining-rod.—A forked branch of hazel, suspended by the two prongs between the balls of the thumbs, supposed by its inclination to indicate the presence of water springs, the locality of precious metals, buried wealth, etc. This has the flavour of the Black Art or old days of Witchcraft. *See* " Witch Hazel."

Djati Wood.—A kind of teak exported from Java. Djati is the Malay name for teak.

Dock Warrant.—A document issued by the Dock authorities as a receipt for goods warehoused. By custom it appears to represent the goods and is freely transferred accordingly.

Dog or Dogs.—A short heavy piece of steel, bent and pointed at one end and with an eye or ring at the other, or two similar pieces of bent steel attached and used scissor-fashion to hoist logs by means of a crane. It is used for many purposes in logging.

Dolphin.—A cluster of piles to which boom logs are secured.

Door.—The frame or barrier of boards or other material usually turning on hinges, by which the entrance way into a house or apartment is closed and opened. The component parts of an ordinary house frame door are as follows : The horizontal pieces of the frame, named respectively, the top rail, the bottom rail and the lock rail (in which the lock is fixed); the outside vertical pieces, known as " stiles "; the intermediate vertical parts termed " munting," and the openings of the frame, which are filled with thin boards called " panels."

Door Casing.—The frame which encloses a door.

Doorway.—An entrance into a building or an apartment in a building, to which a door-frame, or door, are usually fitted. Doorways are prime features in the construction of every country, century, and style of architecture.

Dormer Window.—A window in the sloping side of a roof with its casing set vertically. When the window lies in the plane of the roof it is called a skylight.

Dote or Doat.—A disease that spreads from the ends of logs during certain times of the year, and which will develop right through the log if not dealt with. In certain hardwoods such as birch, maple, hornbeam, ash and beech, the stains of doat can be traced a few months after felling as soon as the ends of the logs are dried by the weather. It is during the hot summer weather that the disease develops rapidly, and if the log remains in the round state twelve months, 3 ft. on each end is touched and stained. On certain hardwoods such as oak, mahogany, rosewood and sycamore, the ends are marred by a brown stain and much valuable wood is lost, as often logs of great value are stored for a considerable time before conversion. A formula has recently been introduced, which prevents dote if applied at the right period. The anti-dote remedy can be obtained of Mr. Wm. Staddon, 38 Shirfield Road, Grays, Essex. Dote is also known as Dosey Stain.

Double Cutting Band Mill.—Machines using wide band saws, having teeth cut on both back and front edges, so as to cut in both directions of the feed.

Douglas Fir or Pine.—*See* "Oregon Pine or Fir."

Dovetail.—A word in carpentry, meaning the fitting one board into another by triangular notches or wedges, which resemble in shape a dove's tail. Hence it is used metaphorically to fit on or fit in nicely.

Dovetailing Machines.—These are of various types for cutting dovetails in the edge of boards for fixing them together for forming boxes, drawers, etc. *See* "Automatic Dovetailing Machines," "Box," "Multiple Spindle."

Dowel.—A cylindrical wooden pin used for securing joints or tenons, otherwise "oak pins," as seen in framed wainscotting. "Dowels" are used in the sense of tenons in the manufacture of "panel doors" and "chair frames." In such instances boring of holes take the place of "sinking mortises" and hardwood dowels of "cutting tenons." Where this "dowelling" is done "oak pins" do not find a place in framing. *In allied carpentry, see* "Drawbore" *and*

"Treenail." A wooden pin used to hold together two pieces of wood.

raft.—A name given to a bill of exchange; also an order for money on a bank (or cheque) or an order by a bank on one of its branches, or vice versa. Also the first rough copy of a document.

rain Tile.—Or "channel tile," mainly used in land drainage. When roofed in or covered they become "drain-pipes" and collared or socketed "sanitary-pipes." In no instance have the variant terms ceased to be interchangeable, the latter being the newest. *See* "Tile."

rammen Standard.—An old-time measure for timber consisting of 120 pieces

$$\left.\begin{array}{l} 9 \text{ ft., } 6\tfrac{1}{2} \text{ in. } \times 2\tfrac{1}{2} \text{ in.} \\ 13 \text{ ft., } 9 \text{ in. } \times 1\tfrac{1}{4} \text{ in.} \end{array}\right\} = 121\tfrac{7}{8} \text{ cub. ft.}$$

raught or Draft of Water.—The technical term for the depth to which a ship sinks in the water when fairly afloat.

rawbore and Drawbore-pin.—A bored hole through the mortised and tenoned part of a piece of framing—large or small. The hole through the tenon is slightly larger and so placed that a "pin" driven into the framing draws the joint up tight. The "try-pin" is of iron or steel, a foot or more long, and driven in tight to draw up the joint, or shoulder of the rail, or munting or post or stud, as the case may be. It is then knocked out and a "drawbore-pin" or treenail is finally driven home. *In allied joinery-work, see* "Dowel."

rawee.—The party to whom a bill of exchange is addressed. If he "accepts" the bill he then becomes the acceptor.

raw-knife or Drawing-knife.—A well-known instrument used in the working of wood. Otherwise "a shave" (*which see*).

ressed and Headed (D and H).—A flooring strip is dressed and headed when it has been surfaced, tongued and grooved, and also had a tongue on one end and a groove on the other so that the board need not join over a rafter.

ressed and Matched (D and M).—Boards which have been surfaced, tongued and grooved.

ressed Timber.—Timber which has been planed, scraped or surfaced on one or more sides.

rive.—A body of logs in process of being floated from the forest to the mill or shipping point.

rop Siding.—An American term for a pattern of lumber used to cover the exterior sides of buildings.

um Sanding Machines.—Consists of one or more drums covered with sand-paper. The wood is held against the surface of the drum and passed along either by hand, feed rollers or a travelling bed.

mken Saw.—A term applied to a circular saw which runs out of the perpendicular when in motion. Used for making large rough grooves in squared timbers, etc., In America called a " wobble saw."

, Cooperage.—Converted hardwood, or softwood, or mixed, not necessarily " dry " in condition, but allocated to the making of " tubs," " casks," " barrels," " kits," etc., for *dry* goods, i.e., not for wines, spirits, oils or liquids, but hardware, crockery, fruit, fish (wet or dry), and the hundred-and-one things that come under the term " merchandise." Like cooperage for liquids, the parts of dry cooperage retain the old nomenclature of " stave," " lag," " hoop," etc.

, Emery Grinder (also known as Moulding Iron Grinder).— A machine in which wheels of emery or other abrasive material are used for sharpening tools, cutters and moulding irons. For the latter purpose a number of wheels are provided, having different widths and shapes on their edges.

, Floated.—Canadian pine and spruce deals that have dried, after having been conveyed on rafts, floated above or on the level of the water.

, Kiln.—A structure in which wood is dried by artificial heat.

, Rot.—Decay in timber brought about by animal or insect action, otherwise the " Furniture Beetle " (*which see*). Another form, which should properly speaking be called " Wet rot," owes its inception to vegetable disintegration. *See* " Fungi," " Worm Holed, Wormy or Wormed."

, Rot Preventive. To arrest the progress of dry rot one authority recommends that the timber be subjected to a heat of 300 , to destroy all reproduction of fungus. Another recommends an ounce of corrosive sublimate (bichloride of mercury) to a gallon of water laid on hot ; no other metallic solution should be mixed with it. A solution of sulphate of copper (commonly called blue vitriol), in the proportion of about half a pound of sulphate of copper to one gallon of water, used hot, makes an excellent wash, and is cheaper than the preceding one. A strong solution of sulphate of iron is sometimes used, but is not so effectual as that of copper, and sometimes a mixture of the two solutions has been used. Coal tar is said to have been found beneficial, but the strong smell is a great objection to its use. *See* " Timber, Preservation of."

Dry Stock.—Sawn wood dried to a condition that admits of it being sold, shipped, etc., in a state for safe travelling or passing into consumption. The drying may be by exposure to the atmosphere termed " weather-drying," or by " stoving " or " desiccating "; the latter system is largely followed by the merchants and shippers of the United States.

Dublin Standard.—An established measure for timber identical with the old London standard, now fallen into disuse. It consisted of 120 pieces, 12 ft. 3 in. × 9 in., or 270 cubic feet.

Duchess Slates.—Those measuring 24 in. × 12 in.

Dunnage.—(1) Wood of a grade below that recognized in market quotations. Cull lumber. (2) Loose wood laid at the bottom of the hold of a ship to rest the cargo upon or in timber yards to pile deals on.

Duodecimal.—*See* " Decimal."

Duramen.—The heartwood of an exogenous tree.

Dutch Balks.—Square timber, generally of spruce, shipped to Holland, 16 to 28 ft. in length and 10 in. to 15 in. square.

Dutch Elm (*Ulmus suberosa*).—A variety of the elm with large thick leaves and a fungous bark. Introduced into England by William III and much used at the time for trimly clipped hedges. Known also as the Cork-barked Elm.

Dutch Wainscot.—In England it implied imported wood. The trade formerly was in the hands of the Dutch, who obtained their supplies from the Upper Rhine and in the Baltic, from Memel and Riga. *See* " Wainscot."

E

Eave and Eaves.—That part of a roof which projects beyond the face of a wall ; the lower border or part of a roof. It is the base-word of " eavesdropper "—an illicit listener, and " eavedropping "—an old legal right of an eave projecting over a neighbour's land, and often the origin of a narrow space, and even a passage between independent properties.

Eaves Board and Boards.—An arris-fillet nailed across the rafters at the eaves of a roof, to raise the slates a little. Otherwise " Tilting-fillet " or " Fillets."

Eaves Gutter and Gutters.—A gutter attached to the eaves ; variantly termed " eaves spout." It may be seated on a wall, and not overhang neighbouring properties, which latter would register the fact that the owner had no "right of eavedropping" over his neighbour's land or properties. *See* "Eave and Eaves."

Ebony.—A hard and durable dark coloured, mostly East Indian, wood, black, green, brown or red, in which the colours may be mixed. The black wood is the product of *Diospyros ebenus*, and is considered the best, but not the most valuable, which honour belongs to "coromandel-wood," varied, particoloured and veined, rarely seen other than in veneer-form for high-class work. Fuller says a negro is "God's image cut in ebony."

Edge Grain.—An American term applied to lumber when it is sawn along the radius of the annual rings, that is the edge of the annual rings shown on the face. Principally used in reference to flooring, which is commonly produced in this way. Synonymous with Comb Grain and Vertical grain (*which see*).

Edger.—A machine used in sawmills to square-edge waney boards.

Edge Tool and Edge Tools.—A steel instrument having a sharp edge, the manufacture of which is a special or distinct class of trade. Its headlines are the coarser or commoner class of tools or instruments, such as "plane-irons," "chisels," "axes," "adzes," "gauges," etc.

Edging Benches.—*See also* "Lumber Trimmer" *and* "Slashers," in which two or more saws, the distance between which is easily adjustable, are used for edging planks and boards, the wood being fed forward by powerful roller feed.

Egyptian Balks.—Small square timbers 3 in. × 3 in. to 5 in. × 5 in. Squareness is here a trade-term only ; in practice a 3-in. balk may have, and usually has, a 3-in. round top. The log may have had a 6-in. or larger bottom, and when hewn possess a 3-in. square butt and hold its square half length up, the top part more or less being waney ; larger squares ditto.

Elm.—The English name of the different species of the genus *Ulmus* of Linnæus. There are many species, about a third of which are natives of Britain. They yield a useful wood whose durability is most marked in water. Operators who habitually work upon it do not claim that its odour is pleasing, as is generally the case with oak. Introduced into England by the Romans. The common elm is *U. campestris* ; the Dutch elm, *U. suberosa* ; the Cornish elm, *U. nitens* ; and the wych elm, *U. Montana*. The last named is mostly found in the North of England and Scotland.

Encaustic Tiles or Floors.—Highly ornamented floors composed of tiles in which patterns of varied colours are impressed or bedded in the face of the tiles ; literally they are " enamelled tiles," in which they differ from self-coloured or tesselated tiles (*which see*).

End Grain.—The transverse section of a log or piece of timber.

Endless Chain Feed Benches.—Saw benches in which an endless travelling chain is used to feed the material past the saw. A type of bench generally used for splitting sleeper blocks into sleepers.

Endogens.—A vegetable class whose substance is formed by successive additions from the inside, as in the palm family.

Ends.—Short pieces of sawn wood cut from the long lengths at the time of assortment and shipment. Firewood, deal and batten ends run from 1 to $5\frac{1}{2}$ ft. ; ends for stowage of cargoes 6 to 8 ft. ; Riga ends, 6 to 9 ft. ; White Sea ends, 11 ft. and under. *See also* " Deal and Batten Ends."

Eng or In (*Dipterocarpus tuberculatus*).—A valuable hardwood timber, the largest forests of which are situated in Burma. It is used sometimes in place of teak.

Engineer and Engineering.—Properly a person employed on the larger kind of engines or in the application of them to various purposes. The trade of the engineer is now specialized ; that connected with " wood " or " timber " is rated " saw-mill engineering " and " wood-working engineering " ; that of building, brick-making, cement and plaster, " manufacturing machinery " ; that of masonry and striking, " stone-sawing machinery." *See* " Machine Sawing " *and* " Machine Saw or Saws."

English Wainscot.—A term applied to selected Dutch wainscot as shipped from Riga. It is one created by the English and their desire to obtain the best of the wood. *See* " Wainscot."

Equilibrium Frames.—Either log or deal frames arranged to deal with two logs or deals at one time. Provided with two saw-frames driven by double crankshaft, so that one frame balances the other, thus permitting the frame to run faster than would otherwise be possible.

Errors Excepted.—Abbreviated thus : E. E. or E. & O. E. (errors and omissions excepted). Sometimes written at the foot of invoices in order that they may be corrected should any error afterwards be discovered.

Escutcheon.—The metal shield to a keyhole.

Evergreen Oak (*alias* " Holm Oak," *which see*).—The tendency of oaks as they travel south or to the sub-tropical climes of the Northern Hemisphere is to retain their leaves through the winter or to become evergreens, and to diminish from forest trees to shrubs.

Ex Quay.—A term signifying that the seller agrees to sell the goods to the buyer as on the quay at bill-of-lading destination.

Ex Ship.—The name applied to the system of selling goods delivered from ship's side, under which the vendor pays the freight to the port of discharge and the purchaser the landing and other charges.

Excelsior.—The American term for wood wool.

Excrescence.—A growth on any part of a living tree ; an abnormal enlargement like a wart or tumour. In the instance of felled or dead trees, or the wood coming into the hands of a timber-manipulator, it is invariably termed a " Burr " (*which see*).

Exfoliate and Exfoliation.—To separate, or separating in itself, as in laminated or flakey matter scaling off. The outer bark of birch-trees and plane-trees, periodically shedding the outer layer of their barks, offer arboreous examples of this terminology.

Exogens.—A vegetable class which augment their woody matter by additions to the outside of that which is first formed. In exogenous trees the medullary rays radiate from the medulla (the pith or marrow of a tree) to the bark. These rays are not as a rule apparent to the naked eye and are said therefore to be " obscure," the exceptions being mainly oaks, beeches and planes.

Export.—Allied to " bearing " or " carrying "—to convey or transport goods from one country to another, the goods themselves in a collective sense being " exports."

Exporter.—A person who exports or sends goods away to markets in distant countries.

Eye Tree or **D.**—The head of the handle of a spade.

F

Face.—The lower concave portion of a saw tooth.

Face and Facing are architectural terms in common use, as "face of a house," "a brick," "a piece of wood," "a block of stone," "inner and outer face of a wall," etc. "Facing" is applied to a substance possessing a face, as "a facing brick," "a facing stone," etc., or a piece of wrought-wood used to face or give a finish to an object it is desirable to hide. A facing may thus be of "plaster," "brick," "stone" or "wood." A "veneer" is a facing of superior quality on a groundwork of ordinary wood.

Face Measure.—*See* "Surface Measure."

Face Side.—That side of a board which shows the best quality.

Facings.—Dressed boards with or without mouldings used in "seen" or exposed places.

Fagot.—A bundle of sticks for fuel ; also applied to a single stick.

Fall, In the Fall.—In the autumn, at the fall of the leaf.

Fall of Timber.—A portion of woodland or area of standing trees marked out for the axe or ready for leading out of the wood.

Fall Shipment.—An American term for shipment after the leaves begin to fall, but before the end of the year, i.e., autumn shipment.

Faller or Feller.—One who fells trees.

"Falling Cut."—This is the first, or "breaking down cut," in a tree or log, and, out of consideration of the labour of getting it on and off the pit, was charged for and paid as two cuts. This custom is still followed with "machine-sawing," but where only one cut is wanted, i.e., one saw put in the frame, it is poor business for the mill. *See* "Machine Sawing."

Falling Moulds.—The two moulds to form the back and under surface of a handrail to finish the squaring.

Fans (Exhaust).—Used for exhausting the air in pipes connected with different machines in a woodworking mill, causing the refuse from the machine to be drawn into the pipe and through the fan, which discharges it into a cyclone or other receptacle.

F.A.S.—(1) A shipping term, "free alongside," which denotes that the price includes delivery alongside the vessel without cost to the buyer. (2) An abbreviation used by American lumbermen to designate the combined grade of Firsts and Seconds.

Fascia.—A band or fillet, or any flat member with a little projection, as the band of an architrave.

Fashion in Woods.—The old English fashionable wood, before the discovery of the great continent of America, was native-oak, which in furniture was inlayed with black or bog-oak and white or yellow woods ; walnut gained a place later in furniture, and then, in the eighteenth century, came the red cedars and mahoganies of Central America, which, with their rich warm colour, created a revolution lasting over a century, the ornament connected therewith being the " roe " and " feather." The nineteenth century closed with " American black walnut " being the fashionable wood. *See* " Figure in Woods."

Fast.—In saw filing, a saw when raised up is said to be " fast " in those places that come up to the straight-edge.

Fathom.—A measure of wood containing 216 cubic ft. ; thus, timber 6 ft. cube, or 12 ft. long, 6 ft. broad and 3 ft. high is a fathom.

Fault and Faulty.—A building term implying that some substance, the ground, a roof or a beam of wood, has developed subsidence, disrepair, or weakness, in some part and is rated as useless, faulty, defective or imperfect either in the plan or design. Also applied to wood, and faulty pieces are common.

Featherboarding.—A covering of boards, in which the edge of one board overlaps a part of the one next it ; and also called Weather Boarding.

Featheredge.—A board thinner on one edge than it is on the other. The term is also used in America to denote an over-sharpened cutting edge.

Feed.—In sawing timber, the linear length of log, expressed in inches, which is cut at each revolution of the saw.

Felloe or Felly.—The exterior wooden rim, or a segment of the rim, of a wheel, supported by the spokes.

Felloe Boring and Spoke Tanging Machine.—The felloe which forms part of the rim of a wheel is fixed to a little table with self-centring apparatus which holds the felloe while being bored. The same machine is used for tanging the spokes of a wheel after they have been driven in the nave, a tanging chuck being used in place of the boring tool.

Felly (plural Fellies).—*See* " Felloe."

Fence, Fencing, and Fencings.—Terms in architecture, trade, landed estates, the forest and the saw-mill ; a fence, if of wood, has a terminology all its own, especially so if treated with some preservatives other than tar or paint, or is "close-boarded," "capped" or otherwise treated architecturally. The material may be oak, fir, chestnut or less-used woods, whole, riven, sawn, rough or square; as a "ring-fence" it may encircle an estate or consist of a wall or hedge as a park-fence, or the palisade or fence of a house. Applied to machinery, it is at once a "guide," as to a saw, and a "guard" or "defence."

nder.—A piece of timber or other substance slung over the side of a vessel to protect it in narrow or confined waters; a "fender-pile," used in open or sheet-piling; to "fend-off" a floating or moving body; a "fire-guard," to limit or counteract the danger or spread of fire in a building.

nestra (in architecture).—*Latin* for a window. A term much used on the European continent. In a building imperfectly lighted it is correct English to say "the fenestration is poor," and in the opposite case, "the fenestration is good."

Idle Back.—A compressed form of figure very pronounced in sycamore wood, hence its selection for "fiddle-backs." *See* "Ram's Horn," an equivalent term.

gure in Mahogany.—"Roe" is that alternate streak or flake of light and shade running with the grain, or from end to end of the log. If the streak be regular in size and unbroken, it is thought little of; but if the flakes be broad and the light and dark parts have a tendency to blend, yet strongly contrast, and are variedly broken in their progress, then it is considered fine. "Mottle" is that mark in the wood which, in a polished board, at first view appears like something raised upon the surface, and a person not infrequently feels to ascertain if it be smooth. It is varied in form so much that many names have been used to designate its several kinds, of which the following are some. "Stop Mottle" chiefly arises from angular grain, and is in broad flashes, frequently diverging from a centre like the foot of a bird, in contradistinction to "Fiddle Mottle," which runs in nearly even streaks, as on the back of a fiddle; and "Ram Mottle" is sometimes similar to Fiddle, only it is in larger and longer marks. Mottle runs even across the grain. There are also "Plum" and "Peacock" mottle; this last resembles the tail of a bird. *See also* "Mahogany."

gure in Woods is an interesting detail. The terms are largely drawn from common objects of a household or familiar character. Oak has the "silver grain" or "plash"; maple, the "bird's-eye"; ash, the "ram's horn"; the "American plane," lacewood, and an Australian tree, "honeysuckle figure" or "wood"; Burr-pollard oak, "cat's-paw" and "fan figure"; "satin wood," from its satiny appearance.

E

See " Sawing, Radial and Tangential," *and* " Silver Grain."
See also " Figure in Mahogany."

Filer.—One who fits saws in a sawmill or other woodworking plant.

Fillet.—A small moulding, generally rectangular in section, and having the appearance of a narrow band.

Filing Machine for Small Band Saws.—A machine in which a file is used for sharpening the teeth of small band saws, generally used when the teeth are too small to be conveniently sharpened by means of an emery wheel.

Fine Grain.—Wood is said to have a fine grain when the annual rings of growth are narrow.

Fir and Firwood.—" Fir " is a North-West of Europe term, its Italian substitute being " pine." This seems to account for the latter taking such strong root in America, where the first white settlers were of Latin stock. In Britain both terms obtain. Instance, " Scots fir " and " Scots pine " is one and the same thing.

> "That pine of mountain race,
> The fir, the Scotch fir, never out of place."—*Scott.*

" Firwood " is thus the produce of the " fir " or " pine." *See* " Pine."

Fireproofing Timber.—Various processes and chemicals have been claimed to render wood uninflammable or to powerfully retard the action of fire. That most in vogue at present is known as " Oxylene," in which the chemicals employed are non-volatile, stable and claimed to be without detrimental effect on any wood, metal or paint with which it is brought in contact.

Firewood.—In the import timber trade, by the term firewood is meant deal, batten, board and planchette ends of from 1 to $5\frac{1}{2}$ ft. in length.

Firewood (*alias* Cook-wood).—Is often brought over as the property of the shipowner, a perquisite of the captain, or as fuel for the ship's cook, and mostly sold on arrival to be overhauled for box-making, the residue or waste passing into firewood. Box-making has grown to such large proportions in the wood trade that entire cargoes are chartered for and shipped from the foreign saw-mills. *See* " Box-wood " *and* " Packing-case Wood."

Firsts and Seconds.—A grading in quality of hardwoods. Also termed Prime Quality in the United Kingdom. In America expressed " Fas " or " F.A.S."

Fissile.—Having the grain in such a direction as to make the wood suitable for cleaving or splitting.

tting, Fittings, and Fitter.—A fitting may be of varied material, viz., house or shop fittings or fixtures of wood ; gas, water and electric fittings. A cognate word, " fitment " (= something adapted to a purpose) is now considered as obsolete. " Fitter " is a skilled workman much in evidence, whose particular calling is his prefix, as " shop-fitter," " office-fitter," " gas-fitter," etc., etc.

ve-ply Veneer.—A piece of built-up veneer composed of five pieces glued one to the other, some with the grain crossed.

akes (*see* " Fleakes ")—Field hurdles.

atting is the process of sawing through the flat or thinnest way of boards, usually called flat-cutting or ripping.

eak, Tray or Hurdle.—With slight exceptions, mean one and the same thing—a portable " wooden fence " or an " improvised gate " ; light constructions of posts, riven rails and struts, each about 6 ft. long, and when fixed, about a yard high. This is a special branch of the wood-trade, relegated to agricultural purposes, one interesting, like the " clog-sole " trade, inasmuch as the operatives go to the woods and there perform their labours, and deliver their finished work. The labour is piece-work.

eam Tooth.—A tooth of a saw shaped like an isosceles triangle ; a peg tooth.

eck and Flecked.—A spot, a dapple, or a variation in pattern or figure, applied to veneers or fancy woods ; thus, maple may be " flecked " with " bird's-eye figure " and oak with " mirror " or " ray figure." In the instance of mahogany, " dapple " is the equivalent (*which see; also* " Figure in Wood ").

exible Arm Sandpapering Machine.—A comparatively small disc is used, over which sandpaper is tightly strained. The disc revolves on a spindle carried by hinged arms attached to a slide. The work is placed on a table and the disc moved slowly over the surface of the work until a smooth face is produced on the latter.

ght.—" A staircase " springing or rising from one floor to another without a landing intervening. In the instance of such a landing the staircase would be in " two flights." *See* " Staircase."

tch.—(1) A large piece of a sawed log ; commonly applied to a part of a log of greater thickness than a plank or board. In the veneer-cutting trade it might be half a log, a third, or even a quarter ; strictly speaking, it is a superior term to " slab." (2) In America, a thick piece of timber with wane on the edge.

Flitch Frame.—*See* " Deal Frames."

Flitterns are young oak trees, the bark of which is richer in tannin than older trees.

Float.—(1) A small raft of wood ; (2) A timber-wagon ; (3) A plasterer's tool of wood or steel—that of wood is used to give a " rough " or " dry face " ; that of steel, a " smooth, glossy face." *See* " Trowel."

Floated Deals.—A term applied to Canadian pine and spruce deals conveyed on rafts for shipment, which are sometimes a little discoloured in transit.

Floating or Floated.—Architectural terms applied to the second of three coats of plaster on walls, expressed (1) " rendered," (2) " floated," and (3) " set " (*see* " Rendered " *and* " Set "). In the instance of plastering on laths, (1) is expressed by " pricking up " (*which see*).

Floating Policy.—The insurance in a lump sum of goods in different places.

Flogging.—The two hardest kinds of work a carpenter was called upon to perform, before machinery in the latter half of the nineteenth century stepped in to relieve him of the major part of it, were " flogging floor-boards," taking them from the saw and preparing them for laying—now done by floor-board planing or chipping machines—and " sticking mouldings," i.e., working them. *See* " Stick and Sticking."

Floor.—The level ground, brick, stone, wood or other substance that forms the lower or horizontal face of a covered building, or an apartment below or above ground.

Floor or Flooring Boards.—Boards of various thickness and fashion in width. In the eighteenth, and first part of the nineteenth, century they were broad, the reverse being the present order of the day. Since machinery has been employed in the " flogging " or dressing, they are usually " planed, tongued and grooved."

Flooring and Matchboarding Machines.—High-speed planing machines for producing tongued and grooved flooring and matching. Usually provided with a fixed knife to give a smooth surface to the face side of the board and fitted with powerful feed gear. The pressures are also different to those used on a moulding machine.

Flooring, A Square of.—In a prepared or manufactured form is 100 superficial feet. The customary square of flooring, which was for many years followed in the London auction sales, is now abolished. The following were the number of lineal feet that were reckoned for the various widths :—

9-inch.	8-inch.	7½-inch.	7-inch.	6¾-inch.	6½-inch.
140-feet.	160-feet.	170-feet.	180-feet.	185-feet.	190-feet.

6¼-inch.	6-inch.	5¾-inch.	5½-inch.	5¼ inch.	5-inch.
195-feet.	200-feet.	210-feet.	220-feet.	230-feet.	240-feet.

4½-inch.	4-inch	3½-inch.	3-inch.
270-feet.	300-feet	350-feet.	400-feet.

For comparative table of actual and nominal measurement, showing the gain for freight, *see* Appendix II.

Floor Joists.—Joists, strong in character, to carry on their upper edges wood and other floors.

Flume.—(1) An inclined trough in which water runs, used in transporting logs or timbers. Flumes are in use on the Pacific coast of North America, Austria, Switzerland, Norway, and other mountainous districts of the world. (2) A water slide.

Flutings or **Flutes** (Lat. *fluo*).—The hollows or channels cut perpendicularly in the shafts of columns, etc. They are used in all the classical kinds of architecture except the Tuscan. In some instances the hollows or flutes are filled with " ovalos " in their lower parts, in which case they are termed " reeds " (*which see*).

Font Cover.—A wooden lid or cover of a font. By certain ecclesiastical injunctions in the Middle Ages such covers were imperative, hence, during the last century of restoration of old churches or monuments, the custom has been revived, followed, and elaborated in altitude and design until they have become important or crowning features.

Foot-power Lathes.—Small lathes worked by foot power.

Fore (in Foreman, Forecourt and Foremast).—As a prefix, implies priority in time, place, order or importance ; hence a " foreman " is the chief servant of a trader or manufacturer, having charge of men or machinery " Forecourt " of a building—the front court, which implies an erection possessing, like certain halls and colleges, more than one court. Foremast, a mast placed in the forepart or forecastle of a ship.

Forest and Forester.—Appear to be terms that landed in this country with the Normans. Original form seems to be preserved in the Italian *Foresto* = wild, savage, foreign. It is curious that in England a forest is read to imply a great tract of woodland, but in Scotland, where a treeless area is viewed as a forest, the reverse is actually the case. " Forester " is an officer appointed to watch a forest, preserve the game, and institute suits for trespasses. *See* " Forest, Science " *and* " Afforest. '

Forest Science.—Knowledge of all things appertaining to the cultivation and management of forests, including the various trees which may be cultivated to advantage and the uses to which their woods may be put, with the mode of their propagation in various soils. *See* "Forest and Forester."

Foxy.—A red tinge in the wood of a tree past maturity, the decay first developing in the butt or root end of the stem, and the tree becomes "stag-headed."

Frame.—An open structure of 6 × 6 × 6 ft., in which to measure small pieces of timber in bulk, such as lathwood, firewood, etc.

Frame Saw.—This machine consists of a fixed horizontal frame, with rollers at short distances apart, in which the wood or tree is laid ; at the end of this is another frame in a vertical position, in which a number of saws are fixed and set as far apart as the desired thickness of the boards to be cut. A rapid up-and-down motion is given to these saws by the machinery, and at the same time the wood is pulled forward on the rollers. This was a common term before machinery came in, and is so now where machinery is not present. It was a large thin-blade pit-saw in a wooden frame, arranged to be worked by two men. In this case it is distinguished from the thicker blade, called the "whip saw."

Free on Board.—Goods placed free alongside and free of all shipping charges or other expenses to the purchasers. Usually contracted to " F.o.b." In French "F.a.b." (Franco à bord).

Freight.—Usually means the price payable for the carriage of goods by sea or for the use of a ship or part of a ship for such purpose. The freight is most commonly fixed by the charter-party or bill of lading ; but in the absence of any formal stipulations on the subject, it would be due according to the custom or usage of trade.

Fret or Fretwork.—Primarily frieze ornamentation or enrichment ; a favourite form of design having its ground or base perforated. The characteristic form of "fret" or "fretwork" in the nineteenth century was that employed for the fronts of pianos, in which it formed the principal ornament. It represents the finest or most intricate form of sawn wood.

Fret Saw Machine.—A saw for cutting fretwork. When driven by power, the machines have a short stroke and run at a very high speed.

Frieze or Frize.—The middle division of an entablature which lies between the architrave and the cornice ; it may be plain or enriched and even sculptured ; sometimes made to swell out in the middle, when it is said to be "cushioned" or "pulvinated." Friezes may, according to situation, be wrought in stone, brick, wood or plaster.

Frieze Panel.—The upper panel of a door of six or more panels, or the upper panel in wainscotting.

Frieze Rail.—The rail next below top rail of six or more panels.

Frith, By Frith and Fell.—" By wold and wild, wood and common." Frith is the Welsh *frith* or *friz*, and means a woody place. Chaucer used the term to connote a wood, which, in the Saxon tongue, from implying *peace*, defined a sacred wood or sanctuary, hence " Frithstool "—a chair of sanctuary.

Frowy Stuff.—A term applied to brittle or soft timber.

Frush.—A term used to describe wood that is short in the grain and brittle.

Fuel.—Is matter which serves as aliment to fire. Wood in a crude state or as charcoal plays a large part, especially so where pit-coal does not obtain. Where wood is plentiful it is, on the score of cleanliness, preferred. " Wood fuel " the world over is an immense business, and the volume of that material consumed is beyond all count or tally, and from " stick " to " yule-log " boasts an extensive vocabulary.

Fungi (the plural of fungus).—Under this name botanists range the mushroom class of plants, a large number of which are microscopic, growing upon other plants or substances, with the appearance of mouldiness and mildew. Instance, the *Merulius lacrymans*, or weeping fungus that is mainly answerable for the destruction of timber placed in damp or humid situations, where its action is popularly termed " Dry rot " (*which see*). The wood in a reduced form has a dry appearance on the face, not unlike burnt or charred wood, and to this extent it is entitled to its popular name.

Furniture.—In architecture, the visible brasswork or ironmongery of doors, windows, shutters, cupboards, etc., in which it is a compound, as " door-furniture," " cupboard-furniture," etc., of a hall, house or building. In a general sense it implies the goods, utensils, etc., of housekeeping, in which ironmongery again finds a place, following in the train of wood, as " drawer," " desk," etc., furniture. Ditto in " coffin furniture."

Furniture Beetle.—Practically a microscopic insect whose larvæ or grub bores in and feeds upon wood ; it is the *Annobium tessalatum* of the naturalist, and superstition has endowed it with the fearsome name of " Death-watch." Its mechanical action is truly the cause of " Dry rot," where the wood is bored and runned, and a dry powder takes its place or is omitted. *See* ' Dry Rot.'

Furrings.—Short pieces attached to the feet of rafters of a roof for carrying the eaves beyond the line of the wall.

G

Gable.—The top of a wall that conforms to the slope of the roof covering or abutting against it ; consequent terms are " Gabled-roof," and, in the instance of a house-end so finished, " Gable-end."

Gambo.—A local term in Mid-Wales and district for a two-wheeled vehicle, with a stiff axle and stiff body without sides. Used almost entirely for carting pitprops sawn to length.

Gang.—A body or batch of men, engaged on time or piece-work to load or unload cargoes of wood, etc., or to store, yard or warehouse the goods.

Gang-board.—The board or way for the rowers to pass from stem to stern, and where the mast was laid when it was unshipped.

Gang Mill.—The American name for a log frame.

Ganger.—The appointed or nominated head or foreman of a gang, when in clearly defined association with a ship or ships loading or unloading cargo ; he may be variantly known as a " Stevedore " (*which see*).

Gang-plank.—Usually a plank not less than 11 in. broad, on which *gangers* and members of their gangs run or carry deals, boards, etc., when piling goods in docks or timber yards.

Gangway.—(1) An alley or way in a timber yard between the piles of deals, etc., so called from being the runs of the gangs in yarding or piling the yarded stocks. (2) The board with cleats or bars of wood by which passengers walk into or out of a ship or steamer.

Gantry.—A sort of raised tramway working on rails laid along the top of two parallel beams supported on two rows of standards.

Gauge.—(1) The thickness of a saw blade. (2) Any instrument to measure the thickness or dimensions of an object to a standard size, such as the size of timber, the thickness of, a saw etc.

Gean.—Another name for the Wild Cherry. *See* " Cherry."

Genoa Prime.—An American classification of pitch pine boards and planks. The boards vary in size from 1 in. to 1¾ in. × 8 and up, the planks from 2 in. to 2¾ in. × 8 and up, and the deals from 3 in. to 5 in. × 8 and up.

Genus, *plural* **Genera.**—In Botany, a genus consists of such a group or assemblage of species as agree both structurally and physiologically, as respects the organs of fructification, reproduction, or perpetuation, and at the same time have a general resemblance in habit. *See* "Natural Order."

Georgia Pine.—A trade name for pitch pine from the Atlantic region.

Gimlet.—A carpenter's tool for boring small holes in wood, as the diminutive "let" or "et" implies. Its initial syllable is possibly another form of "wimble," a larger tool of the kind.

Girder.—A main beam to support the joists of a floor, etc.

Girdling or Ringing.—A method occasionally employed in preparing trees for felling, notably and almost exclusively taken in the case of Indian Teak. The process is to cut completely away a ring of the sap wood at the base of the trunk in order to arrest the upward flow of the life-giving sap. This effectually kills the tree. In the case of teak, the tree is afterwards allowed to stand two or more years, and in the meantime the wood loses much weight and so can be floated on the watercourses. Otherwise its weight when green would debar this method of transport.

Glue Heating Apparatus.—An apparatus for heating one or a number of glue-pots, consisting of a chamber containing water heated by exhaust steam, gas or electricity.

Gnar and Gnarled.—A knot, or knotted, as in *gnarled oak*, i.e., full of knots ; Chaucer wrote it "gnarre," a form now noted as obsolete.

Goat or Saugh Willow (*Salix caprea*).—A native of England. Non-combustible and not liable to split (a heavy blow merely causing an indentation) to a high degree. Used for brake blocks. *See* "Willow."

Goodwill.—An expression signifying the trade connection and name of the vendor, when sold along with any profession, trade or business. In law it appears to mean the probability of the vendor's customers continuing their custom, and the vendor may not solicit their business away from the purchaser.

Gothenburg Standard.—A measurement of pitprops equalling 180 cub. ft.

Gouge.—A carpenter's or woodworker's tool of the "chisel" type, but half circular or partially in section, used where hollows or flutes are required—an important instrument in "wood-carving," or in cutting holes, channels and grooves.

Grace or Days of Grace.—In commerce, a customary number of days allowed for the payment of a note, or bill of exchange, other than those payable on demand. In Great Britain they are *three* days of grace.

Grade and Graded.—Terms in the wood trade, as "high-grade," "low-grade," "poor-grade" and "graded," meaning goods examined or assorted into "grades" or qualities. They are not dictionary words in this advanced sense, but there denote "steps" or "degrees." "Grade" and "Graded" have their equivalents in "Assortment" and "Assorted" (*which latter see*).

Graft.—A small shoot or bud of a tree inserted in a cut or dug into a "stock" or "young tree" intended to be its future support.

Grain.—In wood, a term used with reference to the arrangement or direction of the wood elements and to the relative width of the growth rings.

Granadillo (*Amyris balsamafera*).—A red, figured, aromatic, resinous, hardwood imported from Cuba. Used for turnery.

Gravel Board or Plank.—The horizontal board placed on its edge upon the ground at the bottom of a pale fence.

Gravel Board Stumps.—Supports to the gravel board driven into the ground between the posts to support the gravel board.

Green Oak.—Oak which, owing to the action of fungus under certain conditions, turns vivid green. The colour being permanent the wood is in great request, but attempts to obtain this colour by artificial means have not been successful.

Greenheart (*Nectandra rodiœi*).—A large and important tree, a native of Guiana and tropical America, the wood of which is proof against the action of sea-worms, hence it is largely used for dock and harbour work and ship-building. *See* "Snape or Snape-ended."

Gregorian Tree.—The gallows, so named from three successive hangmen—the Brandons, whose front names were Gregory.

> . . . "And he
> Doth fear his fate from the Gregorian tree."
> —*Mercuitus Pragmaticus*, 1641.

Grinding Machines (for Woodworkers).—A name generally describing the various machines for sharpening saws and cutting tools in which a revolving wheel of abrasive material is used—developments of the old hand- or foot-turned "grindstones" (*which see*).

Grinding Rest.—A rest attached to a grinding machine for supporting a tool while under the action of a grinding wheel.

Grindstone (hand, foot or machine).—A revolving stone used for sharpening tools by abrasion. *See* "Grinding Machines."

Groove.—A long trench or hollow cut or ploughed by a tool, mostly on one edge of a floor or lining board to receive the "tongue" (*which see*) of another board.

Grooving and Rebating Benches.—Saw benches in which the spindle has a rising and falling adjustment to facilitate the operations of grooving, rebating, tenoning, etc.

Grooving-plane.—A joiner's instrument for making small grooves, one of a pair of "tonguing and grooving planes," mostly employed in making tongued and grooved joints ; from the tongues being produced to "match" or fit in the grooves they are variantly termed "matched-joints" and the tools "match-planes," hence "match" or "matched boards" (*which see*).

Ground-off Saws.—Circular saws bevelled off on one side, and of greater gauge at the centre than at the circumference. Straight saws of greater gauge at the front than at the back.

Growing Timber.—Timber trees are those which serve for building or reparation of houses (such as oak, ash or elm), and are of the age of twenty years or upwards. Hedges, bushes, willows, osiers, sallows and ornamental shrubs are not timber, neither are trees which may become timber until they are of twenty years' growth.

Guaiacum.—Another name for lignum vitæ (*which see*).

Gullet or **Throat** is the depth of a saw tooth from the point to the root.

Gum Trees.—*See* "Satin Walnut."

Gummer.—A tool used to cut out the throats of a saw.

Gumming.—To grind out the throats of a saw.

Gun Stocks.—The "stock" or block from which the finished article is evolved. Since the introduction of the gun the chosen wood has been "European walnut," hence in wartime the destruction of that class of tree has been enormous. Beech, and other woods, especially American, have been pressed into that service, but walnut has not been ousted.

Gurjun (*Dipterocarpus turbinatus*).—A dense hard Indian timber.

H

Habitat.—A word used generally by naturalists to express the nature of the situation or locality in which a tree or plant grows.

Hacmatack.—*See* " Tamarack."

Haft and Heft.—Expressive of the handle of a tool. Terms now practically identical, but which may have had different roots in the old Saxon tongue.

Half-timbering.—In " half-timber " houses, etc., meaning framed beams, posts, or studs, with the spaces or panels filled in with clay, stone-slabs, bricks or two-sided lath and plaster work ; a primitive or old form of walling, abandoned in towns after the Great Fire of London in 1666 in favour of stone, brick, iron or concrete. In walls consist of " post and pan or panel work." *See* " Wall " *and* " Post and Pan."

Hammer-beam.—A beam, or really two beams, in the principal of a Gothic roof, occupying the same level as the principal-beam or tie-beam of a " King " or " Queen-post " roof. They represent the latter beam with its central part cut out, or the tie broken ; constructionally it is a weak roof, the gain being confined to obtaining a greater idea of height with the central portion of the tie-beam absent. *See* " Collar-beam."

Hammer Mark.—Distinguishing marks driven into the wood by a blow from a hammer. *See* " Brands."

Hand-barrow.—A barrow or vehicle borne by the hands of men, and without a wheel.

Hand-feed Planing Machines.—Machines in which the material is fed past the cutters by hand, generally referring to a machine with horizontal revolving cutter block and tables to support the work as it is passed over the cutters.

Hand-hawk.—A poetic term ; a tool reserved to the plasterer, and in a minor degree in the kindred trades of mason and brick-layer ; a square, thin, wood board, held in one hand in a horizontal position by a perpendicular wood handle ; the act of using it is figurative of " the hawk in hand."

Hand-hook. A short " steel-hook " with a wooden handle, similar to that of a gimlet ; the point is sharp, and when pressed on the end of a plank or deal enables it to be lifted up, and when on the edge of the piece to be turned over. *See* "Hick and Hicking." Some hand-hooks are entirely of iron, with two hooks, one near the thumb and the other the little finger.

Hand-masts.—Round timber and poles from the Baltic used for masts and other purposes. A technical term applied by the mast maker to a round spar, of at least 24 in , and not exceeding 72 in. in circumference. They are measured by the hand of 4 in.

Handrail. *See* "Staircase."—The master craftwork of the staircase-builder, the "geometrical" or "continuous-hand-rail" being the highest of its class ; like its base, it has an interesting nomenclature, starting with a "newel" or "scroll," "twist," "straight-length," "ramp," "swan-neck," "wreath," "turn," and finishing on a landing. *See* "Scroll," "Handrail-sections," "Staircase," "Balusters," *and* "Rail and Railing."

Handrailing.—The science or craftmanship of making handrails, which embraces the highest reaches of geometry, and con-stitutes a special branch to which few workmen attain. It is a department in woodworking that has called for a number of learned English and American works or publications ; but away from the use of newels, features to which the twentieth-century architects and builders incline, it has not, as a high-art, been so much followed as was the case in the preceding century. *See* "Rail and Railing."

Handrail Punch.—A short steel tool or implement "bull-nosed" at the active end, used for turning the nuts of handrail screws by punching, when the "nuts and washers" are in action, tightening up the handrail-joints in fixing. *See* "Handrail."

Handrail Screws.—Short iron rods with threads for iron nuts at either end nicked on their outer face or periphery to enable them to be turned with a "handrail punch." Such screws are used in making "heaven-" or" butt-" joints, and came into use in the eighteenth century to replace "built-up" or "jointless" handrails. *See* "Handrail."

Handrail Sections.—Starting from the sixteenth century we find them of ponderous size, as indeed were the newels and balusters elaborately moulded, and mostly with a small bead or roll moulding for "hand-hold" on the top. At the opening of the nineteenth century the cross sections were small plain 2½ in. rounds or moulded sides, with little of the Tudor feeling left. They are still usually "ogee," plain or bead-d at the sides, round or double-ogee at the top ; a

term for the latter being "toad-backed," grooved occasionally underside for balusters.

Handsale or **Hansel.**—This term was used to indicate a bargain
ratified by shaking of hands. Afterwards it was called
"hansel," and signified earnest money.

Handspike.—A sort of wooden lever for moving heavy things,
not unlike a heavy spoke. A wooden bar used with the
hand as a lever for various purposes, as in raising weights,
heaving about a windlass, etc. The gunner's handspike is
shorter and flatter than the above, and armed with two claws
for managing the artillery.

Hand Vice.—A little spring vice, worked with a screw and
thumb-nut, i.e., a thumb-screw.

Hanse Towns.—The maritime cities of Germany, which belonged
to the Hanseatic League.

Hanseatic League.—The first union of traders, established for
mutual benefit in the thirteenth century by the merchants
of certain cities in Northern Germany, later extending to
the Netherlands and Russia. The League was broken up
in 1630.

Haskinizing.—A patent method of wood preservation.

Hatch.—(1) A square or oblong opening in the deck of a ship,
forming the communication between one deck and another,
also known as "Hatchway." (2) A door or half door with
an opening over it.

Hatchet.—A small axe with a short handle, to be used with one
hand.

Hatchway.—*See* "Hatch."

Hauling Apparatus.—An apparatus consisting of a chain or rope
drum, round which the rope is coiled by gearing and by
means of which logs are hauled into a saw mill by power.

Haunching Apparatus.—An attachment, sometimes fitted to a
tenoning machine, by means of which the haunch of the
tenon is sawn out usually by means of a drunken saw fitted
to one of the spindles of the machine.

Havana Cedar (*Cedrela odorata*).—One of the many so-called
cedars that are derived from the West Indies, Central
America and other countries. This is the Cuban variety
shipped from all parts of that island. It is almost exclusively
utilized with other descriptions for cigar-box making, especially in the New York and Continental markets, the greater
portion of the supplies being directed to the first-mentioned
port.

Hawthorn (*Cratægus oxyacantha*).—With the Whitebeam the hardest and toughest of native woods, but now of very little commercial value. Used by engineers, millwrights, turners, and walking stick makers.

Hazel (*Corylus avellana*).—A soft European wood, very fine and close grained. Of small size and not durable.

Hazel Pine.—A term used in the American markets for the sapwood of red gum or satin walnut.

Heading.—The pieces of timber from which a keg or barrel head is cut.

Headings.—The word used for the tops and bottoms of casks and barrels.

Heartshakes.—Clefts or splits that follow the medullary rays from the centre outward.

Heartwood.—In Botany, the English term for *duramen*, the central part of the trunk of a tree ; the part that is passive in nature, from having undergone a hardening process (which often protects it from animal, insect or fungoid attacks) by the cells and tissues being sealed with secretionary matter peculiar to the individual species of the " hearted tree." *See* " Spine " *and* " Satin-wood."

Hedge.—Properly a thicket of thorn-bushes or other shrubs or small trees. Such a thicket planted round a field as an enclosure changes its complexion ; it becomes the English " haw " and yields " hawthorn." It is the French " haie " that gave the " hays " in our royal forests, and is identical with the Dutch " hague."

Hedge-carpenter.—A maker of gate-post and rail fences, or other matters connected with hedges and enclosures of land. In *White's Gazetteer of Notts* (1832), ten tradesmen were bracketed at Worksop, as " English Timber Merchants, [hand] Sawyers and Hedge-carpenters."

Helve.—The handle of an axe.

Hemlock.—The hemlock spruce or fir (*Tsuga Canadensis*) is a useful coniferous wood in general use in Canada. The Western Hemlock (*Tsuga Mertensiana*), which grows on the Pacific Coast, is heavier and harder and is considered superior to the Eastern variety.

Hewn.—Cut with an axe or adze.

Hick and Hicking.—Are not dictionary words, hence their origin has not been investigated. " To hick " is to raise one end of a piece of wood ; " hicking " is the work of one man in a gang of men unloading a ship or barge of sawn deals or battens; he has a " hand-hook " (*which see*) in one hand, with which he lifts the wood a few inches until he can grasp the end with both hands, when, with an easy swing, he elevates it as high as he can reach, whereon a " deal-carrier " (*which see*) runs his shoulder under and carries the piece away to the " pile " or " wagon."

Hick-joint Pointing.—In architecture, a term applied to face-joints in brickwork, which have been " raked-out " to a minor depth and repointed with a whiter or superior mortar; a variant term is " Tuck pointing " and to some extent " re-pointing." *See* " Pointing." " Hick-joint," as above, is suggestive of being a late or corrupt form of " brick-joint."

Hickory (*Carya alba*).—An American tree belonging to the walnut tribe, and yielding the nut called *Hickory nut*. A hard wood and coarse grained, used for tools and also as a substitute for ash, though it is somewhat harder than the latter.

Hip.—The external angle formed by the meeting of the sloping sides of a roof, which have their wall-plates running in different directions. *See* " Hip Roof." The opposite of " hip " is " valley."

Hip-knob or Finial.—An ornament, grotesque or pinnacle, fixed at the apex of a " hip " or " gable." In the latter instance it may variantly be termed a " gable knob," " finial," etc.

Hip Rafter.—The rafter which forms the hip of a roof. *See* " Hip."

Hip Roof.—A roof, the ends of which rise from the wall-plates with the same inclination as the other two sides. *See* " Hip."

Hip Tiles.—A special form of tile made suitable for the pitch of a roof, and to work in with a given form or make of roof-tiles. It is not uncommon for " hip-tiles " to be used on slate-covered roofs.

Hoard and Hoarding.—In architecture, the name given to the timber enclosure round a building when the latter is in course of erection, or undergoing repair or alteration.

Hog.—A machine used in America for cutting wood into chips.

Hold of a Ship.—Is between the lowest deck and the keel. In merchant vessels it holds the main part of the cargo.

Hollow.—(1) Joiner's hand-plane, one of a " set," fellow to its opposite the " round "—in " a pair of hollow and rounds "; (2) a place excavated, as " the hollow of a tree "; (3) in architecture, a concave moulding sometimes called a " casement "—usually one-sixth or one-fourth of a circle; (4) " Hollow-wall," one built in two thicknesses, leaving a cavity between, either for saving materials, or for preserving a uniform temperature in apartments.

Hollow-backed.—A board is said to be hollow-backed when a small amount of wood has been removed from the central part of the back side in order to reduce its shipping weight.

Hollow Chisel Mortising Machines.—A mortising machine which cuts a mortise by means of a square hollow chisel. An auger revolves in the centre of the chisel and bores a hole, while the corners are squared out by the chisel as it is fed into the wood. For a long mortise several holes are made one after the other in line.

Hollow Trunk.—Trees decaying in the trunk. Best treated by cleaning out all decaying matter, and when dry painting interior with creosote, then filling up with clean gravel and sand, with a surface coating of cement, adding generally a coat of tar.

Holly (*Ilex Aquifolium*).—A white and hard wood, extremely fine grained. Found all over Europe and Western Asia. Used for engravers' blocks, fancy turnery, etc. It is mainly an ornamental tree.

Holm Oak (*Quercus Ilex*) or " Evergreen Oak."—An oak known but not common in Britain, the wood of which is strong, hard and heavy. *See* " Oaks."

Hook.—The angle between the face of a tooth and a line drawn from the extreme point of the tooth perpendicular to the back of a band saw, or to the centre of a circular saw. Hook is stated in terms of inches. On a band saw it is measured between the two lines prolonged to its back ; on a circular saw it is measured along the opposite side of the triangle.

Hoppus' Measure.—A method of measuring the cubical contents of logs and other round timber. In theory it reduces a round log to its square equivalent.

Hoppus' Measurer, the old standard book of measurement of timber, is one of " customary measure " (*which see*), except in the instance of square logs, when it is " actual measure" (*which see*). The method is by string-girth, reducing the length into one fourth, called " quarter girth," and applying thereto the 144 divisor ; whereas in round timber the " actual measure " should be the 113 divisor. *See* "Customs Measure."

Hoppus' system of measurement by the 144 divisor gives the correct cubical contents of square timber, but is inaccurate in some of the calculations for unequal sided timber, and for round timber the error amounts to 27 per cent.

To ascertain the true contents of a cylindrical body by the quarter girth measurement, the divisor employed should be 113 instead of 144. This gives an exactly correct result

F

if the body measured is absolutely cylindrical, but the trunks of trees are seldom quite perfect cylinders, and therefore some allowance must be made for their divergences.

To ascertain the true contents by measurement at the diameter, the divisor necessary to be used is 183, and the result will be the same as that obtained by the quarter girth measurement with the 113 divisor.

The various systems of measurement may be compared in Mr. Burt's "Round Timber Measurement Tables," as he publishes complete tables or ready reckoners of measurement by Hoppus by the 144 divisor; by H.M. Customs quarter girth system, by the 113 divisor; and by the diameter, using the 183 divisor.

In the home timber trade the Hoppus system has always been in universal use, and both buyers and sellers understand that the percentage of error in true measurement represents 27 per cent., or about the average waste in the conversion of logs, so that measurement with the 144 divisor gives approximately the volume of timber that can be converted out of any given log.

Horizontal Band Saw.—A machine in which the band wheels are placed so that the saw travels in a horizontal plane when cutting.

Horizontal Frames.—These have usually only one saw, although occasionally two are used each on separate slide. The saws work horizontally, and the log is carried past the saw by means of a log carriage to which it is fixed. A rack under the table actuated by a pinion provides the feed motion.

Horizontal Roller Feed Saw Benches.—Saw benches having horizontal rollers driven by power, for feeding the material past the saw.

Hornbeam (*Carpinus betulus*).—A fine, compact grained, hard wood, strong but not very durable. Found in Europe and America. There are four species, the wood of which is used for cogs, handles of tools, mallets and other purposes where toughness and hardness are considerations. "Beam," in this compound word, is a survival of the old Gothic term for a tree; it is high-class wood for fuel and burning into charcoal.

Horse Chestnut (*Æsculus hippocastanum*).—Imported into Britain from Asia. A soft wood of very rapid growth. Possesses whiteness and lightness, but lacks strength and (unless placed underground) durability. Used extensively for temporary buildings and for bobbins; also for wheelbarrows at furnaces and kilns, as the wood is difficult to burn.

Housing.—A trench in a piece of wood made for the insertion and security of a second piece. The term is largely applied in staircase work, especially to the " wall-boards " or " wall-strings," "housed " for reception of the different members of the wooden steps.

Hub.—The central part or nave of a wheel, from which the spokes radiate. *See* " Spoke " *and* " Nave." Also a block of wood which is used to lay to the wheel of a carriage to stop its motion. *See* " Brake-block."

Hulk.—An old ship unfit for service. A great broad ship chiefly in use for setting masts into ships and the like.

Hundred, Long and Ordinary.—The old English or Teutonic hundred is the duodecimal system of computing by " twelves," as against the ordinary decimal one of " tens," hence a long hundred has ten dozen = 120, against the ordinary ten times ten—100. Extended to a thousand (or mille) this gives to the former 1,200 pieces—as in the stave and slate trades—and to the ordinary hundred 1,000 pieces. *See* " Stave " *and* " Slate " *headings or notes.*

Hung Up.—Floated logs or other wood prevented from reaching their destination by want of sufficient water or other causes.

Huon Pine (*Dacrydium Franklinii*).—A valuable Australian timber used for boat building, carving and furniture.

Hurdle.—A temporary agricultural fence of wood. *See* " Fleak."

Hutch.—A variant term for a large box or chest ; it is best preserved in the instance of housing coneys, where it occurs as " rabbit-hutch."

I

Imports and Importer.—That which is imported or brought into one country from another one, the material collectively being termed " imports." A person who imports, otherwise a merchant, who, by himself or his agent, brings in goods from another country. Great Britain being an island kingdom, all imports are by " sea," or " sea-borne." *See* " Export and Exporter."

Impost (Lat. *Impositus*).—The horizontal mouldings or capitals *on the top* of a pilaster, pillar, or pier, from which an arch springs.

In.—*See* " Eng."

Incorruptible Wood.—The cedar-wood of scripture, the pillars of Solomon's Temple, etc., which has won its name for durability from being the material chosen for coffins by the ancient Egyptians. It is an evergreen cone-bearing tree, a fir. The *Pinus cedrus* of the botanist, alias *Cedrus Libani*.

Indemnity.—A letter or document engaging to hold another party free from loss. Where the bill of lading is not to hand goods are frequently released from a vessel without the bill of lading by presentation of an indemnity signed by a banker, such indemnity being handed back to the importer when the bill of lading is forthcoming; and the banker receives the indemnity from the importer in due course, which ends the liability of all parties.

Indorsement (or **Endorsement**).—The term generally used to denote the writing of the name of the holder on the back of a bill or promissory note, on transferring it to another person. The transfer is not complete until the endorsed bill is delivered to the transferee.

Inserted-tooth Circular Saw.—A circular saw on whose periphery are sockets, in which removable shanks or bits are inserted.

Insolvency, or bankruptcy, is the state of a person unable to pay his debts as they become due : but a person does not become a " bankrupt " in England until so declared by the Court.

Insurance.—A contract by which an insurance company or underwriter, in return for a payment known as premium, agrees to bear a contingent loss, during a stated period. Death and loss by fire are the most common forms of insurance, but a quotation from insurance companies or brokers can be obtained against damage from practically any cause.

Interest.—(1) A share in an estate, ship or business; (2) Amount paid for the use of money, usually calculated at an annual rate. Most States formerly had laws fixing the maximum rate of interest, beyond which it became usury and was irrecoverable, but in most countries these have been repealed. A contract to pay a grossly unreasonable and unconscionable rate of interest can be set aside on application to the Courts, who will deal with each case on its merits, looking at the risk involved, without laying down fixed rules.

Inventory.—A list or schedule of goods or property setting forth the particulars so as to inform parties interested.

Invoice.—A detailed account of goods purchased and their price delivered by a seller to a buyer.

Iroko is described as the most useful wood in tropical West Africa. It is sometimes called " African teak " or " African oak."

J

Jack.—A term implying something common-place or ordinary, as in "Jack-plane," "Screw Jack," "Roasting Jack," "Boot Jack," "Jack-tax," etc. Commonly used in the timber and other trades for the hand-screw appliance that is used for lifting or moving trees or timber of any kind.

Jack-rafter.—A short rafter fixed in the hips of a roof ; a piece of timber in a frame cut short of its usual length often receives the name of *Jack*.

Jag.—To notch ; to cut into notches or teeth like those of a saw. In Botany, a cleft or division.

Jam.—A stoppage or congestion of logs in a stream, due to an obstruction or low water.

Jamb (Fr.).—The side of a window, door, chimney, etc.

Janker.—Scotch term for a long pole on two wheels used in hauling timber.

Japanese Oak.—A class of wood uniform in grain and colour, of slow growth and soft texture ; it is the produce of two species, but no difference can be traced in the converted wood. Its arrival on the wood-markets of Europe synchronizes with the opening of the twentieth century, and it finds favour as a companion of, or a substitute for, the European wainscot-oak. It is shipped in log form, also in well-converted lumber, cut radially and otherwise. *See other* "Oaks."

Jarrah (*Eucalyptus marginata*).—An Australian timber of open grain, durable, and one of the hardest and least inflammable woods, and especially useful for paving or piles

Jettison.—To throw cargo overboard from a vessel to lighten it in a storm and prevent it foundering.

Jib Cranes.—Consist of a long jib, which can be raised or lowered, and swivelled round so as to cover a considerable area. By means of a rope passing over the end of the jib, loads are raised or lowered either by a hand or power-driven winch.

Jogged Timber.—Squared logs irregular in their squarage, and made up of different prismatic sections.

Joggle or Stop.—A method of squaring mahogany logs in sections which diminish towards the top of the log. The junctions are termed joggles, and each division requires separate measurement. This method of manufacture is now practically confined to mahogany extracted in Mexico, and principally to wood obtained from the Tobasco districts.

Joggle Joints.—In masonry, stones or other bodies fitted together, especially in arch-work, to prevent them from sliding downwards. In carpentry, the struts of a roof are said to be joggled into the trass-posts and into the rafters.

Joiner.—The man who joins substances together—in a popular sense, "wood" or "timber." His old name was "Housewright" or "Tree-wright"; his fellow, the cabinet-maker, was the "Chest-wright" or "Ark-wright." "Joiner" is glossed by "carpenter," an imported term from our Latin neighbours. In composition, as in "Joiner's bench," "Joiner's stool," "Joiner's chest," "Joiner's tools," "hammer," "mallet," etc., it has a wide field as a prefix.

Joiner's and Box-maker's Cross-cut Saw Benches are provided with an easily traversed table, by means of which boards and planks are moved past a cross-cut saw.

Joiner's Boards.—Specially selected planed boards suitable for joinery purposes.

Joiner's Deals.—First and second quality sawn deals, specially selected as suitable for the manufacture of joinery.

Joiner's Saw Benches have a rising and falling motion to the table, and are used for similar work to that done on a grooving and rebating bench.

Joinery.—The finished hand work of the joiner as an operator in wood. His labour, light and heavy, is now mostly performed by machinery, which during the last fifty years has revolutionized his trade, "machine-made joinery" being the order of the day in this century, the "joiner" (*which see*) being now practically the "fixer."

Joint.—The interstices between the stones or bricks in masonry, brickwork, and timber work are called *joints*. The act of joining timbers or sawn wood together, the main performance of a *joiner*, has furnished his trade-name.

Joisting.—Converted wood suitable for joists. In the hard-wood, or oak days, of the building trade, the sections were usually squares; in soft-wood, of less bearing power, the depths, roughly speaking, are double or treble the thickness. *See* "Joists."

Joists.—The pieces of timber to which the boards of a floor or the laths of a ceiling are nailed, and which rest on the walls or on girders, sometimes on both. The wood or timber collectively is known as "joisting" (*which see*).

Jungle.—In the tropics, land covered with forest trees or less imposing objects, from brushwood to creeping plants.

Juniper.—A coniferous shrub or tree common to the Eastern and Western Hemispheres. The most notable species is the *Juniperus Virginiana*, which exists in North America, but principally in Florida and the S.E. States. This is the variety that is so much sought after for the outside casing of lead pencils, its qualities for this purpose being unsurpassed.

Jury Mast.—A corruption of *joury* mast, i.e., a mast for a day, a temporary mast, being a spar used for the nonce when the mast has been carried away.

K

K.D. Sash.—A knocked down window sash.

Kapp Balks (Norwegian).—Made from timber, about 16 ft. and upwards in length, mostly 20 to 22 in. diameter, free from bark, hewn on two sides to uniform thickness, leaving other sides half round.

Karri (*Eucalyptus diversicolor*).—A hard, tough and strong timber growing in South-West Australia. Sometimes known as "Blue Gum."

Kauri Pine (*Agathis australis*).—A very fine-grained wood, found only in New Zealand; used here as a substitute for Quebec yellow pine.

Kerf.—The groove formed in wood while being sawn.

Key Tapering Machines.—Machines for tapering a railway key. These machines are made with both hand and automatic feed, the work being done by means of revolving cutters.

Keyhole Saw. *See* "Pad-saw."—A small "rat-tail" saw adapted to keyhole work, etc., usually secreted or preserved inside its own handle.

Kick Stamp.—A machine used for splitting up blocks of wood into convenient size for fuel. Short lengths of logs are placed on a die having a number of radial knives, and a falling weight forces the wood on the sharp edges of the knives and splits it into sections, which fall through the spaces between the knives.

Kids.—A term used in some districts in England for fagots, or bundles of heath and furze.

Kiln.—A large stove or oven constructed for the purpose of drying anything. In the instance of drying wood-goods, the term " stove " is generally used, hence " kiln-dried " and " stove-dried " are equivalent terms. *See* " Desiccation " and " Desiccating."

Kiln-dried Saps.—A term applied in America to flooring boards and planks cut from the sapwood of pitch pine and dried in a kiln before shipment.

Kiln-drying.—Drying or seasoning of wood by artificial heat in an enclosed room.

Kindling Wood.—In a popular sense, is another term for " sticks " or " firewood "—a swift burning class of fuel most used for starting or inciting a fire.

King Post.—The part which in a truss extends between the apex of two inclined pieces and the tie beam which unites their lower ends, as in a king post roof. This implies one post only in a principal as distinct from the larger constructions which have two posts and are termed " Queen-posts " (*which see*).

Kingwood.—A species of wood from Guiana and other tropical countries, of a purple colour, hence it is sometimes called " Purple-heart " or " Violet wood."

Kinked.—A " buckled " saw, whose surface undulates or is untrue.

Knag.—A knot in wood, or a protuberant knot, having the same meaning as " Snag " (*which see*).

Knee.—A piece of timber formed with an angle in the shape of the human knee when bent.

Knee-rafter or Knee-piece.—A rafter for the principal truss of a roof, the lower end or foot of which is crooked downwards, so that it may rest more firmly on the walls. Otherwise an angular piece of timber to which other pieces of timber are fastened. Ships have a number of knees—" beam-knees," " head-knees," " carling knees," etc.

Knife.—A cutting instrument with a sharp edge, used in almost every trade : in that of wood it is somewhat obscured by the use of the term " iron "—as in " plane-iron "—but if a like " iron " is fixed, or forms part of a machine, it comes to its own, as in " knife-veneer-cutting machines," rotary or horizontal. *See* " Veneer." The lath-splitter's tools are " riving-knives," and a " circular-saw-guard," in the rear of the saw, is adopting the same term.

Knife Veneers.—Veneers cut with a machine knife ; " fixed-knife " in the instance of the wood moving on a horizontal bed ; " moving " in the rotary veneer cutting or peeling machines ;

i.o., the machines which form the rock-base of the "ply-board " trade.

Knob, Knobs, and Knobstick.—A hard protuberance, well under-stood in the above compound form ; in a milder one knobs furnish artistic finishes to flag-staffs, poles and map-rollers ; as handles on drawers, furniture, doors and fittings they are useful, and form prominent features in wood, brass, and other substances.

Knocked Down.—A machine or article taken apart in order to facilitate shipping. Abbreviated to " K.D."

Knot.—A portion of a branch of a tree that forms a mass of woody fibre running at an angle with the grain of the main stock and making a hard place in the timber. A loose knot is generally the remains of a dead branch, and its bark covered by later woody growth. Knots are classified as pin, standard and large, as to size ; round and spike as to form ; and as sound, loose, watertight, encased, pith and rotten, as to quality. In the pitch pine trade in America the various knots are defined as follows : A watertight knot is one com-pletely interwoven with surrounding wood, but, if a sound or tight knot, will be held by the wood encasing it. A pin knot is sound and not over $\frac{1}{2}$ in. in diameter. A standard knot is sound and not over $1\frac{1}{2}$ in. in diameter. A large knot is one any size over $1\frac{1}{2}$ in. in diameter. A round knot is oval or circular in form. A spike knot is one sawn in a lengthwise direction. A sound knot is one solid across its face, is as hard as the wood it is in, and is so fixed by growth or position that it will retain its place in the piece. A loose knot is one not held firmly in place by growth or position. A pith knot is a sound knot with a pith hole not more than $\frac{1}{4}$ in. in diameter. An encased knot is one surrounded wholly or in part by bark or pitch. Where the encasement is less than $\frac{1}{4}$ of an inch in width on both sides, not exceeding one-half the circumference of the knot, it is considered a sound knot. A rotten knot is one not as hard as the wood it is in.

Knotting.—The process of adzing off the knots on rough timber.

Knuckle.—The working or movable part of a folding metal hinge. In old examples of roofing with stone slabs (from which the term " stone lath " originated, now better known as " tile lath or slate lath ") it is not rare to find the pegs the so-called " knuckle-bones " obtained from sheep's feet, a favourite plaything of schoolboys, variantly called " snobs."

Knysna Boxwood.—A species of boxwood from the Knysna forest, and exported from Knysna, on the southern coast of Cape Colony.

Krabark (sometimes spelt Crabark).—An unidentified hardwood timber exported from Siam.

Kyanize.—To apply corrosive sublimate to timber in order to prevent dry-rot, so called from Mr. Kyan, who invented the process.

L

Laburnum.—A tree of the genus *Cytisus*, the *C. laburnum* of Linnæus, a native of the Alps and much cultivated by way of ornament. The wood of *C. alpinus* is said to be prized by cabinet-makers, but in European commerce it is not prominent.

Lacewood (otherwise the American plane, *Platanus occidentalis*).—A fancy wood that enters the veneer-field. Its speciality lies in the " medullary-rays " or " silver-grain," being somewhat pronounced or exposed to the eye ; but, as usual in oak, beech, etc., only brought out as a fancy-wood when sawn or cut radially or on the quarter. *See* " Plane and Plane-tree " *and* " Figure in Woods."

Lacquer and Lacquering.—A varnish for wood, etc.; a solution of hard gums of different colours in alcohol. It is an old-time Eastern invention in its application to wood, and lacquering is still largely practised in China and Japan. Europe was made acquainted with it through the Dutch about two centuries ago, when wooden clock-cases, etc., were sent out plain and returned lacquered and gilded, as part cargoes in " teaships."

Lacustrine Habitations.—The remains of human dwellings of great antiquity, constructed on certain lakes in Ireland, Switzerland, England, etc. They seem to have been villages built on piles or artificial mounds in shallow waters for defence against wolves, etc.

Ladder Rounds.—The rounded steps of a ladder, variantly called " staves."

Lading.—*See* " Bill of Lading."

Lag or Lagging.—(1) Thin sawn or riven wood or boarding, used as false floors in buildings to carry plaster, daub, sawdust, etc., the object of which is to deaden sound between upper and lower apartments ; another term is " sound-boarding." *See* " Pugging." (2) " Lag," narrow boards laid on the ribs of centring to turn arches upon. (3) Narrow boards, "lags" or "staves" of casks. (4) A board in a fence. *See* "Stave."

Laid Yard of Flooring.—A trade term, especially in Yorkshire, where the buyer only pays for as much tongued and grooved wood as will actually *lay* or *cover* nine square feet ; thus, 5 in. p.t. & g. floor-boards ; this would mean selling them as 4½ in. boards. *See* "Square" *and* "Flooring, a Square of."

Lamao is a Philippine whitewood, with mahogany stripe. It is of very close texture, similar to Bataan, but softer. It can be used for all purposes for which a cheap mahogany is required, as it takes the stain and polish, and when polished is hard to distinguish from real mahogany. It is specially attractive to the furniture trade, where cheap furniture is turned out, and where it is not desired to use expensive lumber. It should also appeal to the railway and shipbuilding trades.

Lamb's Tongue Moulding.—A kind of moulding used principally in the manufacture of doors, windows and casements of sashes.

Laminated.—Layers of one, or various woods cemented together.

Laminated Wood.—Boards built up of several thin pieces or layers of wood glued together ; a variant but not popular term for "three-ply" and "multi-ply" boards.

Lancashire Boilers.—A long, cylindrical-shaped boiler having two flues, side by side, passing through the entire length of the boiler.

Lancewood (*Duguelia quitarensis*).—A very fine and dense-grained hardwood imported from the West Indies.

Landing, or Landing-place.—A place on the shore of a sea, lake or river where persons land or goods are put on shore ; (2) The first part of a floor at the top of a flight of stairs or steps, also the "resting-places," which may occur in any part thereof ; the latter may be called "half-landings" or "quarter-landings," or "half-spaces" or "quarter-spaces," and the main one a "top landing."

Landing Account.—A statement compiled by dock companies of the particulars of goods landed.

Landing Order.—A document authorizing the dock company or wharfinger to receive goods from a ship.

Lap Milling Machine.—A machine in which a small milling cutter is used for tapering the ends of a band saw, forming an overlapping joint, giving it the proper bevel for making a lap joint by means of brazing

Lapboards or **Lapping Boards.**—Thin boards on which bolts of cloth are wound. Also known as "Clothboards."

Larboard and Starboard.—Larboard (now commonly "port side ") is the left side of ship as she advances on her course ; "starboard" is the right, or opposite. The latter is a variant of "steer-board," the board by which a vessel was guided in the water before the mechanism of the helm became common. At the root of this latter we have the "north" or "pole-star" *cynosure*, otherwise the "lode-star" or "leadstar," which served the purpose of the compass before that instrument was invented ; hence a "steer-man " on a ship is properly a "starman."

Larch (*Pinus larix* or *Larix Europa*).—Introduced into this country in the eighteenth century. Flourishes in almost every kind of soil, in cold climates and the most exposed positions. Grows faster and contains more gum and resin than any other home-grown tree. Used by railway contractors (for fences, posts and sleepers), boatbuilders and wheelwrights.

Lath and a Half.—Extra stout laths.

Lathe.—A machine for turning concentric-shaped articles which are caused to revolve while under the action of the cutting tool.

Lathe, or Lathes, Foot Power.—(1) The oldest form is the "pole-lathe," with reciprocative action, i.e., a spring-pole over-head, a cord wrapped round the wood to be turned, and extended to a floor-treadle ; still used for spindle-ends. (2) A lathe, rotary action, which receives its motion by means of a crank and treadle worked by one foot of the operator, or by additional foot-help. *See* "Turner."

Lathes, Gauge.—Lathes specially constructed for turning out a large number of similar articles. One is used for roughing out the piece to the required shape, and a tool of the exact profile required for finishing the article to the exact shape and size.

Lathes, Self-acting.—Lathes provided with a slide rest, which is automatically traversed along the bed of the machine, instead of the cutting tool being guided by the operator's hands.

Lath-river.—*See* "Rive and River," "Rend and Render," *and* "Split and Splitter."

Laths.—*See* "Plasterers' Laths " *and* "Tile Laths."

Lathwood.—Specially selected straight-grained fir-timber suitable for being riven. Imported in half or part-round billets, from which the hearts have been extracted. Sold by the fathom of 216 cubic ft. (6 ft. × 6 ft. × 6 ft). A fathom.

(6 ft. × 6 ft. of wood) contains 3 ft. long, 108 ft. ; 3½ ft., 126 ; 4 ft , 144 ; 4½ ft., 162 ; 5 ft., 180 ; 6 ft , 216 ; 7 ft., 252 ; 8 ft., 288 cubic ft.

Lathwood-culls.—Culls from riven billets lowered in quality, or reduced to firewood value, from being coarse or knotty, but mostly from being twisted in the grain, i.e., interlocked on the edges, and being old, dry and thus difficult or impossible to rive. *See* " Cull, Culls, and Culler."

Lattice and Latticework.—From " latte," a " lath," which, crossing at different angles, form networks or screens. It is a class of work carried to marvellous perfection in the East, an apology for which only exists in the West, and that mostly in fixed or portable plain sheets for garden work.

Lauan.—A Philippine wood used in naval construction because it does not split with shot.

Laurel (*Cerasus laurocerasus*).—An English tree of no commercial importance, but the wood is hard and of good quality.

Lead is the " rake " or angle to which the teeth of saws incline.

Leads.—Deals sawn into twelve or more thin boards.

Lean-to.—A shed or building annexed to the wall of a larger one, the roof of which is formed in a single slope with the top resting against the wall of the principal building. In the South it is sometimes called a " to-fall." It has much the same meaning as " pent-house " (*which see*).

Legal Tender.—The tender of not more than twelve pence in copper or forty shillings in silver to settle a debt. Gold and Treasury Notes are the only legal tender for amounts over £2, and Bank of England notes are a legal tender for amounts exceeding £5, but the creditor cannot be compelled to give change, whether for gold or notes.

Letter Wood (*Amanoa guianensis*).—A striped fancy wood imported from Guiana. Called by the French " Lettre rouge." Also called " Snakewood."

Level.—An instrument by which to find or draw a straight line parallel to the plane of the horizon, as the " carpenter's level," " mason's level," etc. The " spirit level " has of late become the most popular.

Lever.—From the French or Latin tongue " levier " = to raise. A bar of wood or other substance, turning on a support called the fulcrum or prop. It is an instrument much in use as affording one of the mechanical powers. Ash is a favourite wood for conversion into levers.

Lightning Fixed Knife Planer.—Sometimes called Hazeland Planer. Consisting of fixed knives, the edges of which slightly project above the table level. The wood is passed over the knives by means of a large rubber-covered roller. They are called lightning planers owing to the very high speed at which the work is performed.

Lignine is the incrusting matter contained within the cellular tissues, which gives hardness to wood.

Lignum Vitæ.—The *Guaiacum officinalis*—a tree, native of the warm latitudes of America and some of the West Indian islands. The wood is firm, heavy, resinous, the heartwood blackish. Used in medicine; wrought into wheels, cogs and many articles, tools, and turnery.

Lilac (*Syringa vulgaris*).—A hard native wood, beautifully marked, and used by the turner and cabinet-maker, but of little commercial importance.

Lime (*Tilia Europea*).—A tree that is common to Europe but not indigenous to this country. It is plentiful, however, in the southern counties, being largely used for park and street planting. It produces a soft, light and close-grained wood, which in former times was principally used for wood carving. At the present time, however, its chief employment is for making boards for the leather cutters, and for action work in pianoforte making. Much used in Russia for the manufacture of bast matting. Known also as the Linden. The wood imported from the United States as Basswood is produced from a species of lime.—*Tilia Americana.*

Linden.—*See* "Lime."

Linings.—Narrow strips of wood dressed with groove and feather, for the inside boarding of houses, usually $\frac{1}{2}$ in., $\frac{5}{8}$ in., $\frac{3}{4}$ in., and $\frac{7}{8}$ in. in thickness. They vary with their use, as sash-linings, window-linings, etc.

Lintel.—A horizontal piece of timber to be placed over an opening.

Live Rollers.—Rollers which are driven by power, and used to convey timbers, boards and slabs from one machine to another in a mill.

Liverpool String Measurement.—A method of measuring the cubic contents of logs and other round timber. All timber in the log at present sold on Liverpool string measure is sold and measured $\frac{1}{4}$ in. in girth, $\frac{1}{2}$ ft. in length, and contented out to cubic feet and twelfths, measurers using either girthing-tape or string. Girth is ascertained by tape as far as possible, otherwise by string at the option of the seller. In the case of round timber, if measured over bark, allowance is made for bark $\frac{1}{2}$ in. on $11\frac{1}{4}$ in. and under, 1 in. on 12 to 17¾ in., and an additional ½ in. for every 6 ins. or part thereof over. Allowances for defective logs as customary.

Lloyds.—The headquarters of the underwriters, especially of marine risks, so called as their original meeting place was Lloyd's coffee-house. Lloyd's-rooms now form part of the Royal Exchange, and are under the management of a committee. *See* "Underwriter."

Load.—A load of timber unhewn, 40 cubic ft. ; squared softwood timber, 50 cubic ft. ; 1 in. plank, 600 sq. ft. ; 1½ in. plank, 400 sq. ft. ; 2 in. plank, 300 sq. ft. ; 2½ in. plank, 240 sq. ft. ; 3 in. plank, 200 sq. ft. ; 3½ in. plank, 170 sq. ft.; 4 in. plank, 150 sq. ft. In the Board of Trade Returns and other Government statistics timber is always returned by the load and not by the standard.

Lock.—Anglo-Saxon *loc*, a fastening. (1) Applied to an instrument for fastening a door, a lid, a trunk, etc., also to fasten with a lock and key. (2) Among engineers, a place where the current or stream of a river is stopped, variantly a lockpit.

Lock Rail.—The middle or horizontal rail of a door to which the lock or fastening is fixed.

Locust Tree.—*See* "Acacia."

Loft.—A room in the roof of a building ; a gallery or small chamber raised within a larger apartment, or in a church, or a music loft (musician's gallery), a singing loft, or a rood-loft. It is the final syllable in "cock-loft," i.e., the "top-loft."

Log.—An instrument for measuring the rate of a ship's motion. The trunk of a tree ready for conversion.

Log-board.—A couple of boards shutting like a book on which the logs are entered. It may be termed the waste-book, and the log-book the journal.

Log Run.—In softwoods, merchantable lumber of all grades, as it comes from the saw ; in hardwoods, the full run of the log with No. 3 common out.

Log Saws are of four classes : band, horizontal and vertical, reciprocating and rack benches (*which see*).

Logwood (*Hœmatoxylon campechianum*).—A very hard wood found in the West Indies and Central America. Used as a dyewood, but not of much commercial value.

Lorry.—*See* "Lurry."

Lower Ports.—Shipping places in Canada, broadly speaking which are situated in the Gaspe Peninsula, New Brunswick and Nova Scotia.

Lumber.—A term used in America for timber sawed or split for use.

Lumber Gauge.—A tool used to measure the thickness of a board, or to determine the accuracy of the manufacture of the tongue and groove which have been cut on a piece of planed timber.

Lumber Jack.—One who works in a logging camp.

Lumber Trimmers.—A name given to a series of cross-cut saws, each on a separate hinged carriage, and so arranged that any one or more of them may be brought into cut and so trim off the ends of a plank and cut it into the required lengths.

Lumper and Lumpers.—A "lumper" is a labouring man whose office it is to load and unload ships in harbour. Lumpers are a body of men so employed who usually do the work "in gross," or for a "lump-sum" ; such bodies are called gangs, their head man "a ganger," but alternatively a "stevedore" (*which see*), each of which, as men of business, may be actual employers of the "lumpers" or "gangmen."

Lurry.—A timber wagon. Also known as lorry.

M

Machine-saw or Saws.—Consist of thin blades, discs or bands of steel with teeth cut on their edges. There are three types : (1) Worked with a reciprocating motion, cutting in one direction of the stroke only. *See* "Horizontal Frame," "Fretsaw," etc. (2) Circular saws used in a large number of different machines. *See* "Rack-bench," "Joiner's Benches," "Roller-feed Benches." (3) Band-saws : endless ribbons of steel running over top and bottom or pairs of horizontal pulleys. *See* "Band-saws," "Plain Bandsaws." *See* "Engineer."

Machine Sawing.—A term used to distinguish it from hand sawing on the pit ; it takes various forms with different machines from log-frames to fretwork machines, and so embraces the whole field of sawing, cutting, ripping, etc. *See* "Falling Cut." *See* "Engineer."

Machinist.—An operator of wood-working machines, as distinct from a "mechanic "- a maker of machines.

Magnolia (*Magnolia grandiflora*).—A tree indigenous to the Southern States of America. The wood is used for cabinet work and interior decoration.

Mahogany is possibly a native Indian "tree-name" that came to the surface—early fifteenth century—after the wood was handled by white-men as "cedar," which latter made its appearance in Britain in the last half of the seventeenth century. This old name "cedar" clings to the soft "Havana cedar." With the opening of the twentieth century the trade largely changed its ground to West Africa, where woods, somewhat related to the true Central American mahoganies, abound: the characteristics are medium and hard wood, red in colour. *See* "Havana Cedar" *and* "Fashionable Woods."

The beauty of mahogany arises from its being cross-grained, or presenting the fibres' endways or obliquely on the surface—these positions on the fibres, as well as their different colours, give a clouded and mottled variety to the surface; and when some of the parts are partially transparent, they give rise to a variety of lights and shades, as the observer shifts his place, and reflect them in the most varied manner, like the surface of a crystal. This overlapping of the fibres, and their varied colours, are the occasion of the singular appearance which the surface of a dining table will present to two persons when seated opposite to each other. From one side of the table portions will seem to be quite light, but in the same seen from an opposite point of view the contrary effect of deep shade will be produced; and this is the reason why no painter can correctly imitate mahogany.—(From *The Mahogany Tree*.) *See also* "Figure in Mahogany."

"*Expensive Mahogany*—Specimen of the finest Honduras mahogany in regard to figure and quality ever grown. This single tree contained 390 cubic ft. broker's measure (i.e., 4,684 ft. of inch), and was bought unopened by Messrs. Broadwood for the manufacture of pianos at the price of £1,781, in 1849, supposed to be the most valuable tree in the world, and after it was opened, £2,000 was offered for it and refused."

The above inscription is framed in the London office of Messrs. Broadwood

Mahogany Measure.—A special measure for mahogany which allows 1½ in. in 12 in. width and thicknesses, and also makes allowances in the length for defects in the log. The difference between Mahogany and Calliper measure usually runs to from 25 to 30 per cent.

G

Maiden Wood is a term principally associated with ash-trees. One young and fairly endowed with full meed of elasticity is termed "a maiden ash": by the side of an older or fully developed tree it may be said to be in the company of its mother, for all trees, poetically and otherwise, are of the feminine gender. *See* "Ash." *See* "Stool and Stooled."

Main Tram Pieces.—*See* "Solebars."

Mall or Maul.—A wooden hammer, a variant of which is "beetle" and "mallet" (*which see; also* "Plank, Deal, or Board Stower").

Mallet.—A wooden hammer, originally a military weapon of known but now varied size: it is another term for "beetle" and "mall" or "maul" (*which see*).

Malodorous Woods.—Or woods which in a converted form emit offensive odours. An example of this class is the round (so called) mahogany, shipped from Gaboon in West Africa. A mill-man sawing such wood is apt to endow it with an Anglicized form of a well-known but unidentified Biblical wood. The nomenclature of wood, in and belonging to America, is expressive on this point, instance: "Fetid Buckeye," "Fetid Yew," "Stinking Ash," "Stinking Cedar," etc. This, if a shortcoming in Nature, is there counterbalanced by a number of sweet and "odoriferus woods" (*which see*).

Mandrel.—*See* "Saw Arbor."

Mangle Rollers.—Maple, sycamore, and lignum vitæ, cut to the desired lengths out of quartered wood and into octagonal blocks of regulated size, for the wringing machine industry, an important market for which is Keighley in Yorkshire.

Manifest.—A ship's document, being a detailed statement of a cargo of goods, imported or laden for export, to be exhibited at the custom-house by the master of the vessel or the owner or shipper.

Mansard Roof.—A roof formed with an upper and under set of rafters on each side, the under set less and the upper more inclined to the horizon. It is a favourite French form, taking its name from François Mansard, said to be its inventor. It is variantly called a "curb-roof," from the double inclination of its sides.

Mantel-piece.—A modern "fire-place" fitment that grew out of the older "mantel-tree" and "mantel-shelf" (*which see*) ditto "Over-mantel."

Mantel-shelf.—A domestic shelf of prime importance fixed on the "mantel-tree" (*which see*) when those beams were low, and the articles stored were within easy reach. The old idea is retained in the modern and less picturesque " mantel-piece."

Mantel-tree.—A beam that forms the head or front of a fire-place, reminiscent of the days when fires were heaped on the floors or hearths. It is a by no means solitary instance of " tree " being used as a variant of " wood " or " timber." *See* " Mantel-shelf."

Maple (*Acer*).—A hard fine-grained wood similar, but harder than sycamore. The tree attains no great size in this country, and supplies are principally derived from North America. A great part of the import to this country consists of manufactured flooring, for which purpose it has few rivals, minor supplies comprising planks and boards in lumber form. Its uses are confined to objects used in the textile trades, to the manufacture of rollers and in a limited way to articles employed in the printing trades. From this American grown tree the beautiful bird's-eye figured wood is obtained, and quantities of syrup that is afterwards made into sugar are extracted in Canada and the United States.

Margin.—A variation mutually allowed by custom or practice in the precise conditions in a contract, generally expressed by the word " about " Referring to quantities the margin is generally understood to mean 5 to 10 per cent. more or 5 to 10 per cent. less than the quantity stated in the contract. The percentage of margin varies according to the custom of the particular port of shipment. In f.o.b. and c.i.f. business the margin is understood to be allowed for convenience of chartering, and when several vessels are loaded under a particular contract it only applies to the last vessel loading under such contract. In present-day contracts for North European wood goods the margin allowed is expressly defined and limited to a certain quantity irrespective of the quantity sold.

Marquetry.—The art of inlaying wood with wood of other colours, or with various other materials, as metal, ivory, shell, etc.

Mast.—(1) A piece of timber elevated perpendicularly on the keel of a ship, from which comes the term " mast-piece," a suitable piece for a mast, and " mast-hunter," a pioneer in a fir-wood forest marking or " blazing " the cream of the trees. (2) The fruit of certain forest trees : acorns, nuts, etc.

Match.—A splint of wood, capped by a combustible composition · much reduced in size from the old " brimstone-match " by the introduction of the Congreve and Lucifer matches in the first half of the nineteenth century, of which the " safety match " is an outgrowth.

Match Boards or **Matched Boards.**—Boards, variantly called "matched-linings," grooved and tongued on the edges, the tongue being formed in the solid, expressed "p.t. & g."; or, if **V**-jointed, "p.t.g. & **V**-joint," with the substitution of "B" if "beaded" instead of "**V**-joint"; others are rebated instead of tongued and grooved and expressed "R."

Match Splints.—Thin wooden sticks for making matches. They are cut double the length of matches and are crosscut after the ends have been dipped and supplied with the striking material.

Matched.—Any form of joint in wood; usually applied to tongued and grooved jointing; or "matched in figure," with fancy or ornamental wood in veneer form.

Matched Linings.—*See* "Match Boards."

Mattress Scantling.—Wood (generally pitch pine) cut to size, for making the frame to which mattress wires are attached.

Mauerlatten.—A German word, formerly employed to signify wood used for the framing of buildings. Small logs, mostly 8 × 9, 10 × 10, and 11 × 11, exported from the Baltic; chiefly from Riga and neighbourhood.

Measure and Measurement.—*See* "Customs Measure," "Customary Measure," "Actual Measure" *and* "Hoppus's Measure."

Medullary Rays.—Compressed cellular tissues which usually run continuously from the pith to the bark. They are present in all exogenous trees, but only become apparent to the naked eye in a limited number, at the head of which stands the oak and includes the beech and plane. This constitutes the beauty of figure termed "Silver-grain" (*which see*). In other trees the rays or figure from this source are said to be "obscure."

Merblanc.—A special form of charterparty for shipments from the White Sea.

Merchantable.—In general commerce a term applied to goods fit for market; or such as are usually sold in market; or such as will bring the ordinary price. In the timber trade it is used as a technical designation for a particular kind of assortment. Oregon fir, for instance, is graded for export as prime (clear), select and merchantable, and a lower grade of pitch pine timber, sawn and planed lumber is called merchantable.

Metric Foot.—This is strictly a *façon de parler*, as a foot is not a metrical measure. In many French, Dutch and Belgian contracts a clause is inserted that "Lengths be cut in metric feet, thicknesses and breadths in English measure." Taking the metre as 3·2809 ft., a metric foot is one-third, i.e., a little over 13 in., and the wood is adjusted accordingly to comply with Continental demands.

Middle Cuts.—Lengths cut from the middle of the tree or log.

Middling.—A term used in connection with wood-goods, of middle rank or quality; for instance, in Danzig timber, "best," "good middling" and "common middling."

Mill Culls.—An American expression for the poorest quality of wood produced, practically refuse.

Mill Run.—The product as classified by the particular mill. In America all saleable timber which the log makes and which is sold without being sorted.

Mill Webs.—Straight saws employed in sawing machines with a reciprocating motion.

Mille (Latin *mille*, a thousand).—Used in the "stave" and "Welsh-slate" trades to imply "twelve hundred"; those trades retaining the now nearly obsolete Teutonic "long-hundred" of *six-score*, against the more popular *five-score*. *See* "Stave" *notes and* "Slate" *notes.*

Millwright.—Properly a wright or artificer in wood, who made or constructed mills; the term has of late extended to "smiths" or "workers in iron," who should, to be exact, be called "mill-smiths."

Mitre.—A junction, usually at an angle acute or obtuse; the line formed by the meeting of mouldings or other surfaces, which intersect or intercept each other as an angle.

Mitre-block.—A wrought block of wood usually of hard texture, rebated as the seat of wood to be operated upon or cut into mitre form—practically a "saw-guide." *See* "Mitre-plane."

Mitre-plane.—A special hand-plane made to traverse on its side, and true or plane the mitres as they come from the saw.

Monger.—A trader; a dealer; chiefly used in composition, as ironmonger; cheesemonger; and fishmonger; of this type the wood-dealer was until a century or more back, when he honoured the call of "wood-monger" (*which see*).

Monkey.—The hammer of a piledriver. Known also as "Ram."

Montants.—The intermediate stiles in a piece of framing which are tenoned into the rails. Variantly called mountins.

Mora (*Dimorphandra excelsa*).—A dense, strong wood imported from Guiana and Trinidad. chestnut brown or red in colour.

Mortise or Mortise-hole.—A cut or hollow place made in timber as the receptacle of a "tenon" (*which see*).

Mortise-chisel.—A hand-power or machine tool or implement specially made and shaped for cutting or sinking mortises.

Mortising and Boring Machine.—A machine capable of boring a hole or of cutting a mortise in a piece of wood. These are of different types: actuating chisels, chains, hollow chisels, and revolving bits.

Mottle.—Figure transverse of the fibres, doubtfully caused by the action of wind upon the tree. Distinctive names are given to the various forms the figure takes. *See* "Mahogany Figure."

Mould.—(1) The short or abbreviate of "moulding" (*which see*). (2) A matrix of sand or other substance in which to found or cast objects in brass, iron, lead, plaster, cement, etc. *See* "Stick and Sticking," "Planting Mouldings" *and* "Scratch Mouldings."

Moulding.—A general term applied to all the varieties of outline or contour given to angles of various subordinate parts and features of buildings. The varieties are legion, the most popular worked in wood are the *stragal* or *bead*, the *Ogee, Reverse Ogee, Ovalo, Scotia,* and *Torus.* In high-class work they are capable of considerable enrichment ; instance, "Egg and Tongue" and "Egg and Spear" mouldings.

Moulding Iron Grinder.—*See* "Dry Emery Grinder."

Moulding Machines.—Machines capable of cutting on four edges at one time, and with pressures specially designed for dealing with mouldings. *See* "Moulding Machines—Single and Double Spindle."

Moulding Machines—Single and Double Spindle.—In which one or two vertical spindles are used for planing and moulding wood. More generally used for wood of irregular form. The object of two spindles on one machine is to enable irregular work to be planed as nearly as possible with the grain. This is achieved by running the spindles in opposite directions.

Mountain Ash (*Sorbus aucuparia* or *Pyrus aucuparia*).—A firm and fine-grained wood found in Europe, Asia and N. America, but more cultivated for underwood than for timber. Thrives best in mountainous districts even at an altitude of 2,500 ft. Used by wheelwrights, turners, and (when in sufficient size) for the same purposes as ash ; also for hop poles. broom and rake handles, bows (for archery) and hoops, Known as the Rowan Tree, Roan Tree, Wiggen Tree, Quicken Tree. Roddan, Wichen Tree, Quick Beam, Fowler's Service Tree and the Wild Sorb.

Mounting.—A term used for the intermediate vertical parts of a door.

Mouse.—A crooked bar of lead about the length of the body of a mouse, with an eye for a string at one end. In hanging sashes or replacing broken cords it is an essential tool or instrument. In use, it is put over the "sash-pulley," allowed to fall in the box of the sash-frame and be recovered at the "sash-pocket." The "sash-cord" is fastened to the tail-end of the mouse-string and is pulled down into place after it. *See* "Sash-pocket."

Mulay Saw.—A long stiff saw which is worked by a pitman attached to the lower end. The upstroke is accomplished by means of a spring pole or some similar device.

Mulberry.—An English ornamental tree, with smooth wood of rich colour and beautiful grain. The wood is durable and used by cabinet makers. It is probably better known for its leaves which are used as food for silkworms. Grows well in towns even when exposed to smoke.

Mullion.—A vertical division between the lights of windows, screens, etc.

Multiple Spindle Dovetailing Machine.—In which a number of spindles are used for cutting all the dovetails required in the edge of a board at one operation. The cutters used are dovetail in shape and act on two boards, one laid on a table horizontally and the other fixed vertically enabling dovetail and pin to be shaped at the same time.

Multi-ply Boards.—*See* "Three-ply, Plywood or Built-up Boards" *and* "Built-up Boards or Stock."

Muntin.—*See* "Drawbore."

Myall.—An Australian acacia. The wood is dark brown, beautifully marked and violet scented. Used for fancy work and tobacco pipes.

N

Nailing Machines for Boxes.—Machines by means of which boxes and packing cases are nailed together. The nails are placed in a hopper and are automatically driven into the wood in the required positions.

Natural Order.—In Botany Linnæus divided known plants into two divisions, one of which he divided into twenty-three classes, or in all twenty-four classes ; those classes he sub-divided into orders, or " natural " orders, which serve as the practical working bases in particularizing trees ; instance, an oak—*natural order*, " Cupuliferæ," or " Corylaceæ " ; *genera*, " Quercus " ; *species*, " Robur." Since his time changes in classification have taken place. The English oak, *Q. Robur*, embraced a variety which has been advanced to a species, the two now stand *Q. pedunculata* and *Q. sessili-flora. See* " Genera " *and* " Species."

Nave.—(1) The block in the centre of a wheel, from which the spokes radiate and through which the axle passes. Called also hub or hole and stock. (2) The middle of the church (excluding the aisles).

Nave Mortising and Boring Machines.—Machines specially con-structed for mortising the naves of wheels ready to receive the spokes.

New Style.—The reformed or Gregorian Calendar, adopted in England in 1753, when eleven days were dropped or left out.

Newel.—A post at the end of a flight of stairs, to carry the hand-rail or for the steps to work round.

Nib, Lip or Tongue.—A term applied to the upper back part of an earthenware roof-tile ; it is a projection or lip, a feature in " hanging tiles," by which the tile is hung on the " tile-lath." *See* " Tile " *and* " Pantile."

Nick and Notch.—To cut in notches or make indentations on wood, especially in the instance of " tally-sticks " (*which see*). " Notch " is another term for " trench " cut in the " wall-strings " of staircases to receive and hold the ends of the wooden steps—hence a " string-board " may variantly be called a " notch-board."

Nogs.—Wooden bricks, introduced here and there into walls, for the purpose of fastening internal fittings, window frames, etc.

Nominal Horse-Power.—A term used to denote the approximate horse-power of an engine. As the name does not give any exact rating it has been generally discarded. The actual power of an engine is generally expected to be $3\frac{1}{2}$ times its nominal power. *See* " Brake Horse-Power."

Nominal Measure.—The full measure of a board before it is planed or dressed.

North Carolina Pine.—*See* " Pitch Pine."

Nosed.—Rounded on one edge.

Nosing.—The projecting edge of a moulding " step," " tread," or " drip." *See* " Scroll-step."

Notch.—*See* " Nick."

Notch-board.—*See* " String-board."

Nursery.—A plantation or group of trees, mechanically trained, attended, or nursed into regular order until they approach maturity

Nursery-man.—A person whose office it is to attend upon a nursery of plants or young trees, also applied to the proprietor of a business in which such are grown and sold.

Nut Gall.—An excrescence caused by insect action on oak trees, otherwise called " oak galls," " gall nuts."

Nut-tree.—The hazel tree, *Corylus avellana.* Linnæus found this growing in a wild state in many woods and coppices in Great Britain. The wood is employed for hoops, fishing-rods, walking-sticks, crate making, and other purposes. The nuts are articles of food, and produce oil little inferior to olive oil.

O

Oak (*Quercus*).—A genus of trees of the natural order *Cupuliferœ,* bearing a round nut called an acorn, natives of temperate and tropical countries. Europe produces a few species, but many are found in America. It also grows in mountainous districts of the torrid zone and at low elevations in the Himalayas, while some even grow at the level of the sea in the Malay Peninsula and Indian islands. None are found in the peninsula of India, Ceylon, tropical Africa, Australia or South America. *See* " Japanese Oak," " Evergreen or Holm Oak," " Red Oak," " Scarlet Oak," " Willow Oak," " Turkey Oak "—others, not here noted, as " Austrian Oak " (*Q. Austriaca*) ; " Spanish Oak " (*Q Hispanica*). The name " oak " is sometimes popularly applied to trees of a different genera, as for instance " African Oak," which is another name for African teak. In like manner the " Swamp Oak " of Australia is an alias for beef-wood ; the Stone Oak of Java is specifically the *Lithocarpus juvenensis.*

Oak Apple.- *See* " Nut Gall."

Oak Tree Leafing.—The tradition is, if the oak gets into leaf before the ash, we may expect a fine and productive year. In 1831, 1832, 1839, 1853 and 1860 the two species of trees came into leaf about the same time. In 1818, '19, '20, '22, '24, '25, '26, '27, '33, '34, '35, '36, '37, '42, '46, '54, '68 and '69 the oak displayed its foliage several weeks before the ash. *See* "Ash Trees Leafing."

Oaks (noted) in England.—Owen Glendower's oak, Cowthorpe oak, Fairlop oak, the Bull oak, the Winfarthing oak, William the Conqueror's oak, Queen's oak, Sir Philip Sydney's oak, the Ellerslie oak, the Greendale oak, the Swilcar oak, etc. *Vide* "Brewer's Phrase and Fable."

Oddments.—A term applied to the remainder of stocks or shipments, otherwise broken specifications. In the Canadian trade the term is applied to all goods under 12 ft. 3 in. by 11 in.

Odoriferous Woods (from "odour," smell, scent, fragrance, a sweet or an offensive smell) are numerous. There are few woods which, in a newly split, sawn, or riven state, fail to emit some distinctive odour; instance, the oak, the elm, and the lime. Amongst those of a specially fragrant type is the "American pencil-cedar," the Australian "Raspberry-jam" and "Rio Rosewood." It may be noted that odoriferous woods are not favoured as happy hunting grounds by wood-boring insects. *See* "Malodorous Woods."

Offer.—*See* "On Offer" and "Offer Off."

Offset Device.—Used to set the log clear of the saw on the backward motion of the carriage. Usually automatic in its action.

Ogee or O.G.—A moulding of two members, one concave and the other convex. A contraction of "Old Greek."

Old Style.—The unreformed calendar, still in use in Russia. There are now thirteen days difference between Old Style and New Style, *e.g.*, Jan. 1st O.S. = Jan. 14 N.S.

Olive Tree (*Olea Europea*) **and Wood.**—Considered the emblem of prosperity. David says, "I am like a green olive tree in the house of God" (Ps. lii. 8). The wood is beautifully veined and works with a pleasing odour. Objects from the Holy Land are invariably wrought or turned in this wood. This species is more valued for the fruit and oil it yields than for its wood.

On Offer, and Offer Off.—Popular terms in the *wood* trade, especially in the import department or section; they relate to goods sent out on offer which, although still unsold, the offer either to sell or to buy for some reason is withdrawn or declared off.

Order.—In architecture, a column entire, base, shaft, capital, and entablature ; usually said to be five : Tuscan, Doric, Ionic, Corinthian and Composite, the latter called also Roman The term is also applied to the divisions, ribs or recesses of an arch in Gothic architecture.

Oregon Pine or Fir (*Pseudotsuga Douglasii*).—One of the largest coniferous trees in existence, reaching 200 to 300 ft. in height and with a diameter of from 27 to 120 ft. It exists in extensive stands in British Columbia and Vancouver in Canada, and also in Washington and Oregon in the United States. The wood is largely used in all parts of the world for shipbuilding, piles, sleepers and constructive work of all kinds. Also known as Columbian and Douglas pine or fir.

Orel Poles.—A local name amongst farmers in the Worcestershire district for Alder Poles.

Orham Wood.—This name is probably a corruption of the French word " orme," a term for elm. It is a species of elm and imported from Canada. The wood is of a light brown colour, and has many of the characteristics of the common elm of this country. The moderate supplies that come forward to these markets are principally utilized for coffin making.

Osage Orange (*Maclura aurantiaca*) —A tree found in Arkansas and Texas, formerly used for bows and arrows, now used for wheelwright work and turnery. Called by the French " Bois d'arc."

Osier or Crack Willow (*Salix fragilis*).—An English wood, seldom allowed to reach the timber stage, but cut while underwood for basket making and wickerwork. *See* " Willow."

Out of Wind.—True or free from twist.

Over.—As in " overdraw," " overdue," " over-trade," " overboard," " overcharge," " overweight," " overfreight," " overgrown," " overhaul," " overheated," " overladen," " overmeasure," " overplus," " oversold," " overstock," " overweight " and " overwork " are understood trade-terms in daily use, implying excess. *See* " Under " *for their opposites.*

Over and Under Planing Machine.—A machine similar to a panel planer but provided with a top table also, so that the work may be passed over the cutter by hand, and trued up, taking out any twist, and afterwards passed under the cutter by means of a roller feed, and finished to a uniform thickness.

Overhead Price.—A single price for all classes, instead of separate prices for different sizes, qualities, etc.

Overhead Travelling Crane.—Consisting of girders spanning a building, etc., and provided with wheels to run on rails. Supported on overhead gantries, along which it travels by hand or power gear. The lifting is effected by means of a crab which traverses across the span on the main girders of the crane. Modern cranes of this type are often provided with three electric motors, one for lifting, one for cross traverse, and a third for moving along the gantry.

Over-mantel.—A special fitment in wood, stone, or plaster, to which sculpture, carving, and painting may be added, that occupies the space intervening between the mantel and the ceiling of an apartment ; it is usually found to be the most ornate part of an interior dating from the fifteenth to the nineteenth century. *See* "Mantle-tree," "Mantel-shelf," *and* "Mantel-piece."

Ovolo.—A moulding, the vertical section of which is in Roman architecture a quarter of a circle. In Grecian architecture it is elliptical, or, rather, egg-shaped.

Oxylene.—A process claimed to render wood uninflammable. *See* "Fireproofing Timber."

P

Packing Cases.—Large boxes used for packing goods or merchandise for transit, mostly in the export trade. Those of small size are usually termed "boxes," or "cases." Plywood is now playing an active part in this branch of the wood trade.

Packing-case Wood.—Sawn wood, not of a high class, used in making "packing-cases." Some large consumers elect to use "logs" or "square whitewood sleeper-blocks" and convert them into boards. *See* "Packing Cases." *See* "Firewood."

Packing and Packing Pieces.—Mainly used in sawmills in connection with "circular saw beds" to pack or steady the saws when running or cutting. They vary from hempen matter to wood.

Pad Saw.—A small narrow saw fitted to a handle or pad, into which it can be telescoped when not in use. *See* "Keyhole Saw."

Padouk (*Pterocarpus indicus*).—A hard wood found in Burmah, Siam and the Andaman Islands. In use for furniture and decorative purposes

Pale = a narrow piece of wood.—Otherwise a "lag" (*which see*), used in the boarding of fence-rails, open or close order. It is the Latin "*palus*" which coincides with the English "pole" and "pale," giving "palisade," "pale-fencing" and the plural form "paling."

Paling.—A row of pales, pickets or stakes fastened together. Also a vertical object or figure, as in heraldry.

Pan.—A piece of timber used in a building, otherwise called a wall-plate.

Pane.—(1) The hewn or sawn surface of the log in sided timber. (2) Implying a "panel," as in "post and pane" walls, i.e. timber posts and stone, brick and plaster panels.

Panel.—A piece of board, whose edges are inserted in a frame. The short of this, especially in old half-timber buildings, is "pane" and "pan"—hence "post and pan," a wall of post and panel.

Panel Planing Machines.—Machines for planing wide boards and panels, sometimes called Thicknessing Machines as they reduce the wood to a uniform thickness. The wood is passed under a revolving cutter head by means of feed rollers, which are fitted both in front and at the back of the cutters.

Panel Raising Machines.—A machine for forming raised panels, generally consisting of a horizontal spindle fitted with suitable cutters. The panels are gripped in a carriage working on a slide extending along the table of the machine, the slide acting as a guide for the material as it is passed over the cutters.

Panelling.—In architecture (1) the operation of covering or ornamenting with panels. (2) Panelled work, i.e. formed with panels. *See* "Panel."

Panels.—Thin boards used for filling in strong framing, as in doors, shutters, etc.

Pantile.—A tile in the form of a parallelogram, straight in the direction of its length, but with a waved surface transversely, usually about $13\frac{1}{2}$ in. × 7 in. × $\frac{1}{2}$ in. It has a small tongue or projection to hook to the lath. The ridge and hips of roofs covered with pan or plain tiles are finished with large concave tiles, called hip or ridge tiles. *See* "Tile."

Paper Wood.—Round whitewood timber, cut to short lengths, for the manufacture of wood pulp for paper making.

Parget and Pargetter.—Obsolete terms in architecture, for which we may now read "plaster and plasterer"; the latter obscures the still older English trade names of "daub and dauber." "Parget" appears to have reached us from Spanish sources, possibly from art workmen being imported in Tudor times. "Parget-work" of an ornamental character for inside and outside decoration, especially of half-timber buildings, occupied an important position in the day of Queen Elizabeth, examples of which remain. It is only now known as rough-work in chimney-flues.

Parquet.—Flooring made in geometrical designs with coloured hardwoods.

Parting Bead.—A slip inserted into the centre of the pulley stiles of a window, to keep apart the upper and lower sashes. *See* "Sash Window."

Parting Slip.—Properly a "lath of wood" fixed at its head only in the box of a sash-frame to keep the "sash-weight" (*which see*) apart when the casements are working. *See* "Sash Window."

Patten-sole.—A wooden sole mounted on an iron ring to raise it above the wet ground. It is distinct from the "clog-sole" (*which see*), although wrought in the same class of wood, inasmuch as it is not intended to be used in direct touch with the ground.

Pavers, Setts or **Road-pavers.**—Usually the "paving-stones" or "cubes" of roadways; occasionally extended as "floor-pavers," "floor-tiles." The term "paving-setts" seems to refer more to *number* of cubes than to their ultimate purpose. *See* "Tile."

Paving Block Cross Cut.—A machine having a number of saws equally spaced. These saws have a rising and falling motion, cutting the wood blocks into suitable lengths. In some cases the sliding motion is horizontal, or even the saws are attached to a swinging arm.

Pear Tree (*Pyrus communis*).—Its wood is similar in its properties to the apple tree and used for the same purposes, but sometimes preferred to it, being very slightly superior in quality.

Pedestal.—(1) In architecture, the base or foot of a column or statue on which the upright work stands; (2) in machinery, a pillow block.

Peel and Peeling.—In the wood trade to remove the bark or outer covering of a tree. These terms have of late attached themselves to the "rotary-veneer cutting machines," formerly "scale-board cutting machines," now in the plywood trade "peeling machines," as they slice,* slive,* or slash* thin layers of wood off the round or tangential face of the tree ; by which, as in "Bird's Eye Maple," the "eye" or "slash-grain" or "slash-figure" is obtained. *See above as headings.

Peeled.—Logs from which the bark has been removed.

Pencil or **Virginian Cedar.**—Otherwise "Red," etc , cedar (*Juniperus virginiana*). Largely a cabinet-maker's wood in the last century, prized for its durability and its proof against the worm, possibly from its strong odour or perfume, but now practically a thing of the past. Its scarcity has produced a class in the land of its birth, called "pencil-men," to hunt and buy up cedar posts, rails or any old-time uses to which it has been applied, the "pencil factories" of the world claiming every available stick.

Pendulum Cross Cut Saws.—Consist of an arm with a saw spindle at bottom running in suitable bearings and hinged on the same centre as the countershaft which drives the saw. The saw is fed on to the wood, by swinging the arm pendulum fashion, hence its name.

Pent Roof.—A roof formed like an inclined plane, the slope being all on one side. Called also a shed roof. The covering of a "penthouse."

Pent-house.—Old forms "pentee" and "pentice," an open shed or projection over a door, window, flight of steps, etc., to form a protection against the weather ; a shed standing aslope from the main building. It has much the same meaning as "lean-to" (*which see*).

Per Procuration.—The authority given by a merchant, or other principal, to his manager or agent to sign his name on letters, etc., is called "power of procuration," and letters and documents are signed either "per pro. J. Robinson & Co.," or "p.p. J. Robinson & Co.," with the name of the authorized person underneath.

Perch or **Perk.**—(1) A pole, as a measure of length or square ; (2) a staging in a builder's yard for storing on-end boards, planks, poles or ladders. In this sense it implies something erect.

Periphery.—*See* "Circumference."

Persimmon (*Diospyros virginiana*).—Known as "Date Plum." A strong and tough wood imported from the Eastern States of America and used for shuttles, etc.

Petrograd Standard.—*See* " St. Petersburg Standard."

Pickets.—Narrow strips of wood used for fencing.

Pilaster.—A debased pillar ; a square pillar projecting from a pier or a wall to a portion of what would otherwise be its square. It suggests the place of a detached pillar or column if the wall was not there.

Pile.—(1) A large stake or piece of timber or " reinforced concrete," pointed and driven into the earth, as at the bottom of a river, or in a harbour, or for a foundation, where the ground is soft, for the support of a building, a pier, or other super-structure, or to form a coffer-dam, etc. *See* " Pile-driver " *and* " Beetle." (2) An iron column with a screw at its point for screwing into the ground, often used in pier work where the soil is tenacious clay = " a screw-pile."

Pile-driver.—A machine worked in a vertical position, on which an iron " ram " or " monkey " is hoisted, by steam or hand power, to a set height, where it is released to fall on the head of the pile placed in position for driving or sinking into the ground. In the instance of concrete piles, a block of wood intervenes between the ram and the head of the pile. *See* " Pile " *and* " Beetle."

Pin Knots.—Small knots not above half an inch in diameter.

Pine and Pinewood.—" Pine " is the Latin *pinus*, supposed, from the form of the leaves, to imply " pin " ; a tract of arid land in America is known as a " pine-barren." " Pine-wood " is not such a common term in Britain as " firwood " (*which see*).

Pinetum.—A collection of living pine trees made for ornamental or scientific purposes.

Pinholes.—Small holes in the wood caused by worms or insects.

Pipe Stave Oak.—A standard stave of a certain size, namely 6 ft. × 3 in. × 6 in., used by coopers. Riven on the quarter from selected oak, these and other staves of different dimensions were once largely used in the cabinet trades, but with the advent of American oak in lumber form a rapid decline in their use took place. *See* " Stave (oak) Standard Stave."

Pit-chocks.—Short square sawn blocks of birch, beech or oak, used in coal mines.

Pit-saws.—Large two-handled saws worked by two men, one of whom stands on the log and the other in the pit beneath, hence the name. The man who works on the log is called the " top sawyer " and the man underneath is called the " pitman " or " bottom sawyer."

Pit-sawyer.—Workman who saws timber in a pit.

Pitch.—The angle between the back of a tooth and a line drawn from the extreme point of the tooth in the back of a bandsaw, or to the centre of a circular saw.

Pitch (of a Roof).—The inclination of the sloping sides of a roof to the horizon. Its relation to the "span of a roof" is very important. In a "lean-to" roof, that is where the apex of the roof leans against another building, "a pitch of one half" would be *the horizontal span,* the result a " pitch," "rake" or slope of 45 degrees. "One-third pitch" is the most common one in roofing, i.e. 33⅓ degrees. *See* "Roof."

Pitch Pine, a species of trees, is known in America as yellow pine. A wood reddish in colour resembling Scots fir, but heavier and more resinous. The Gulf Coast classification comprises the following : Loblolly Pine (*Pinus talda*), Longleaf Pine (*Pinus palustris*), Cuban or Slash Pine (*Pinus heterophylla*) and Short Leaf Pine (*Pinus echinata*). The last named is known in commerce as "North Carolina Pine."

Pitch Pockets are openings between the grain of the wood in pitchpine containing more or less pitch or bark, and are classified as small, standard and large pitch pockets. A small pitch pocket is one not over ⅛ of an inch wide. A standard pitch pocket is one not over ⅜ of an inch wide or 3 inches in length. A large pitch pocket is one over ⅜ of an inch wide or over 3 inches in length.

Pitch Streaks in pitchpine are well defined accumulations of pitch at one point, and when not sufficient to develop a well defined streak, or where fibre between grains is not saturated with pitch, it is not considered a defect.

Pith or **Medulla.**—The cellular tissues in the centre of a tree stem, which rarely runs perfectly straight, but usually snake-like along its entire length, only a portion continuous with the bark.

Pit-props.—Small round timber used in coal mines. Long props are from 10 ft. up in length or 15 to 16 ft. with 3 in. tops. Short props are from 2½ ft. up to 7 and 8 with 2½ in. and up tops.

Pixpinus.—A special form of charterparty used in chartering for cargoes of pitch pine.

Plain Band-Saw.—A name given to the smaller type of band-saws, used for cutting sweeps and other work which can be fed on to the saw by hand.

Plain Sawed.—All timber which is not quarter sawed, such as flat grain. bastard grain, slash grain.

H

Plain Tiles are simple parallelograms, generally about $10\frac{1}{2}$ in. × $6\frac{1}{4}$ in. × $\frac{5}{8}$ in., and weigh about 2 lb. 5 oz. Each tile has a hole at one end to receive the wooden pins to secure it to the lath. In England they are usually termed flat-tiles or Staffordshire tiles, and have "nibs" or "tips" to hang them on the roof laths—they are two colours, "red" and "brindled."

Planchettes.—Narrow boards under 6 in. in width, and from 1 to $1\frac{1}{2}$ in. in thickness.

Plane.—A joiner's and carpenter's hand-tool. Of prime import-ance, the working of which reduces rough or uneven surfaces to plain, level or smooth faces; planes are of different lengths, forms and sizes, their number, especially "mould-ing planes" and "match planes," has of late years been reduced by the intrusion of machinery. *See* "Shot," "Shooting Plane," "Trenching Plane" and "Toothing Plane." Planes of iron or steel are now finding favour in working high-class woods.

Plane or **Plane-tree.**—A tree of the genus *Platanus*, two of the best known of which are the "oriental" and the "occiden-tal." The former is known as an introduced tree into England, that can thrive in the heart of London town, and is a favourite tree in our streets, but is strange in shedding its bark in patches. The wood is white, like that of its false offspring, the sycamore. The wood of the Western or American plane has a browner cast, partly produced by the medullary rays or silver grain, somewhat prominently displayed, being darker than the ground or field of the wood. *See* "Lacewood" *and* "Figure in Woods."

Plane-stocks.—Beechwood blocks, quarter sawn, the radial face being the near side of the plane when in work, the wear-ing face, unlike that of pitchpine flooring boards, being the unfigured or tangential one. The blocks are usually steamed to aid seasoning, a process that gives the wood a warmer tint in colour.

Plank, or **Planks.**—In London and the South implying sawn wood 10 inches and over in breadth. In the North "deal," as distinguished from "batten," covers 9 inches and up. This word has many front names to distinguish it in various trades, as "gang-plank," "running-plank," "deck-planks," "scaffold-planks" (*which see*).

Plank-, Deal- or Board-stower.—Usually a member of a gang employed to "stow" goods in a ship, or in stocking a timber-yard; a man who is something of an artist, if not an expert, for his finished work in piling deals, etc., with no assistance further than a " hand-hook " (*which see*) and a " mall " or " mallet " (*which see*) is a wonderful performance.

Plant.—The equipment of a mill or factory, specially applied to the machinery necessary for the trade carried on therein.

Plantation.—A piece of ground planted with trees or shrubs for the purpose of producing timber or coppice wood.

Planting-mouldings.—The opposite of " stuck-mouldings." *See* " Stick and Sticking " *and* " Scratch Moulding." These terms a century ago had more meaning in the joinery department of the wood trade than they have to-day, the principal field of their application being " panel-framing " ; if the moulds were " stuck " on the framing, as in old wainscotting, they were described as being " stuck on the solid." The modern system of " planting " loose mouldings in or around the panels gave the name of " planting moulds or mouldings."

Plasterers' Laths.—Thin and narrow riven strips of wood, nailed to the rafters, studs or floor beams, in order to sustain the covering or plastering. Of late years machine-sawn laths have come into very general use. The usual dimensions of laths are $1\frac{1}{8}$ in. × $\frac{3}{16}$ in., 1 in. × $\frac{1}{4}$ in., 1 in. × $\frac{3}{16}$ in., in lengths of $2\frac{1}{2}$, 3, $3\frac{1}{2}$, 4 and $4\frac{1}{2}$ ft. Sawn laths are sold per bundle of 500 running feet, and hand-split laths per bundle of 360 running feet.

Plate.—A general term applied to almost all horizontal timbers which are laid upon walls, etc., to receive other timber-work, hence " wall-plate," etc.

Platter or Platter-board.—An ancient article of domestic use, a large shallow dish of turned sycamore or maple-wood, the use of which is now retained on the table as a dish or stand for bread and cheese, or other dry food substances. The term is allied to the wood-plate or " Trencher " (*which see*).

Plinth.—(1) A member serving as the base of a column or wall, or collectively members which serve as a base (*which see*). (2) A board running round a room next the floor, known also as " Washboard."

Plough.—A joiner's instrument for grooving or trenching, worked after the manner of a plane. Its finished work is a " plough-groove "—a groove invariably larger than that wrought by a " grooving-plane " (*which see*).

Plugs.—Pieces of wood driven into the log to hide defects. Large pegs driven into logs for making some attachment for hauling or rafting.

Plywood or Built-up Boards.—Terms for a new trade—one not possible until powerful " peeling machines " could be pressed into its service. They cover the now ubiquitous " Three-ply-boards," and those of higher number or count. *See* " Three-ply " *and* " Multi-ply Boards."

Pneumatic Apparatus for Wood Refuse.—An apparatus consisting of an exhaust fan connected by piping with the various machines in a mill, and by exhausting the air in the pipes draws off the chips and shavings with it, which after passing through the fan are blown into a cyclone, where the refuse drops from an opening in the bottom and the air escapes from an opening in the top.

Pointing.—In architecture, the finish given to the mortar-joint in bricklaying, "Towel pointing," "Tuck pointing," etc. *See* " Hick-joint pointing." The " raking-out " of the mortar from between the joints of a stone or brick wall and replacing the same with new mortar. This latter, in new work, is usually termed " tuck pointing," and is carried out with raised joints, made specially prominent in church restorations, where the original plaster, inside or out, is removed and the stone or " rubble-work " is left exposed.

Points.—Small saw teeth are reckoned by the number of teeth points to the inch.

Pole.—(1) In forestry a tree from 4 to 12 in. in diameter breast high. A " small pole " is a tree from 4 to 8 in. in diameter breast high. A " large pole," a tree from 8 to 12 in. in diameter breast high. (2) A measure of $5\frac{1}{2}$ yds. long or $30\frac{1}{4}$ yds. square.

Pole-lathe.—An early form of lathe worked by a pole under-foot, and a cord wrapped round the wood or object to be turned, the cord attached to a spring pole above—on the reciprocative action of the bow-drill ; such lathes are still in use by chair-makers in turning spindles, especially so at their ends. They antedated the rotary foot-lathe of the late eighteenth century.

Pole-plate.—A small kind of wall-plate used in modern *roofs* to receive the feet of the rafters.

Pole-wagon.—A four-wheeled pair-horse or ox wagon worked with a pole instead of a pair of shafts after the manner customary with coaches and large or family or state carriages.

Policy of Insurance or Assurance.—A document evidencing a contract of " Insurance," *which see.*

Poling Boards.—Short boards used to line the insides of tunnels during construction, and the sides of trenches for sewer-laying, etc. ; they are held up against the soil or loose or doubtful ground by horizontal lines of trees, poles, planks, deals, or battens, as the case demands. The latter are termed " whalings " (or " wale "—as in gun*wale* of a ship).

Pollard Oak.—*Alias* " Red " or " Brown Oak." The former from " polled " or maimed oaks deepening in colour by age or incipient decay to brown, red and even partially black ; hence a tree never polled, if it takes on colour, is termed " a pollard." Occasionally protuberances, or " Burrs " (*which see*), form or swell on or from the stem or near the roots, which, if coloured, yield pollard-oak veneers of value, should the taste or fashion in wood incline that way, as it did in the latter half of the nineteenth century. *See* " Pollards."

Pollards.—Trees which admit the crowns being cut off, leaving them to send out new branches from the top of the stem, By constant cutting the heads swell and become deformed features known as a " Todds " or " Old Todds," possibly from " Tod," an obsolete term for " a bush." *See* " Pollard Oak."

Polled Trees.—*See* " Pollards."

Pontoon.—A flat-bottomed or shallow draught boat whose primary purpose was a temporary bridge, or part of a " pontoon " bridge, as the Latin name " *pons* " = a bridge. implies Originally of wood or plank construction ; of late *buoyant* cylinders of iron have taken their place in constructing floating landing-stages, etc., otherwise " pontoons."

Poplar (*Populus*).—Introduced into Britain by the Romans, and many species are known here, though only three (the White Poplar or Abele, the Black Poplar and the Lombardy Poplar) are of commercial value A very soft, light wood, which does not easily splinter or ignite by friction. Used by clogmakers, wheelwrights and hurdlemakers.

Poppy Heads.—The tops of seat ends in churches, etc. Some of these made in the Middle Ages are extremely ornamental.

Portable Jib Cranes.—Consist of a jib crane mounted on a carriage and capable of motion along a railway track. These are usually driven by steam power, with engine and boiler mounted on the carriage, which not only propel the crane along the track, but also lift the load.

Port Orford Cedar (*Cupressus lawsoniana*).—A fine wood exported from the Pacific Coast of America.

Post.—An upright timber in a building. Those used in modern roofs are called *king-posts* or *queen-posts*, according to their number and position. It is a term coupled with " rail," to form a fence or defence. Posts were used in thorough-fares and seized upon as bill-posting stations, hence " bill-posting," etc. *See* " Post and Pan."

Post and Pan.—Another and popular term for a " half-timbered " building. It consists of upright grooved posts placed at inter-vals, the spaces or " panels " between being filled with slabs of stone, brick, clay, or other like material. The " pan " is the horizontal head or lintel. *See* " Half-timber-ing."

Post and Pane.—A term implying " post and panel," allied to " post and pan " (*which see*).

Post and Petrail.—A term implying " post and stone panels," hence " petrean "; allied to " post and pan " (*which see*).

Premium.—(1) The annual or other payment for keeping up a policy of insurance ; (2) a lump sum present payment for a lease or other benefit.

Prepared Boards.—Boards that have been passed through a planer or other finishing machine.

Presentation of a Bill.—Presentation of a Bill for Acceptance signifies the handing of a bill to the drawee for pay-ment. A bill must be presented on the day it is due, and during the usual business hours ; otherwise the previous indorsers, if any, are not responsible should it be dis-honoured.

Pricking Up.—An architectural term—the first coating of plaster in work of three coats upon laths of wood, etc. *See* " Float-ing or Floated " *and* " Rendered and Rendering."

Prick Post.—An intervening post of light scantling in " post and rail " fencing, deriving its name from being pointed at its lower end and " pricked " or driven into the ground to give strength to the rails.

Prima Vera.—A Central American timber resembling mahogany but of a lighter colour. Much used in the United States for cabinet work and sometimes called " White Mahogany."

Prime.—The " first " or " best " part ; a superior classification.

Prime Cost.—The full or total cost of goods with every charge added.

Prime Quality.—A United Kingdom term for the grading of a quality in hardwoods, generally known as " Firsts and Seconds."

Principals.—(1) The framework supporting the purlins, which again carry the common rafters, and thus the whole weight of the roof is sustained by the principals. *See* " Roof-timber Terms." (2) Also the partners in a firm.

Progressive Kiln.—A drying arrangement with openings at both ends, and in which the material enters at one end and is discharged at the other.

Pugging.—In architecture, any composition, generally a coarse kind of mortar, laid on " lagging " or " sound-boarding " under the boards of an upper floor, to prevent the transmission of sound.

Pulley Block.—A block fitted with a pulley or shiver, or a sheaf of pulleys or shivers, to distinguish it from a block without pulleys known as " a *Dead-eye* " (*which see*).

Pulley Stiles.—The inner sides of a " sash-frame " (*which see*). They derive their name from carrying the " sash-pulleys " (*which see, and* " Sash-window ").

Pulpwood.—Short lengths of whitewood or spruce 3 in. and upwards in diameter, used for grinding into pulp to make paper.

Punky.—A term applied to wood affected by rot, arising from a large fungus of the genus *polydorus*.

Purlin.—A piece of timber laid horizontally, resting on the principals of a roof to support the common rafters. Purlins are sometimes called ribs.

Putlog Holes.—Holes in the wall for one end of the putlog to rest, the other resting on the ledger of the scaffold.

Putlogs.—Short pieces of timber, generally about 7 feet long used in scaffolds to carry the floor. They are placed at right angles to the wall, one end resting on the ledgers of the scaffold, and the other in holes left in the wall, called putlog holes. Birch putlogs are largely imported from Finland.

Pyroligneus Acid or Wood Vinegar.—A form of acetic acid made by the destructive distillation of wood.

Q

Quality and Shipping Marks.—Floated timber or wood in the log is usually hand-marked by " screeve " or scribe or stamp, i.e. " hammer mark." Archangel, Petersburg, (now Petrograd) and Canadian sawn goods are "chalk-marked" on the side or edge, the exceptions being "hammer-marked." Swedish, Norwegian and Finnish goods are largely stencilled in red or blue with shipper's marks of quality on the ends. Certain known marks, as "BSSC," indicate the names of the ports from which they are shipped and become their trade names. *See* "Quality or Qualities" *and* "Brand and Branded." *See* "List of Shipping Marks on Timber," published by William Rider & Son, Ltd.

Quality or Qualities.—In sawn goods, timber and lathwood. (*a*) Merchantable—the commercial standard. (*b*) Unmerchantable—the wrack, culls or inferior qualities, now largely imported and traded in. Riga wainscot oak is classified (*a*) English crown; (*b*) Dutch crown; (*c*) wrack; now but little observed; the Riga, Austrian and Odessa shipments being understood as "crown" only. *See* "Quality and Shipping Marks."

Quants.—*See* "Boathook Shafts."

Quarter Sawn Lumber.—A term, implying wood sawn in a direction transverse to the annual rings, or in an approximately radial direction; a log is approximately quartered as the first step in the sawing process. Where figure, as in oak, is only obtained by quarter-sawing it follows that in other woods, such as the pines or firs, their figure, known as "slash-grain," is won by cutting on the line of the annual rings, i.e. tangentially.

Quartered.—Cut into four parts across the grain, same as quarter sawn; radially, as distinct from tangentially.

Quartering.—Square timber of small scantling, from 3 in. × 3 in. to $4\frac{1}{2}$ in. × 4 in.

Quarters.—The upright posts of timber partitions, etc., used for lathing upon.

Quebec Standard.—An established measure for timber consisting of 100 pieces 12 ft. 11 in. × $2\frac{1}{2}$ in. = $229\frac{1}{6}$ cub. ft.

Queen-post.—The suspending posts in the framed principal of a roof, or in a trussed partition. A principal with two posts, as distinct from "King-post" which implies one post only. *See* "King-post."

Quercus (*see* "Oak").—*Quercus*, the botanical equivalent of "oak," is the old Latin classic term for that tree, and where it occurs in old writings is translated "oak." The dominating British oaks are *Quercus pedunculata* and *Q. sessiliflora*, the former only having "stalks" to their flowers or fruit, the wood produced by each species being practically the same.

Quicken Tree.—Another name for Mountain Ash.

Quilting.—Ridgy marks sometimes seen on the sawn surface of wood. The ridges are generally shallow and do not follow the line of the cut, but zigzag across it in rather a mysterious manner. Reciprocating saws are more liable to "quilt" than circular saws.

Quirk.—A deep indentation, the hollow under the abacus of a column

Quirk Mouldings.—Mouldings whose apparent projection is increased by the addition of a quicker curve.

R

Rabbet.—*See* "Rebate."

Rack-benches.—Circular saws, usually of large diameter, with travelling tables, each consisting of two plates, one on each side of the saw, resting on rollers and actuated by pinions and racks fixed under the tables. In some cases, instead of the plain tables, "carriages and dogs" are provided; the logs then overhang the carriages, which are traversed by racks and pinions.

Radial Arm Feed or **Roller Feed, for Saw Benches.**—Usually fitted to circular saw benches, consisting of a feed roller driven by gearing and carried in an arm pivoted at the back end of the machine The arm can be turned out of the way when automatic feed is not required.

Raff Merchant.—An obsolete or variant term for an importer of foreign timber, whose goods, far more so than in this century, were "floated" or rafted, hence they were called "raff." *See* "Timber Merchant." "Monger" *and* "Wood-monger," *also* "Raft."

Raft.—A float of timber passing down a river from a forest to a saw-mill or a shipping station, from which is derived "raff" and the merchant dealing with rafted goods a "raff merchant" (*which see*). When rafts are carrying other goods or hardwoods which will not readily float of their own accord they are apt to become "floats."

Rafters.—Pieces of timber which form the framework of the slopes of a roof. Common rafters are those to which the slate boarding. or lathing is attached, a variant term for which is "spar" or "roof-spar." *See* "Spar."

Rail and Railing.—Usually a horizontal bar of wood attached at either end to a post in the ground by way of forming a fence ; further, in playing an important part in wood framing of doors, shutters and panelling. As handrailing to a staircase it becomes an art work, fixed on a wall as a substance to hold by, or forming the baluster capping to the open end of a step or stair ; it there freely departs from the horizontal plane. *See notes headed* "Handrail."

Rails.—The horizontal bars in panelled wood-work, such as doors, shutters, etc., which enclose the panels (the upright pieces being termed "stiles"), and horizontal bars in wood gates and fences.

Railway Keys.—Hardwood wedges mostly of oak or teak, made to special designs, bevel edges one side and rounded edges the other, to fit between the steel chair and the rail.

Railway Timber.—A general term for all woods purchased wholesale for railway work.

Rake, in saws, is the angle or "lead" to which the teeth are inclined. A variant term is "set."

Rake or **Raking.**—Anything that inclines from the perpendicular, as a mast *rakes* aft.

Raking Mouldings.—Those which are inclined from the horizontal line, as in the sides of a pediment.

Ram.—*See* "Monkey."

Ram's Horn.—A lateral grain or figure, peculiar to European ash, the result of compression or contortion of the vertical fibres, known as "ram's horn" or "fiddle back" from its resemblance to the ram's horn, or the figured sycamore used in the backs of fiddles. This contorted grain is best seen in the Austrian and Hungarian billets imported for ornamental purposes, sometimes in wainscot oak logs.

Ramp.—Literally a spring or bound, any sudden rising interrupting the continuity of a sloping line, commonly used to denote a sudden upward curve in the handrail of a stair.

Raze Knife.—A sharp instrument for scribing the contents on timber. *See* "Scribe."

Rebate (or **Rabbet**).—A longitudinal channel, groove or recess cut out of the edge or face of any body, especially one intended to receive another member, so as to cover the joint, or more easily to hold the members in place ; thus the groove cut for a panel, or for a door, is a "rabbet" or rebate. *See* "Shiplap Joint."

Rebate Plane.—In a technical sense to "rebate" is *to reduce*, hence the rebating of a door-casing is a sensible reduction made for " housing " the edge of a door. Like all planes in Europe, except it may be a "cooper's-stave-plane," it is, unlike the Asiatic or Japanese plane, worked by a push action. *See* "Rebate" *and* "Shiplap Joint."

Reciprocating Cross-cutting Machine.—A machine used for cross-cutting logs into lengths by means of a saw blade having a reciprocating motion, impelled either by a connecting rod and crank, or by means of steam acting directly on to a piston, the rod of which is attached to the slide carrying the saw.

Reciprocating Saw.—A saw moving alternately backward and forward or up and down

Red Cedar.—*See* "Pencil Cedar."

Red Gum or Gum-wood.—A term now practically confined to America, but represented in Europe by "satin-walnut" and "hazel-pine" (*which see*). The name is also given to a Western Australia wood.

Red Heart in pitchpine is the result of a fungous disease which in a certain stage of progress affects the quality of fibre of the wood and its strength.

Red Oak.—The red oak (*Q. rubra*) is a native of the States and Canada ; remarkably porous in its character, so much so that it is the favourite wood of " spile-peg " makers Known also as brown oak. *See* "American Oaks."

Red Pine, Canadian (*Pinus resinosa*).—Called in Canada and the States "Norway Pine." A hard resinous wood not unlike Scots fir.

Red-rot.—A defect in the heartwood of a tree, which may be sometimes discovered by the presence of fungi at the base, or by tapping the trunk, when a hollow sound is emitted.

Redwood (Sequoia).—*See* "Californian Redwood."

Reed or Reeding.—Small convex moulding. A " reed-moulding " is half a circle in section, and such mouldings when worked in the flutes of columns become ovolos; such "reeds" are occasionally placed side by side until a broad space is formed, instance in sets of architraves, in which case they are said to be " reeded-architraves " or to be " reeded." *See* "Flutings."

Refinery Poles.—Oak poles of small girth which are burnt in furnaces for refining copper and other metals.

Reglet.—A small moulding rectangular in its section, a fillet or lintel.

Regulars.—A Canadian term, applied to pine 12–16 ft. long, 3 in. × 11 in., and to spruce 12 ft. and upwards long, 7, 9 and 11 in.

Rejects.—Wood thrown out of a parcel as not equal to the classification or description required. In some cases a distinct classification of itself.

Rend and Render (as Lath-render).—*See* " Rive, River and Rived " *and* " Split and Splitter."

Rendered and Rendering.—Architectural terms. " Rendered and set " is a term applied to two coats of plaster on walls, " rendered " being the act of laying the first coat of plaster on walls, but not on lathwork, where it takes the form or title of " pricking-up " (*which see*).

Resaw.—A circular or band mill that is used to resaw boards and other wood products.

Re-sawn Timber.—Timber sawn on all four sides, as distinguished from rough-edged timber.

Reticulated Moulding.—In architecture a member composed of a fillet interlaced in various ways like network.

Return Bead.—One which shows the same appearance on the face and edge of a perpendicular piece of stuff forming a double quirk.

Return Moulds.—A moulding on the end of a step continued from the front ; in like manner a mould on a square cap of a pillar or column, mantel-shelf, etc.

Reveals.—The sides of an opening for a door or window between the framework and the face of the walls.

Ribs.—In carpentry and joinery are curved pieces of timber to which the laths are fastened, in forming domes, vaults, arches, etc. ; another name for purlins (*which see*).

Ridge.—The highest part of a roof of a building ; as a substantive—a " ridge board " or a " ridge-tree."

Ridge Piece.—A piece of timber against which the top of the common rafters or spars abut ; otherwise, ridge-board or ridge-tree.

Ridge Tile.—A convex tile made for covering the ridge of a roof.

Rift-sawed Wood.—Practically means " quarter-sawed," tho latter being more expressively applied to quarter-sawed oak.

Riga Last.—A measure of timber consisting of 80 cub. ft. of sawn deals or square timber or of 65 cub. ft. of round timber.

Rimu (*Dacrydium cupressinum*).—A New Zealand timber used in building construction.

Rindgall.—A defect in a tree caused by a blow or concussion, which may penetrate no farther than the bark but the concentric layers at the part affected are not solidified on each other. There is usually no decay of the fibre.

Ring Rot.—Decay in a log, which follows the annual rings more or less closely.

Rio Deals.—An American classification of pitch pine lumber cut to deal sizes, 3 and 4 in. × 9 to 12 in.

Rip.—To cut a board lengthwise, that is parallel to the fibres.

Ripping.—A term applied to sawing with the grain of the wood, i e., lengthwise, but usually to " flat-cutting " of deals and boards ; the act of cutting wood the shallow way. *See* " Cutting " The number of " rips " and " cuts " is thus defined in a saw-mill.

Riser or **Raiser.**—The vertical surface of a step, where the horizontal is the " tread."

Rive, River and Rived.—As in " lath-river " = a " splitter " or " render " of laths (*which see*) ; " to rive," " to split " and " to rend " meaning one and the same operation ; they are thus variant or interchangeable terms, and

> " The scolding winds
> Have *rived* the knotty oaks."—*Shakespeare.*

Riving Knife.—An attachment to open the cut in timber after it has passed the saw, to prevent it jamming the saw ; but as a hand instrument, a form of axe used by " lath-rivers."

Robur.—*Robur* is an old specific term used to define the British oaks, *Q. pedunculata* and *Q. sessiliflora,* under one heading, when, as in the time of Linnæus, they were viewed as " varieties " and not " separate species," as *Q. robur,* i.e., English or European oak. In the Middle Ages the Latin scribes used this term to imply dead or leafless oak trees— gifts of the kings from their forests.

Rock-laths.—A variant term for a strong slate or tile-lath. The name is drawn from the custom of roofing or covering buildings in some districts with " rock " or " stone-slabs " or " slates."

Roe Figure.—A peculiar figure caused by the contortion of the woody fibres, and takes a wavy line parallel to them. *See* " Figure in Wood," *also* " Figure in Mahogany."

Roll Moulding.—A round moulding divided longitudinally along the middle, the upper half of which projects over the lower.

Roller Blocks for Wringing Machines.—The dual office of the " wringing and mangling machine " brought to the front a new branch of the wood-trade, that of " roller blocks " or " mangle rollers," made of English and foreign sycamore, until other woods not so suitable in whiteness had to be brought on the market. It is an ever expanding line of business, one largely supplied in the twentieth century by Canadian birch. In instances where one of a pair is hardwood "lignum vitæ" is used. *See* "Wringing Machine Rollers."

Roller Bearings.—Bearings in which steel rollers are used to reduce the friction. In some cases the rollers are hollow, but the best types have short rollers of hardened steel, accurately ground to size and running between two hardened steel concentric rings.

Roller-feed Benches.—Circular saw benches fitted with power rollers to grip the wood being operated upon and force it to the saw. They have largely replaced the earlier "rope-feed benches."

Rolling Machine for Band Saws.—A machine in which the saws are squeezed between hardened steel rollers, so as to expand the steel in the centre, and to put into the saw what is known as tension.

Rood-beam.—A horizontal beam, usually the capping of a church-screen, on which the holy-rood is fixed, where a stage or gallery is formed at its level. The term is merged into "rood-loft," of which it forms part.

Roof.—In architecture, the cover of a building, irrespective of the material of which it is composed. The forms are numerous: amongst them are house, barn, shed, gable, hip, conical, ogee, curb, wagon, pent-house (*which see*), span, saddle, hammer-beam (*which see*), *also* mansard (*which see*) *and* "Pitch (of a Roof)."

Roof-tile.—Roof covering of earthenware tiles varied in form, "flat" or "concave," and in colour "buff," "red" or "black," "glazed" or otherwise. A mixed colour is termed "brindled." *See* "Tile."

Roof-timbers.—Consist of the main and minor parts; the former being "the principals," each of which, as frames, is called "a pair." The most common is the "king-post" form, with one central post; the less common and usually the largest span is the "queen-post" form, with two posts and "a loft" or space between.

Roof-timber Terms.—Tie-beam, hammer-beam, king-post, queen-post, principal rafters, braces or struts, ridge piece, tree or board, purlins, collar beams or collars, common rafters, pole plates, wall plates, hammer brace, side-post, straining-beam, etc. *See* "Hammer-beam," "Collar-beam," "King-post," "Queen-post," "Principals," "Struts," "Ridge-piece," "Purlin," "Common Rafter," "Pole Plate," "Roof" and "Roof Timbers."

Rooky Wood.—Not the wood where rooks do congregate, but the misty or dark wood. " Wallace " speaks of the " rooky mist."

"The crow
Makes wing to the rooky wood."—*Shakespeare,* " *Macbeth,*" iii. 2.

Rope-feed Benches.—Circular saw benches fitted with power rope and grips to force the wood being operated upon to the saw. This invention followed on the " man-fed benches," but is now largely superseded by the " roller-feed benches."

Rosewood (*Dalbergia*).—A very hard and durable wood, in great request for high-class furniture and formerly for pianos. Many species are in commercial use. Found in India, West Indies, Brazil, etc.

Ross.—Local terms in parts of England and the United States *for the accumulation of matter on the bark of trees.*

Rosser.—One who removes the bark from logs.

Rossing.—Taking off the bark.

Rotary Veneer Machine.—A machine that cuts or peels a thin endless sheet of wood from a round log.

Rough and Rough-hew.—Wood goods from the saw having small inequalities on the surface, not smooth or planed, as a " rough " board. To hew coarsely without smoothing, as to " rough-hew timber."

"There is a divinity that shapes our ends
Rough-hew them how we will "

Round (of a Ladder).—A rundle, the little cylindrical step of a ladder, otherwise " a rung."

Round Shake.—*See* " Shake."

Round Timber.—A term applied to timber in its natural state.

Rounding Machines.—Employed for turning round rods such as broom handles, curtain poles, etc. The headstock has a hollow mandril, and the cutter revolves at a high speed. The wood does not revolve, and is fed through the machine by means of feed rollers or by hand power.

Rounds or Rundles.—*See* " Staves."

Roup.—A Scotch term synonymous with auction.

Rowan Tree.—Another name for the mountain ash (*which see*).

Rubble and Rubble work.—Stones of irregular shapes and dimensions, walls built of rubble stones ; when coursed the stones are roughly dressed and laid in courses, but random in the height of the courses ; when uncoursed the stones are used as they occur, the interstices between the larger stones being filled in with smaller pieces. *See* " Pointing."

Rundle.—A round; a step of a ladder; the drum of a capstan. *See* "Round."

Rundlet or Runlet.—From "Round." (1) A unit of capacity equal to about 18 gallons. (2) A small cask barrel of no certain dimensions, it may contain from 3 to 20 gallons.

Rung.—A floor timber in a ship; one of the rounds of a ladder; one of the stakes of a cart; a round heavy staff; a cudgel. *See* "Round."

Runners.—Deals, etc., drawn out from the ends of piles of yarded stocks, on which to rest the ends of "gang-planks" or "running planks," used on the occasion of goods being yarded. This is also a cabinet-maker's term, *runners* being the guides and supports of the drawers in "nests of drawers," "chests of drawers," etc.

Running Plank.—A variant term for "gang-plank" (*which see*).

Russpruss.—A special form of charterparty for shipments from the Baltic and Russia.

S

Sabicu.—An extremely hard wood found in the West Indies. The wood was used to construct the stairs of the Crystal Palace in Hyde Park in 1851, and after six months' use the steps hardly exhibited any signs of wear.

Sabot.—A kind of wooden shoe much used in France and Belgium.

Saddleback.—Rail at the top of a fence. Generally known as "capping rail."

St. (Saint) Petersburg Standard (or Petrograd Standard).—The most generally used measure for timber, consisting of 120 pieces—

$$12 \text{ ft. } 11 \text{ in. } \times 1\tfrac{1}{2} \text{ in. } \atop \text{or } 6 \text{ ft. } 11 \text{ in. } \times 3 \text{ in. } \Big\} = 165 \text{ cub. ft.}$$

Sal (*Shorea robusta*).—A heavy, tough, hard timber in general use in India.

Sandalwood (*Santalum album*).—An extremely fine-grained wood, found in India and Malaysia. Of little commercial use here.

Sanders-wood, Red (*Pterocarpus santalinus*).—A tree growing in India, Ceylon, China, Java, etc. Used for images, turnery, etc., also as a red dye soluble in alcohol, but not in water.

Sandpapering Machines.—Machines for sanding wood to save hand labour. They are made in several types. *See* " Flexible Arm " and " Bobbin Sandpapering Machines."

Sap Stain.—A discoloration of the sapwood which cannot be removed by a reasonable amount of dressing.

Sapling.—In forestry, a tree 3 ft. or over in height. A " small sapling " from 3 to 10 ft. in height. A " large sapling " 10 ft. or over in height.

Saps.—A term used in the American hardwood trade for pieces containing all or part sapwood without any limit.

Sarking-boards.—An old term from the Saxon " sark "—a shirt. Covering board of a roof fixed under the slates, often wrought and seen underneath where the timbering is wrought or exposed. A Scotch term for thin sawn boards, usually ⅝ in. thick, used as roofing boards.

Sash.—The framed casement part of a window in which the glass is fixed. *See* " Sash Window."

Sash Cord.—A twisted or plaited hempen-cord, used for hanging sashes or casements in a sash frame ; in large " sash windows " copper cords or chains of metal are used as superior articles *See* " Sash Window."

Sash Fastener.—A piece of mechanism in brass or iron, the subject of many patents, to fasten and unfasten the casements of a " sash window " (*which see*).

Sash Frame.—The outer frame with sill, in which the sliding sashes or casements are suspended. *See* " Sash Window."

Sash-head.—The top horizontal part of a sash frame in an ordinary building ; but in superior work often " circular-headed " and even circular in plan. *See* " Sash Window."

Sash Linings.—The inner and outer facings of a sash frame (*which see*) affixed to the " pulley stiles " (*which see*), and the " heads " of these are the " inside lining " and the " outside lining," the latter the broadest, as it projects about two-thirds of an inch, and is generally beaded on one edge on the face. *See* " Sash Window."

Sash Pockets.—Portable openings in the lower parts of " sash stiles " to admit the insertion or removal of " sash weights " (*which see*) ; the piece cut out is usually made to cover the same hole, and to be secured in place with a screw. *See* " Sash Window " *and* " Mouse."

Sash Pulley.—Formerly, or in the seventeenth century, a block of oak mortised for and receiving a turned boxwood pulley or sheaf. They were inserted but not screwed or fastened

I

in their places, fitted to the bottom casements only, the top ones being "fast." Modern examples are of iron rising to brass and are variantly termed "frame pulleys." *See* "Sash Window."

Sash Sill.—The bottom horizontal part of a sash frame, properly of hardwood (oak), grooved on the underside for an iron-tongue, weathered and rebated on the upper side. *See* "Sash Window."

Sash Weights.—"Balancing weights" in the cavity of the sash frame, usually of cast iron, but formerly of lead; in section round or square, the former working the best on twisted "sash line" (*which see*). In the top glazed sash the pair of weights are heavier in proportion to or in comparison with the bottom sash. *See* "Sash Window."

Sash Window.—Is sluice window; a window that moves up and down like a sluice (Dutch, *sas* = a sasse, or sluice). The "sash" (*which see*) is the moveable portion; the other is the "sash frame" (*which see*; *also* "Sash Cord," "Lining," "Pocket," "Sill," "Stiles" *and* "Weights" *headed* "Sash").

Satin Walnut.—The European name for American red gum, the product of the *Liquidamber styraciflua* of Linnæus. The sapwood has become known in England as Hazel-pine (*which see*).

Satin-wood (*Chloroxylon Swietenia*, natural order *Cedrelaceæ*, latterly re-named).—A light orange-coloured wood, a native of the mountainous parts of the East Indies. As in the instance of other valuable woods brought from far-off and mostly inaccessible lands, we only trade in "the heart-wood" or "*duramen*," the "sapwood" or "*alburnum*" being dressed off and left behind as worthless. *See* "Spine" *and* "Heartwood."

Saugh Tree.—The Scottish name for the willow tree. Sometimes spelt "sough."

Saw.—A joiner's tool or working instrument operated by hand. Varies in size and shape, defined by rip (as rip-saw), hand, panel, sash or frame, dovetail, keyhole, bow, fret-saw, rat-tail, etc. *See* "Machine Saw."

Saw or Saws (*Variety of*).—European "hand-saws"—the original form—are worked by the "push-action," those of Asia or Japan by the "pull-action." Those of the former are prin-cipally "pit-saw," "frame-saw," "whip-saw," "cross-cut-saw," "rip-saw," "hand-saw," "panel-saw," "sash-saw," "dovetail-saw," "bow-saw," "pad- or keyhole-saw," "rat-tail-saw," "fret-saw," etc. The modern machine-saws, although varied in size and form, do not range much beyond the "web-saw," "jigger-saw," "veneer-saw," "circular-saw," "swage-saw," "drunken-saw" and "band-saw."

Saw (*Inventor of*).—Dædalos, a Greek, who formed the Cretan labyrinth, etc., is said to have invented the saw, the axe, the gimlet, and other carpenter's tools.

Saw (*in Christian art*).—The saw is an attribute of St. Simon and St. James the Less, in allusion to the tradition of their being sawn to death in martyrdom.

Saw Arbor.—The shaft and bearings in which a circular saw is mounted. Also called "Mandrel."

Saw Doctor.—A mechanic skilled in the care, repair, and management of saws.

Saw Falling.—The sizes and quality cut from the log according to the judgment of the sawyer. Without selection; unclassified.

Saw Guide.—A device for steadying a circular or band log saw.

Saw Kerf.—The width of cut made by a saw.

Saw Logs.—Logs after they have been cut down and before they reach the mill to be sawn up.

Saw Pit.—An excavation in the ground used for sawing purposes, in which the under-sawyer stands.

Saw-sharpening Machines.—Used for sharpening saws, working either automatically or only partially so. It is usual to use an emery-wheel for grinding the teeth ; a file when very fine saw-teeth have to be dealt with.

Saw through and through.—To make all cuts on the log parallel.

Saw Timber.—Logs suitable in size and length for the production of merchantable lumber. In America all trees which would make a log 8 in. and upwards in diameter and 8 ft in length.

Sawing, Radial and Tangential.—Details of prime consideration in certain woods, and their behaviour in seasoning, etc., independent of the question which plane is the best to develop the figure or beauty of wood. "Radial" is the line followed in "quartering" wood (instance oak, to obtain "facial figure"), or to saw on lines suggested by the radiation of spokes in a wheel; oak-veneers, other than pollard are "radially-cut." "Tangential" is cutting at an angle of 90 degrees from the radial plane, on which line the "bird's-eye figure" in sugar-maple is found or won. Veneers from a "rotary-cutting" machine are tangential, the tangent there being a circular line, hence "three-ply" and "multi-ply" boards are "tangentially cut." *See* "Figure in Wood."

Sawn.—Cut by a saw, but not otherwise manufactured.

Scaffold.—A term applied to a temporary wooden stage used in the operation of building, or as an instrument of execution.

Scaffold Boards.—Stout boards, bound at the ends with hoop iron and used to form platforms on a scaffold.

Scaffold Plank or **Planks.**—Planks $1\frac{1}{2} \times 11$ in. and 9 in., used as floors or stages of scaffolds or as " walking planks." This term is occasionally extended to 2 in. $\times$ 7 in., which properly are " batten size." *See* " Plank."

Scaffold Poles.—Perpendicular, horizontal and other poles, used in scaffolding. The white, or spruce poles of the Baltic are principally used for this purpose in England and in Europe.

Scaffolding.—Material (mostly wood) of which scaffolds are erected. In London small square timbers are largely used on important buildings.

Scale-boards.—Thin soft-wood boards, " scaled " off with a knife, used for making " match," " hat " and other light boxes, and as a substitute for pasteboard, especially so when a duty obtained on paper ; knife-cut veneers are of this class, so are " 3-ply " and " multi-ply " boards, built up of sheets, not cut by the scale-board machine but by the " rotary peeler." *See* " Rotary Veneer Machine."

Scalper.—An American term for one who sells, for a commission, lumber in which he has no direct financial interest.

Scanfin.—A special form of charterparty, applying to Scandinavian and Finnish wood goods.

Scant.—A verbal term for wanting in size or substance, applied to wood goods sawn bare, narrow or thin in measure or gauge ; it is sometimes extended to waney goods, as " scant at the corners." *See* " Cant " *and* " Wane."

Scantlings.—" Scant " or " small " sizes, often applied to anything under 2 in. $\times$ 6 in. The following sizes of sawn wood are really regarded as scantlings: 2×3, 3×3 and $3\frac{1}{2}$, $3\frac{1}{2} \times 3\frac{1}{2}$ in. Sometimes 2×3, 4, $4\frac{1}{2}$, 5 and $5\frac{1}{2}$ in. are styled scantlings or " two-inch."

Scarf.—To join two pieces of wood together longitudinally, usually with a slanting transverse cut at the join.

Scarfed Lengths.—Two or more pieces of wood fastened together to make the aggregate length required.

Scarlet Oak (*Q. coccinea*).—A native of the States and Canada, which derives its name from the beauty of its autumnal foliage.

Schedule.—As " of prices," a form or an appendix to a contract for work or material : thus (*a*) a contractor may agree to do certain work on a " prime-cost " basis, the work on completion to be measured and priced according to the schedule of prices given, and an agreed trade profit added ; (*b*) a contract may be arranged and a schedule of prices made a part of it, the object of which is to adjust a final settlement—a reduction for what may be left out, and an addition for what is extra or over that covered by the contract amount.

Scoots.—An American term for culls thrown out from mill run in hardwoods.

Scotia.—The hollow moulding in the attic base between the fillets of the Tori. It takes its name from the shadow formed by it, which seems to envelop it in darkness. It is sometimes called a casement, and often from its resemblance to a common pulley " Trochilus."

Scots Fir (*Pinus sylvestris*).—A quick-growing British conifer, thriving on the poorest soils. Used for pit-props, temporary sleepers and building construction.

Scraper.—A " hand-tool " for putting a finished face upon hardwood, especially with cabinet-makers on veneer-work ; it is usually an oblong plate of steel about the size of a post-card, the sharp edges of the metal being dexterously turned over in " setting " to produce a keen edge.

Scraper Grinding Machine.—A machine for sharpening scraper knives. Emory discs of small diameter hollow grind the cutter, while it is automatically passed to and fro in front of it. The edge of the cutter is also turned over by a special tool and thus forms a scraping edge.

Scraping Machine.—This machine is used for scraping boards after planing, which have to be highly polished The boards are fed through the machine by powerful roller feed gear and scraped by means of a cutter, having a turned edge like a hand-scraping tool.

Scratch-moulding.—A moulding worked on the stiles of early wainscot panelling with a " scratch," a piece of steel, shaped for the moulding stick in a block of wood, and worked by hand after the manner of a " spokeshave " or " draw-knife," so worked that the moulding ran out on the surface before the point of a rail was arrived at. Such moulding can only be " scratched " on hardwood like oak. In some degree they resemble the " stop-chamfer " (*which see* ; *also the later* " planting mouldings ").

Screed.—(1) A long thin narrow strip of board, such as are used by plasterers in running moulded plaster cornices. They are temporarily nailed on the walls, ceilings, angles, etc., as " runners " or " guide-rails " for their " moulds " ; (2) narrow edgings in a saw-mill.

Screen.—(1) A partition; an enclosure, separating a portion of a room; usually fixtures, but folding ones of minor importance are common. (2) A riddle or sieve for sifting sand, lime, gravel, etc.; sometimes large rectangular wooden frames with longitudinal and transverse wires. In working position it is propped up at one end to an angle of about 70 degrees; the sifting is done by casting the material against it, when the finer particles pass through the wires.

Screeve.—*See* " Scribe."

Scribe.—An iron-cutting instrument or knife for marking or scoring timbers, commonly termed " scribing iron " or " scribing knife." The chases of the tool are " screeve-marks " (*which see*).

Scribe or Screeve Marks, denoting cubic contents on log timber. *See* "Timber Measure." It is customary in the timber trade in London to mark the solid and superficial contents of masts, trees, spars, timber, and planks of all descriptions with Roman characters; but this is not generally adopted at all the outports. A table of those characters is subjoined, commencing at unity, and ending at 100 ; all higher contents are usually marked in common figures.

TABLE OF NUMBERS RAZED ON TIMBER, ETC., DENOTING CONTENTS.

—From " The Standard Timber Measurer," by Mr. E. A. P. Burt, published by Wm. Rider & Son, Ltd., London. 8s. in cloth.

Scroll.—(1) An initial feature in a handrail starting on a newel and balusters. Eighteenth-century examples were imposing features in mansions, taking turn after turn. *See* " Handrail." (2) A name given to a large class of ornaments characterized generally by their resembling a narrow band arranged in convolutions or undulations. They are prominent features in the capitals of Corinthian and other columns, where they are termed " volutes." *See* " Scroll-step."

Scroll-step.—The first or bottom step in a staircase intended to have a scroll handrail base ; the step has a " scroll-end," formed of a built-up " scroll-block," round which the riser, thinned to the consistency of a veneer, is wound and glued round it ; a board, or boards, forming the " tread " and " nosing " covering or completing the step *See* " Scroll " *and* " Baluster."

Season.—To dry timber, either in the open or in a dry kiln.

Season Checks.—Cracks which appear on the exterior faces of timber during the seasoning process.

Season's Cut.—The output of a sawmill plant for that portion of the year the mill is operated.

Second Growth.—The term " second growth " is applied to certain trees which have grown from the stumps of felled trees, such as hickory or ash. It is also applied to trees of a new growth which have grown up from seeds where the older forest has been cut or otherwise destroyed. The trees produced from shoots of the stumps of older hickory trees grow rapidly, and are held to produce tougher and more pliable wood.

Secret Nailing.—Nailing boards through thin edges where the nail holes are not seen.

Selections, Selected, and Unselected are terms in the wood-trade closely associated with " sorting," " sorted," and " unsorted," and apply to goods that are " graded," or " ungraded." *See* " Graded." Selection may apply to a portion of any known quality or grade of goods where a buyer, paying an extra price, may have the pick of the stock. Unselected means shipments of goods capable of being selected or graded which are dealt with in trade without sorting being resorted to.

Self-acting Cross-cut Saws.—In which either the saw, or the material, has a self-acting feed motion actuated by power.

Self Log, or Cut Log.—Logs, usually mahogany, put aside and sold separately.

Semi-portable Engines.—Engines of the locomotive or portable type, but without road wheels for transporting them from place to place.

Sequoia or Californian Redwood (*Sequoia sempervirens*).—*See* "Californian Redwood."

Serayah.—A Borneo timber resembling mahogany, strong, tough and easily worked.

Serrated (or **Toothed**).—From the Latin *serra*, a saw; a term in various forms that enters the technological field of Botany, as descriptive of leaf forms that clothe certain plants and trees.

Set.—The deflection of the teeth of saws which causes the saw to cut a kerf wider than the thickness of the blade. *See* "Set and Setting."

Set and Setting.—The word "set" is used in various connections, as (1) "To set" or place a house-wall, etc.; (2) "to set up" in business; (3) "to plant," as a shrub or tree; (4) "to set straight" or in "decent order"; (5) "to fix," as "to set a machine, a door-frame, step, stone, or brick"; (6) "a set-time" for completing a contract; (7) "number," as "a set of carving tools"; (8) "to set a fine edge" on cutting or shaving tools; (9) a tool, a "saw-set"; (10) to "set-straight," to hammer out a bend, etc.; (11) in navigation, "to set the compass"; (12) "set-off" (*which see*); (13) "setting a saw" (*which see*); (14) in architecture, the quality of hardening in plaster or cement; (15) "setting-coat" (*which see*). The term "set," like "Joseph's coat," has many colours.

Set Gauge.—A tool used by a cross-cut saw filer to regulate the amount of set given to each tooth.

Set-off.—The part of a wall, etc., which is exposed horizontally when a portion above it is reduced in thickness; its variant name is "off-set." In a legal sense "set-off" represents a counterclaim.

Setting a Saw.—The process of bending saw teeth alternately to the right and left, to give clearance to the sawdust or to cause the saw to run cool and free. *See* "Set and Setting."

Setting-coat.—The third or finishing coat of "three-coat plaster-work," otherwise called the "skimming" (*which see*).

Shaft.—(1) The body of a column or pillar; the part between the capital and base; "a shaft," from the instance of an arrow shaft, is understood to be light in character, hence they may, as in Gothic architecture, be attached, detached, or clustered; (2) a wooden handle of a hammer, spade or other tool; (3) the "shafts" of a cart, wagon or carriage; (4) "iron shaft" of an engine, or for conveying power.

Shakes are distinguished from checks in having been caused within the tree while standing, by frost, wind or other obscure causes, while checks are a cracking of the timber in the seasoning process, due to the fact that all woods shrink in a larger, though varying, proporton in a transverse than in a radial direction. *Round shake* is a separation of the wood along the entire line of an annual ring, usually rather close to the heart, so that a round core of wood enclosing the heart is loose from the rest of the tree. By *through shake* is understood a shake that extends throughout the tree from heart to circumference, although it might be applied to manufactured product and here would merely mean a shake extending through from face to face of the stick. *Boxed shake* is applied only to manufactured product and indicates that the interior shake is entirely enclosed within the piece and nowhere reaches the surface of any side or edge. *Growth* or *heart shake* is sometimes referred to as *star shake* and refers to cracks extending outwardly in one or more directions from the heart. These cracks tend to close rather than open in the seasoning process, because as this process produces tension at the circumference of the piece it must produce compression in the centre.

Shave.—An instrument with a long blade and a handle at each end for shaving hoops, a variant term for a " drawing knife " —used in dressing telegraph poles—(*which see, also* " Spoke- shave.")

Shavings (*of wood, etc.*)—Thin slices pared, peeled, scaled, or shaved off with a shave, a knife, a plane, or other cutting instrument.

Shaw.—A provincial term for small wood or plantation.

Sheathing, Open and Matched.—Tongued and grooved boarding for roof covering under slates, tiles or shingles. " Open " stands for square-edged boards; " matched " may be vari- antly expressed by " tight sheathing." This terminology is American. " Sheath " is an old Saxon word for " a covering," *as of a sword*, and is not common to wood, instance " metal " or " copper sheathing " to a ship's bottom ; " ar- mour plates " to a ship's side ; or ship's planking fixed to the ribs.

Shed, Shedding, and Shedded.—Popular terms in the sawn-wood trade which embrace important subjects and need little descriptive text, their office being to protect goods from damage by sun and rain.

Sheeting.—A lining of planks or boards for protecting an embank- ment and trenching for culverts, otherwise termed sheet- piling ; in working in sand the planks are often tongued and grooved on their edges ; (2) " sheeting " is covering wrought wood-goods with waterproof sheets when travelling on rail in open wagons.

Shelving.—Broad boards suitable for making shelves.

Shimer Cutter Heads.—A form of cutter head usually employed for tongueing and grooving the edge of boards. This is an American product, although much used in this country.

Shingles.—Flat, thin, oblong pieces of wood with one end thinner than the other in order to lap lengthwise, used in covering roofs and outer walls of buildings. A straight-grained, readily splitable wood is cut into blocks, the longitudinal faces of which are of the size intended for the shingles, which are then regularly split off in thicknesses of about a quarter of an inch.

Shiplap and Shiplap-joint.—An overlapping joint in boardings, mouldings, floorings, etc. This may be instanced in " covering boards " of houses, etc., where one board " cloaks," " hides," or " overlaps " another at the joint, the lower edge of the upper board being rebated for that purpose. *See* " Rebate " *and* " Rebate-plane."

Shipping Culls.—A grade of wood above mill culls.

Shipping Days.—The number of days agreed upon by the owners and engagers of the vessel to be devoted to loading, beyond which " Demurrage " is reckoned (*which see*).

Shipping Documents.—All necessary documents appertaining to the shipment of a parcel or cargo of goods to enable the receiver to deal with it.

Shipping Marks.—*See* " Quality and Shipping Marks," *also* " Brands."

Shipping Season.—That period of the year during which it is customary to make shipments from a specified district.

Shives (Cooper's).—Pieces of wood used by coopers as bungs to casks.

Shooks.—A bundle or set of staves sufficient in number for a cask or barrel ; a set of boards for a box. Also called Boxboards, or Caseboards.

Shooting Plane.—A joiner's " hand-plane " of extra length in the stock, used for jointing boards together for tables, countertops, etc. It works on the edge of the boards, its extra length over other like planes enabling it to make truer or finer joints ; of late years the stocks have been shortened and the planes adapted to run on their side like mitre-planes. *See* " Plane."

Short Leaf Pine.—*See* " Pitch Pine."

Shortness of Grain.—May be illustrated by a charge brought against Californian redwood, that when jointed in dovetailing the " pins " break or snap off with a touch , an allied term—not a dictionary word—is " crapply," applied to " softwoods " in like circumstances, or where the wood is dry and " breaks off short."

Short Bills.—Bills with less than ten days to run before maturity.

Shorts.—An American term for small sizes in mahogany 4 in. and over, 2 to 5 ft. long.

Shot, Shoot and Shooting.—Terms in working or handling wood the carpenter and joiner has preserved from a remote past, but which are now obsolete or beyond the reach of modern lexicographers. " Shot " here means a piece of wood, as a door stile, planed and finished straight on the edges, i.e., " shot straight " ; to " shoot " is to straighten, hence a jointing or long shooting-plane, a tool now rarely seen, is the instrument of " shooting " ; it is reflected in a good sportsman, " shooting straight.",

Shutter.—A board or framed and panelled piece of wood whose purpose, like that of a door, is to close a *hole* in a wall, or assist to that end where a window is concerned. For other purposes *see* " Boxing Shutters."

Shuttering.—A term used to describe the boards for making the moulds and shapes used in reinforced concrete construction.

Shuttle.—An instrument used in weaving cloth, with a backward and forward movement.

Shuttle Blocks.—Hardwoods cut to sizes ready for turning to make shuttles.

Siding and Drop-siding.—Siding is a new term little known outside the Canadian " white " or " yellow pine " trade, which literally means " boards." It was not in use with importers when logs, balks and deal sizes of 3 in. in thickness held the European market. It follows that to-day the " pine-sidings " from 1 to 2 in. in thickness are important factors. In the United States this term extends to " prepared feather-edged rebated boards " used for outside boarding of houses, etc. In the broadest of such covering boards the term " Drop-siding " is used.

Sidings.—Boards sawed from the outer portion of a log when the central part is made into timber.

Sight Bills.—Bills payable at sight, or on demand or presentation.

Silky Oak (*Stenocarpus salignus*).—A fine cabinet wood from New Guinea and North-East Australia.

Sill, Sills or Cills.—The base of a door, window or sash, or pieces of timber on which anything rests ; its variants are " syle," " sole " and " sule." That on the lowest level is often termed the " groundsel " or " groundsol."

Silo or Silos.—Term applied to a collection of bins for storing in bulk uncleaned or partially cleaned wheat. Made of (1) timber (*see* " Timber Silos ") ; (2) reinforced or ferro-concrete ; (3) steel cylinders.

Silver Fir (*Abies pectinata*), or Swiss pine.—A resonant wood. Imported chiefly for making the sounding boards for pianos.

Silver Grain.—The medullary rays of the botanists, being compressed cellular tissues, which usually run continuously from the pith to the bark. This figure has other names, as " mirrors " (American), " pith-rays " (ditto), " flecks " (ditto), " patches of silvery-wood " (ditto), " figure."

Silver-grained.—Quarter sawed timber with conspicuous medullary rays.

Silver Spruce.—*See* " Sitka Spruce."

Sitka Spruce (*P. Sitchensis*), known also as " Tideland Spruce " and " Silver Spruce."—A Pacific Coast timber, extensively used during the late war in the manufacture of air-craft. Its wood is clear and of a silky texture and yields large sizes.

Skid.—An American term signifying the drawing of logs from the stump to the skidway, landing or mill.

Skidway.—The prepared road along which logs after being cut are passed to a special point in the forest.

Skimming.—(1) Correctly speaking, the " third " or " setting-coat " (*which see*), the last or finishing coat of " three-coat plaster-work." In " two-coat work " it may not obtain, as the second or finishing coat may be " trowelled-off," that is, given a " smooth or a steel-face " to otherwise rough floated-work, i.e., work " tooled " with a wood-float. (2) Fine plastic material, otherwise " putty."

Skin-dried.—Surface dried only.

Skirting.—The board, usually moulded, running round a room next the floor. Also known as " plinth " or " washboard."

Slab.—The cut taken first from a log in process of reducing it to square form for the sawing from it of lumber with square edges. A slab has one flat surface, while the other surface is the bark or outside of the log. *See* " Flitch."

Slab Edging.—Taking the outside cuts off the log.

Slack Cooperage.—Packages or cases consisting of two round heads and a body composed of one or more staves held together with hoops, which are used as containers for non-liquid products.

Slash.—An American term for the débris left after logging, wind, or fire.

Slash and Slashing.—Implies "cut at random or cut into long strips or slits." It has come to mean parting one annual ring, zone or layer of wood from another, a process finely illustrated by the "rotary veneer" or "peeling machines"; hence the figure shown on the face of such veneers is called "slash grain," and should not be confused with the "silver grain" of oak obtained by radial sawing. *See* "Peel and Peeling," "Slash Grain or Slash Figure," "Slive and Slivering."

Slash Grain or Slash Figure.—Terms in the veneer trade not yet fixed as dictionary words. To be correct, they should not be applied to figure such as the "silver grain" or "mirror figure" of oak obtained by "quarter" or "radial sawing," but be confined to figure yielded by rotary knife cutting, or peeling veneers off the round or tangential face of the tree, the figure being the play of the knife in the hard and soft light and dark parts, *ergo* the spring and summer wood (*which see*).

Slashers.—An American name for "trimmers" or edging saws. The term is usually employed to describe a number of saws on one spindle which cannot be quickly placed in and out of action independently, as is the case with the trimming machine.

Slat and Slats.—(1) A narrow piece or pieces of timber, whose meaning is well defined in "bed slats"—strong narrow spaced boards notched into and reaching from side to side of a bed-frame, to form a floor or stage for the mattress and the bed proper. "Slat" appears as a close relation to "lath." (2) In America a term for a sawed piece of wood $7\frac{1}{2} \times 2\frac{1}{2} \times \frac{1}{4}$ in., used in pencil manufacture.

Slate or Slates.—As roof covering, an *argillaceous* stone, highly crystallized, but not cleaving on the line of its bedding as originally; a sedimentary deposit; it varies in colour from a bluish-grey to a greenish-black. *See* "Welsh Slates," *and* "Slate-slabs," produced by splitting in thicknesses like the "school-boy's slate," to "3-in. slabs," and from a few inches in length to about 7 ft.

Slate-slab or Slabs.—An important branch of the Welsh slate-trade, being slabs from $\frac{1}{2}$ in. to 3 in. in thickness, wrought for sills, steps, troughs, billiard-table beds, sinks, lavatory tops, tanks, urinals, mangers, chimney pieces, shelves, tombstones, cisterns with galvanized bolts and nuts, ridge rolls, ridge wings, etc. The slabs are sold random sizes, or cut to specified dimensions. *See* " Slate or Slates."

Slates.—The various sizes of slates are thus named :—

Doubles	..	..	..	..	13 × 7 in.
Ladies ..	..	..	..	..	16 × 8 ,,
Countesses	..	..	..	..	20 × 10 ,,
Duchesses	..	..	..	..	24 × 12 ,,
Imperials	..	..	..	..	27 × 36 ,,
Queens ..	..	..	..	..	27 × 36 ,,

The mode of trading in this century inclines to work upon sizes, and not titles or state-names. *See* " Westmorland Slates " *and* " Welsh Slates."

Slating Battens or **Slate Laths.**—Small strips of wood upon which the slates are fastened. *See* " Rock Laths."

Sleepers or **Sleeper Blocks.**—In railway construction, one of the pieces of timber placed across the permanent way, to which the rails are fastened in order to keep them in position.

Sleeper Joists.—The joists used on the ground floor of houses.

Sleeper Saw Benches.—Powerful endless-chain feed benches, in which sleeper blocks are fed forward by strong chains having dogs at intervals, usually sawing the block down the centre, forming two sleepers at each cut.

Slice and Slicing.—Implies " a thin broad piece " and " to cut or to divide." It is curious that these terms have not attached themselves to rotary veneer-cutting, where " peel and peeling " have found lodgment. *See* " Slive and Slivering," " Slash and Slashing," *and* " Peel and Peeling."

Slide Rule.—A mathematical instrument consisting of two parts, one of which slides into the other, for the mechanical performance of addition and subtraction, and, by means of long arithmetic scales, for multiplication and division.

Slings.—The material for transporting wood from ship to shore or from one point to another.

Slive and Slivering.—Terms related to " slash and slashing," or " slice and slicing," and imply long, thin riven shreds of wood. Their meaning is plainly seen in " firwood flooring-boards " unquartered in the sawing, or cut tangentially where the hard part of the grain (the summer wood) wears into long splinters. Where the edge of the grain is presented to wear, the flooring wears without slivering and more evenly. *See* " Peel and Peeling " *and* " Yellow Pine Flooring."

Sloates.—The narrow pieces of wood which hold a framework together, as the slats or sloates of a gate or cart.

Slot Mortising Machine.—A machine which cuts out mortises by means of a revolving tool. This leaves the ends of the mortise circular in form　Gate and fence posts are usually mortised in this manner.

Smoked Beech.—Used in the manufacture of sabots or wooden shoes in Germany ; to render it proof against decay, it is first converted to the smallest sizes required for practical purposes, and then steamed and smoked over branches and chips of beechwood, or, in other words, charged by fumigation with the pyroligneous acid common to the beech.

Snag.—A rough piece of timber. The term is generally used for pieces floating or accidentally fixed in water. It has the same meaning as " knag " (*which see*).

Snake.—In sawing, to make a wavy cut in a log. It is a sign of poor saw fitting.

Snape or **Snape-ended.**—A term applied to square or partially squared logs, especially of mahogany, which have been dragged overland before shipment, and, to ease their motion, have had their front lower sides somewhat rounded, sledge fashion ; such ends, as in Greenheart, become special lines in the timber trade, where they pass into various trades ; one is in connection with " hydraulic oil-presses." They are invariably bored for pegs, for haling-ropes, or chains. *See* " Snipe-ended."

Snath.—*See* " Sned."

Sned or **Snath** (*variously written* " snead," " sneed," " sneath ").—The handle of a scythe.

Snedding.—Dressing a tree.

Sneeze-wood (*Pteroxylon utile*).—One of the most valuable woods of South Africa for engineering work, furniture and carpentry. It is difficult to work, as its dust provokes violent sneezing.

Snigging.—Dragging the logs on the ground. Called locally " tushing."

Snipe-ended or **Snake-ended.**—Hewn logs tapered at the butt end in felling for the purpose of facilitating being drawn through the bush. *See* " Snape-ended."

Soffit.—The under side of the lintel or ceiling of an opening, also the under horizontal surface of an architrave between the column and the under surface of the corona of a cornice.

Softwood.—A term applied to the produce of needle-leafed or coniferous trees.

Sole Bars.—Longitudinal pieces of oak used in the framing of railway wagons. Also known as "Main Tram Pieces."

Solignum.—A timber preservative, brown in colour, much used for preserving timber from decay and insects.

Sorting.—Dividing lumber into its various qualities and dimensions.

Sound Merchantable.—A loose general term more often applied to logs than to sawn wood, and intended to include all logs that it will pay to saw.

Sound Wormy.—Wood affected by worm holes, but otherwise sound. Used in America as ground for veneering upon.

Spade Tree.—The handle of a spade.

Spall or Spale.—A term seldom met with. Applied to a shaving or chip of wood wedgelike in shape.

Spandrel.—The irregular triangular space comprehended between the outer curve or extrados of an arch, a horizontal line drawn from its apex and a perpendicular line from its springing.

Spanish Chestnut.—*See* "Sweet Chestnut."

Spars.—Mainly used as masts for ships. Also a small beam or rafter. In architecture, spars are the common rafters of a roof, as distinguished from the principal rafters. *See* "Rafters."

Species (*in Botany*).—Usually defined as a collection of individuals that are precisely alike in every character, not capable of change by any accidental circumstance, and capable of uniform, invariable and permanent continuance by natural propagation. *See* "Genus" *and* "Natural Order." All species have a tendency to form "varieties" (*which see*).

Specification.—(1) The document stating the sizes and particulars of a number of pieces or cargo of wood. (2) The statement of what is required, prepared by an architect for the guidance of a builder.

Specific Gravity.—The weight of wood is sometimes expressed by a comparison of the weight of a given volume with that of an equal volume of water, or by what is known as "specific gravity." If the specific gravity of a certain kind of wood is stated to be ·300, it means that a given volume of this wood weighs ·300 times as much as an equal volume of water. Since a cubic foot of water weighs 62·5 or 1,000 ounces, a cubic foot of wood of specific gravity of ·300 weighs ·300 $\times$ 62·5 or 18·75 pounds.

Spigots.—*See* "Spiles."

Spile Boards.—Boards used in mines for shoring up passage-ways.

Spiles or Spigots.—Wooden pegs for casks containing fermenting liquid. Usually made of American red or porous oak and termed " Spile-pegs."

Spindle Machine.—A vertical moulding and shaping machine, so called because the cutter spindle is visible for a greater portion of its length than in other machines.

Spine.—A trade-term, especially amongst ship-carpenters, for the heart-wood of oak, as distinct from the sapwood. *See* " Satin-wood " *and* " Heart-wood."

Spinney or Spinny.—A small thicket or grove with undergrowth ; a clump of trees.

Spiral.—Implies a round or cylindrical substance, associated with the sense of a twist. This is a form observable in certain plants and the stems of forest trees. *See* " Spiral Grain." In architecture it is an ancient form of staircase twisting round a newel, the latter in modern instances being deleted and its place taken by an open " well " or " well-hole " *See* " Staircase "

Spiral Grain.—A rounded, twisted grain. This may often be seen on the outside of a round bole of a tree, or on the crown of a wainscot log or billet, possibly traceable on the outer bark also. *See* " Spiral."

Splay.—A large chamfer.

Splice and Spliced.—Refers largely to wood, beams, etc., joined or married in lengths, instance " tie-beams " or " principal beams " in roofs of abnormal span, " crane-beams," etc. ; in a lesser but more popular degree splicing is pursued in fixing handles to " cricket bats," where the art is brought to great perfection.

Splint and Splinter.—(1) To split or rend wood into long thin pieces ; (2) a piece of wood split off, or broken away from a saw, or wrought into serviceable form as a surgical appliance. In the instance of a tree struck by lightning the pieces may be " splinters " or " shivers," the latter reminiscent of the sailor's term, " Shiver my timbers."

Split and Splitter, as Lath-splitter.—*See* " Rive and River."

Splits.—Ordinary pit-props split in the middle. By splits and back is meant ordinary splits from which a thin slab has been sawn off the back, thus being an intermediary between sleepers and splits.

Spokes (*of a wheel*).—The rays of a wheel; small bars inserted in the hub or nave of a wheel; the round of a ladder; a handspike. *See* " Hub," " Round," *and* " Handspike."

Spokeshave.—A finer or superior tool to the " draw-knife" (*which see*); a two-handled instrument of hardwood with a cutting iron inserted, to work after the manner of a plane.

Spool.—A wooden cylinder or reel used to wind thread or yarn upon.

Spool Bar.—Small squares of timber from which spools are turned.

Spoolwood.—Hardwood imported in small squares for turning into spools and similar material.

Spout or **Spouting.**—Horizontal wooden, leaden, or iron gutters running along the eaves of buildings to carry off rain-water; spouts fixed perpendicular are called " wall-spouts," " fall-spouts," or " down-spouts." The latter are now rarely made of wood; the metal ones (iron and zinc) are called " wall-pipes," " stack-pipes," etc.

Spout Adze.—An adze shaped like a gouge, to chase the hollow or trough of the spout in hand-made wooden spouts, which instruments have been practically obsolete since the introduction of machinery for spout-making.

Spout-head or **Heads.**—Head or heads of " wall-spouts," " fall-spouts," or " down-spouts." In the case of wood they are made square in plan, but " hopper-shape " on the front and sides; where of lead, variant in size and pattern, often highly ornamented, bearing dates, initials, heraldic signs, etc. Those of the seventeenth and eighteenth centuries are prized and collected as art objects for museums. The modern cast-iron heads are occasionally ornamented and dated.

Sprag.—A billet of wood used to check the motion of a carriage on a gradient. Used also in shunting operations on the railways.

Spring-set.—A saw is spring-set when one tooth is sprung slightly to the right and the next one to the left, and so on alternately throughout the saw.

Spring-wood.—Formed in the spring of the year, and is the inner, lighter coloured and most porous part of an annual ring, layer or zone of wood in an exogenous tree, as the outer, darker and less porous part is the summer-wood (*which see*; *also* " Slash Grain "). It is the joint growth of the " spring " and " summer " woods, and knives, as in rotary veneer-cutting machines, slicing through them that produce the figure known as " bird's-eye " in the sugar maple, and "feathery figures" from other woods, features so largely worked upon in American veneered stock. *See* "Slash Grain."

Spruce Fir (*Abies excelsa*) or **Common Spruce.**—A soft wood, but the English variety is of little commercial value, owing to competition with the foreign variety which is imported from the North of Europe cut into convenient sizes. Used for temporary sleepers and temporary fences. *See also* "Black Spruce" and "Sitka Spruce."

Spunk.—Rotten wood; touchwood; wood decomposed by vegetable action, the work of fungi.

Spur or **Spurs.**—(1) The principal root of a tree. (2) A post used to strengthen a rafter. A variant of this is "sper."

Square.—One hundred superficial (or surface) feet of wood, irrespective of thickness.

Square-edged.—A piece of wood in which all the edges are practically square. Sometimes loosely taken (if not described as absolutely square-edged) as admitting some wane.

Square Frame.—In joinery, a work is said to be square-framed or framed-square when the framing has all the angles of its stiles, rails and mountings square without being moulded or chamfered.

Square-jointed.—Cut square at the ends and on the sides, as in flooring-boards, to distinguish from "tongued and grooved."

Square Staff.—A square fillet used as an angle staff in place of a bead moulding.

Stack.—A stack of wood measures 12 ft. × 3 ft. × 3 ft. and contains 108 cubic ft., being exactly half a fathom.

Staff and Staff Bead.—"Staff," in a primary sense, is a hand-staff to ease or assist in walking.

> "A staff his right hand bore,
> And blue the colour of the frock he wore."

For staff bead *see* "Angle Bead."

Stage.—(1) A slung platform at the bow porthole of a ship, on which men stand when discharging goods from a ship. (2) The part in a theatre on which stage-plays are performed.

Stagheaded.—A tree past its maturity, the topmost branches and branchlets of which are dead.

Staircase.—Or "flight of stairs," a "storey" of which may be in one or more parts broken by "landings." Being a fitment of many parts it has an interesting nomenclature; instance, "riser," * "tread," * "nosing," * "step," * "winder," * "flyer," "half-landing," "quarter-landing" or "space" or "pace," "newel" * (if omitted, "a well" or "well-hole,") "string-board," * "cut-string," "carriage" (*which see*); *also the above terms marked* *, "Scroll Step," "Handrail," *and* "Spiral."

Stand.—(1) All the growing trees of a forest ; (2) a construction or stage, to stand upon—instance "band-stand," "race-stand," "procession stand," etc.

Standard Dozen.—In Russia sawn timber is calculated by the standard dozen or 12 pieces 12 ft. 11 in. $\times$ 1½ in.

Standard Hundred.—An established measure for timber consisting of 120 pieces (the Long Hundred or 10 dozen), except the Quebec Standard, which contains 100, of a certain size. The Petrograd or St. Petersburg Standard is the one most generally used in this country. In the early days of timber importing, each of the principal ports had its own standard, but most of these have fallen into disuse, as have the London and Dublin Standards. The following are the principal standards :—

Christiania :
   120 pieces 11 ft. 9 in. $\times$ 1¼ in. $= 103\frac{1}{3}$ cub. ft.
Drammen (Dram) :
   120 pieces 9 ft. 6½ in. $\times$ 2½ in. $\Big\}= 121\frac{7}{8}$ cub. ft.
            13 ft. 9 in. $\times$ 1¼ in.
St. Petersburg (or Petrograd) :
   120 pieces 12 ft. 11 in. $\times$ 1½ in. $= 165$ cub. ft.
Quebec :
   100 pieces 12 ft. 11 in. $\times$ 2½ in. $= 229\frac{1}{6}$ cub. ft.

Standard Lengths.—An American term for lengths into which rough lumber is cut for general use. The standard lengths in pitch pine are multiples of 2 ft., from 4 to 24 ft. inclusive. Hardwood standard lengths run from 4 to 16 ft. inclusive. In Quebec the standard lengths are 12 and 13 ft.

Standard Stave.—*See* "Stave (Oak)," *and other* "Stave" *notes.*

Stave (Oak) "Standard-stave."—*The unit of computation* is understood to be 5½ ft. long, 5 in. broad or wide, and 1½ in. thick. All other sizes traded upon are brought up, or reduced down to that *one standard-stave*. A *mille* of staves is 1,200 pieces (based on the old Teutonic "long-hundred" of "six score") and those "pieces" the "computed standard-staves." *See* "Pipe-stave Oak" *and other* "Stave" *notes.*

Stave (Oak) "Standard-stave" in Computations.—175 standard-staves are equal to 50 cubic ft. 1 in., 6¾ parts, practically one load of 50 cubic ft. Hence 1,200 "standard staves," owing to the variations in the breadths, are viewed or considered equal to 13 loads. *See* "Standard-stave" *and* "Pipe-stave Oak" *and other* "Stave" *headings.*

Stave-trade.—A complex department of the wood-trade, now largely conducted as a separate branch. The small consumer, or home brewer, has dropped out in the face of the brewing trade being specialized and centred in certain districts, a movement that has led to the "stave-trade" being conducted on wholesale lines, or in the hands of a few operators.

Staves.—(1) Narrow pieces of wood, of oak or fir, birch and beech, from which casks, tubs, etc., are made. Largely used in the manufacture of cement casks, in the chemical and china clay trade and for making herring boxes. Large quantities of fir staves are shipped from Sweden, Finland and Russia. (2) Little cylindrical staves in a ladder or hayrick are known as "Rounds" or "Rundles."

Staves, Freight of.—A mille standard of oak-staves is taken at six times the rate charged for timber per load. *See* "Stave (Oak) 'Standard-stave.'"

Staves (Oak), Customary Lengths and Names (about).

EUROPEAN.

	Ft. In.	Ft. In	
Memel Pipe	5 6	6 0	The longer lengths, 5 in. or more broad, the shorter descending to 4 in.; the thicknesses (on the thin edges) ranging from 1 in. to 3 in.
Brandy Pipe	4 6 to	5 5	
Hogshead	4 3 „	4 5	
Brandy Hogshead	3 7 „	4 2	
Long Barrel	3 2 „	3 9	
Short Barrel	2 10 „	3 1	
Long Heading	2 4 „	2 9	
Short Heading	1 6 „	2 1	

AMERICAN OR QUEBEC.

	Ft. In.	In.	
Pipe	5 6 long	5 broad	From 1 in. to 3 in. thick on the thin edge.
Hogshead	4 6 „	4½ „	
Barrel	4 0 „	4 „	
Heading	{2 6} / {1 6} „	5 „	

Staves 5 ft. 1 in. long, and all heart-wood, if only 4½ in. broad, shall pass in the trade as 5 in., or as being of merchantable size.

Staves for Dry or **Slack Casks.**—Have no special mode of extraction in relation to, or with, the radial lines shown by the "medullary rays" or "figure" of oak in the cross or end-section of a tree. They are consequently cut any way, the essential mode imperative in the instance of the "Liquor staves," being ignored. See "Staves for Liquid Casks" and also "Stave" entries. Their source is largely Sweden and Norway.

Staves for Liquid or **Tight Casks.**—These are specially riven and hewn oak, the sides synchronizing with the radial lines of the wood, and the edges with the tangential lines. They are the most valued and costly staves in the trade. See "Staves for Dry Casks" and also "Stave" entries. Their source is the Baltic ports of Danzig, Memel, Stettin, Riga and Libau, and from Russia and N. America.

Stay.—In carpentry, a piece of timber performing the office of a brace to prevent the swerving of the piece to which it is applied.

Steam Cant Lifter.—Consisting of an arm actuated by steam power in a similar manner to a steam nigger, but used for shifting about timbers instead of logs.

Steam Feed for Log Carriages.—A long steam cylinder with piston actuated by steam. The piston rod acts directly on to the log carriage, giving a very rapid feed motion, for which reason it is sometimes known as "shotgun" feed.

Steam Jump Saw.—Consists of a circular saw fitted to the top of a vertical post. The saw is situated immediately under the log or timber to be crosscut, and is fed into the work by means of steam acting against a piston attached to the bottom of the beam, causing it to rise.

Steam Nigger.—Known under various other names, such as "Log Canter" and "Log Turner." Consisting of arms actuated by a piston which are thrust against a log by means of steam power, pushing the log to more into any required position. It is used near to the carriage of a saw when it is desired to turn a big log.

Step or **Stair.**—A block of stone, concrete or wood, of a uniform height, a number of which form a "stairway," or "flight of stairs." In the instance of being built up of boards it becomes a "staircase," which see.

Stepping.—A grade of timber suitable for steps.

Stevedore.—A term much heard at shipping ports, and there consisting of a man whose business it is to act as contractor for the loading and unloading of vessels with their cargoes, or has...

gang of men undertaking such work. It is a corruption of the Spanish *estirador*, a woolpacker, from the Latin *stipare*, to press together.

Stick.—A thin strip of wood placed between boards when piled to facilitate seasoning. The straight trunk of a tree; a log; a piece of wood; a piece of kindling; or the "stick" or "splint" of a match. *See* "Tally-stick."

"Stick" and "Sticking" (*of thrust*). Terms used in working "wood-mouldings" by hand. It is another term for "working mouldings," hence "sticking mouldings" or "beads." It was not uncommon, before machinery was adapted to this work, for a builder to employ a man to do nothing else but "stick mouldings," who, with "heavy mouldings," would have a strong youth in front pulling the hand-plane with a cord; "stuck moulds" now little used. *See* "Planting Mouldings."

Stile or Style. (1) The vertical or upright piece of a sash or door; (2) the vertical part of a piece of framing, into which timber the ends of the rails are fixed by mortises and tenons, sometimes written "styles"; (3) a contrivance for allowing people to pass over or through fences without permitting animal stock to follow them.

Stinkwood (*Ocotea ballata*). A South African tree, its wood somewhat resembling walnut, giving off a strong peculiar odour when worked. It is valued for its strength and durability.

Stobs.—Rough uprights used in fencing.

Stock, or Stocks. (1) The stem or main body of a tree or other plant; (2) the stem of a tree in which a graft is inserted; (3) a post, a log, something fixed solid, as in "village stocks," instruments for punishing transgressors; (4) the handle of a tool; (5) the wooden portion of a musket (*see* "Gun-stock"); (6) capital, or the money invested in trade, in insurance, etc.; (7) the goods on hand of a merchant or trading company; (8) a tool, as in "stock-drill" and "stock and dies" for tapping or cutting threads, "stock and bit" or "brace and bit." It is the root-word of "stock-ade," "stock-lock," etc.

Stock Sizes.—Sizes for which there is a constant demand and which are usually kept on hand.

Stool, and Stooled.—"Stool" is another term for "stump"—the part that remains in or on the ground when a tree is felled, when a stooled maple that has commenced to decay, but has put forward new life in the form of one or more shoots seated between the wood and the bark, and may again produce its like in a forest-tree or trees.

Stooled-Ash.—Second growth from the original roots. There are other species than that of ash endowed by nature with this gift of reproduction. *See* " Ash."

Stop.—A projection or point where the girth measurement of a log suddenly alters.

Stop or **Stop-chamfer.**—An elaboration of " chamfer " (*which see*). A chamfer is a narrow face cut back at an angle of 45 degrees from each face of a corner at right-angles. It is a common mode of treatment of the edges of panelled framing, but capable of great elaboration in larger works in wrought wood, stone or plaster.

Storey.—A horizontal division in a building. The cellar or basement is sometimes so-called, but invariably the ground (level) storey, followed by the higher in number or chamber stories. In important buildings there are occasionally intermediate stories termed " entresols " or " mezzanine."

Stow, and Stower.—*See* " Plank, or Deal, or Board Stower."

Stowage.—All kinds of goods that make up the cargo of a ship ; but in thus loading or stowing vacant places occur, caused by cross-beams, masts, pumps, etc., which for the benefit of the ship-owner is filled up with goods supplied by the merchants or bought at the ports of loading by the captains ; such goods are termed " broken stowage," and where wood is shipped may consist of log-ends, " deal, batten and board ends " (*which see*), or " firewood, *alias* cook-wood " (*which see*).

Stowage Planks.—A poor quality or classification of planks for stowing wood or other goods in vessels. In cargoes of hewn pitchpine timber they filled vacant places in ships' holds and were usually common in quality.

Straight Grain.—The wood of a tree or log is said to be straight grained when the principal wood cells are parallel to the axis of growth. A piece of lumber is said to be straight grained when the principal wood cells are parallel to its length, that is with the grain running from end to end of the piece and parallel, not twisted, with its length.

Straps.—Small pieces used and fastened internally on stone walls on which to nail laths for plaster, otherwise termed " screeds."

Strickle or **Strike.**—A piece of straight wood, variantly termed " a straightedge," used to " strike " grain to the level of a measure ; other uses for like instruments are (*a*) with

plumbers to gauge the thickness when casting sheet-lead;
(*b*) with plasterers in getting even-faces on wall, etc., when
" rendering " or " floating " their work.

Striking Gear.—An attachment of levers to regulate the starting
or stopping of machinery, by throwing the driving belt on
or off the pulley.

String-board or **String-piece.**—Another term for the " wallboard " of a staircase, " housed " or prepared to receive
the ends of the " steps." It extends to, or embraces, the
" box " or " boxed " string at the opposite end of the step
(if no wall is there present); a variant form of the latter
is " cut-string," which means that part is cut away for the
step-ends to run over. In one case the balusters stand on
the " string "; in the other on the exposed " step-ends."
See " Staircase " *and* " Nick and Notch."

Stringcourse.—A projecting horizontal band or line of moulding
in or on a building, used to denote floor-lines, or continued
sill-lines. In some periods of Gothic architecture they
were developed into chaste and beautiful features. In later
brickwork it is often a flat band.

String Measure.—A measure of timber taken to half-inches by
a string round the centre of a log and doubled twice to
quarter girth; lengths are taken to feet only and allowances for defects are made in the length. *See* " Liverpool
String Measurement."

Stringers.—Pieces of wood into which other pieces are fitted and
which hold the whole together, as, for instance, the side
pieces of a ladder.

Stringy Bark is a name given to various Eucalypts growing in
South Australia and Tasmania.

Structural Timbers.—Timbers used for a framework or for the
essential parts of a whole structure.

Struts.—In carpentry, any piece that keeps two others from
approaching, and is therefore in itself in a state of compression, the opposite of " tie." In flooring, short pieces of
timber about $1\frac{1}{4}$ in. thick, and 3 to 4 in. wide, inserted
between flooring joists, sometimes diagonally to stiffen
them. In roofing larger and varied in size. *See* " Bridging."

Stub, and Stubbing.—A stock, a stem, a log, a block, usually
applied to a stump with a root, such as are grubbed up,
or " stubbed up " Its diminutive is " stubble."

Stud, or Studs.—(1) The intermediate posts in partitions of wood-
work. They are also called *uprights* or *quarters*. In this
position they are modern representatives of the older and

larger " posts " in " post and pan " (*which see*) or " half-timbering " (*which see*). Allied, or consequent terms, are " studding " and " stud-partition." (2) A nail with a large head inserted in work chiefly for ornament ; an ornamental knob.

Stuff, Thick and Thin.—Common terms in the converted wood-trade, which extend to the carpenter, joiner and cabinet maker, and even to the makers of wood-working machinery, for the moulding machines. Lightning-planers, etc., are not constructed to deal with " thick stuff." Timber trees, standing, felled, or *en route* to the sawmills, have not taken on these terms, hence, this heading presents itself as the English equivalent of the mysterious American term—" Lumber." *See* " Thick Stuff " *and* " Thin Stuff."

Stump.—(1) The stub or part of a tree remaining in the earth after the tree is cut down. (2) One of three round pegs, 2¼ ft. long, three of which form the wicket in the game of cricket.

Stump Orator.—In America, a person who harangues the people from the stump of a tree or other chance elevation ; a mob orator.

Stumpage, and Stumpage Prices.—American terms which relate to the current values of standing or felled timber or timber-trees. They are variant terms for " timber " and " timber values," and are distinct from the ubiquitous one of " lumber " which only comes on the scene when the timber trees in the hands of the millmen pass into converted stock. *See* " Lumber."

Styles.—Upright pieces in panelled work. *See* " Rail."

Sugar Pine (*Pinus Lambertiana*).—A tree growing on the Pacific Coast of North America, known also as Pumpkin Pine. Wood resembles Canadian yellow pine.

Summer, or Sommer-beam.—A horizontal beam or girder, otherwise " summer-tree," usually a beam mortised for joists. It is one and the same with " Brest-sommer," and implies a beam above the ground level, otherwise its proper name would be a *sill*.

Summer Shipment.—Shipments during the summer, which, in the United Kingdom, is regarded as extending from 21st June to 22nd September.

Summer Wood.—The outer, darker coloured and least porous part of an annual ring, layer or zone of wood in an exogenous tree, as the inner, lighter coloured and most porous part is the " spring wood " (*which see*). The annual rings or

accretions are faintly marked by colour lines in lime trees
and sycamores.   They are on the other hand pronounced
in the firs and pines; instance, the "pitchpine, or "yellow-
pine" of America.   *See* "Slash Grain."

Surbase.—The crowning, moulding or cornice of a pedestal, a
border, or moulding above the base as the mouldings immediately above the base of a room.

Surface Measure.—The area in square feet on one face of a board.
When boards are 1 in. in thickness the term is synonymous
with board feet.

Surfaced.—A board or other piece of timber planed on one or
more sides.

Survey and Surveyor.—A "survey" is an attentive view, a look,
or a careful examination of an object, usually made in connection with fixing or assessing its value.   A "surveyor" is
a qualified and experienced person, who views and examines
for the purpose of ascertaining the condition, quality or
quantity.   This work, and the expert associated with it,
form an important detail in the timber and wood trades
touching the forest growth, the felled trees, the floating
rafts, the mill-stocks, and the converted goods through
their every phase; wood being a damageable class of goods,
and a prey to fire, Surveyors, Lloyds-marine, and others,
are established at most ports and centres of trade.

Swage.—A tool used to spread the points of teeth of a band or
circular saw.

Swage-set.—A saw is swage-set when the ends of the teeth are
spread to a width greater than the thickness of the saw.

Sweet (or **Spanish**) **Chestnut** (*Castanea vesca*).—Introduced into
Britain by the Romans.   A hard durable wood, much
resembling oak. but can be distinguished from it by the eye
not detecting the medullary rays.   The wood is more durable
young than old and diminishes in value after reaching the
age of sixty, though it may live for centuries.   Used by
cabinet makers, undertakers and turners, and when young
as a substitute for oak.   Its failing is ring or heartshake
when approaching maturity.

Sweet-woods.—Embrace trees that produce edible fruits; they
are mostly hardwoods inclined in colour to brown and even
darker shades.   They rank as perishable woods from being
prone to the attack of the worm, or *larvæ* of the furniture-
beetle, after the wood is seasoned and placed in work.
"Walnut" and "pear-tree wood" may be taken as examples; exceptions, with regard to the fruit, are offered by
the ash and the lime, but the sweetness of the latter is
noticeable in the odour of its blossom.

S.X. Board.—A wallboard with a white mat surface, consisting of wood and vegetable fibres compressed into layers.

Sycamore (*Acer pseudo platinus*).—A fairly hard, close-grained white wood, valuable artistically as well as commercially. Used for printing and mangle rollers, also by manufacturers of dairy utensils, toymakers, brushmakers, bobbin turners, also for musical instruments (especially violins).

T

Table.—An article of furniture consisting of a flat surface raised on legs. It is a term endowed with an extensive application, not restricted to a horizontal plane or position, as " altar table," " table of the laws," etc. Its most common use is " dining table," " kitchen table," " dressing table," e.g., where it is allied to " board " ; instance, H.M. " Board of green cloth," primarily a table covered with that material. *See* " Board " *and* " Abacus." This term has travelled to machinery, instance " saw-table."

Taint.—(1) To imbue or impregnate, as with some extraneous matter which alters the sensible qualities of the substance. (2) To be infected or corrupted, or to be touched with something corrupted ; a term often used in connection with sawn-wood goods out of condition, spotted, damaged with rot or decayed, often engendered in the hold of a ship or by close piling.

Tally (French, *tallier* ; Spanish, *tallar*).—To cut ; its equivalent in the Teutonic languages is *nick* and *notch*. Throughout its ramifications as a verb, active or neuter, it is associated with wood ; primarily it is a *cut* or *incision* on a piece of wood, but in the timber-trade, especially the heavy part connected with shipping and handling cargoes, the lead-pencil takes the place of the knife. *See* " Tally-stick," " board," *and* " man."

Tally-board.—A piece of soft white board, about 2 ft. long, 9 in. to 11 in. broad, and 1 in. thick (when new), on which tally-men mark the various sizes, etc., of the goods to be tallied, indicating them in fives, made by five pencil strokes, thus: |||| ; or in tens—X, or twenties—XX ; working and counting on fives being the most practised. Such tallies are only kept a short time in the offices, when the boards are re-planed and re-used or worn thinner.

Tally-man.—One who records or tallies the measurement of logs or the number of pieces in each sling as they are discharged from the ship ; one who keeps the " tally " or marks or cuts the numbers on a " tally-stick " (*which see, also* "Tally" *and* " Tally-board ").

Tally-stick.—A piece of round or square wood on which notches or marks of number and value were or are cut ; the latter, usually hazel, and which had writing added on the uncut sides. The principal form, after the notches were made, was to split the stick into two parts, the buyer and seller or the borrower and lender each retaining half, one the counterpart of the other. A notch for £100 was the breadth of a thumb , for £1, the breadth of a barleycorn ; a penny was indicated by a slight slit. This clumsy contrivance was effectual in preventing forgery, and survived in the Exchequer until 1834, when several cart-loads of old " tally-sticks " and " counters " in the cellars of the Houses of Parliament were destroyed in the fire which consumed that national building.

Tamarack (*Larix Americana*).—A species of larch found in Canada and the United States. Its wood is reddish grey in colour, moderately heavy, strong and durable as oak. Crooked pieces are used for knees in shipbuilding. Sometimes called " Hacmatack " (*which see*).

Tapped Trees.—Trees that have been boxed for resin.

Teak Wood (*Tectona grandis*) —A tree of the East or East Indies, which furnishes an abundance of high-class durable timber for ship building, railway rolling stock, etc. Its habitat extends to Burmah and the islands from Ceylon to the Moluccas.

Tellar, Tillar or **Tellow.**—A sapling or selected coppice shoot left to stand for a timber tree when the underwood is cleared.

Tenon.—The end of a piece of timber so formed as to be fitted into a *mortise* (*which see*).

Tenoning Machines.—Machines for forming tenons. These are of various designs, and are sometimes provided with automatic feed. Others are arranged to cut a tenon at both ends of a board at the same time. The smaller patterns are used for cabinet and joinery work and the larger for railway wagon construction.

Tension, or Strain.—To make a circular or band saw more loose in the centre than on the cutting edge One of the technical tests applied to wood to arrive at its power of resistance to strain or stretch longitudinally. A tie-beam, whose office it is to keep the feet of rafters from spreading out, illustrates wood as a substance in tension. *See* "Tie Beam." In the instance of iron it is clearly expressed by "tie-rod." "Tension" is the opposite of "compression" (*which see*), and both are distinct in action from "transverse strain" (*which see*).

Tesselated Tiles or Floors.—Highly ornamented floors, composed of self-coloured tiles or *tesserœ* worked into geometrical patterns. The *tesserœ*, not always cubical in form, may be marble, precious stones, ivory, glass, wood or mother-of-pearl. The mosaic floors, etc., of the ancients were of the above materials, and they are still being wrought of the highest artistic order ; instance, the chapels, etc., of Westminster Cathedral. *See* "Encaustic Tiles."

Tewart or **Tuart** (*Eucalyptus gomphocephala*), or "White Gum."—A West Australian strong and heavy wood.

Thack-tile or **tiles.**—An old term, the origin of which is worn on its sleeve, and came to be applied to their substitutes or successors—" tiles " and " slates." *See* "Thatch," "Thatchpeg," "Tiles," "Slates."

Thatch or **Thack.**—A primitive covering or protection against the weather. "Straw," "rushes," "reeds," "heath," etc., used for roofing or covering buildings, or stacks of hay or grain ; a form of roof-covering not allowed in towns, and disappearing in rural districts from the difficulty of insuring such property against fire. *See* "Thack-tile" *and* "Thatchpeg."

Thatch or **Thack-peg** or **pegs.**—Small stems or branches of trees riven or entire, used in connection with thatch cord—usually tarred for pegging down thatch as security against the action of wind. *See* "Thatch" *and* "Thack-tile."

Thicket.—A wood or collection of trees or shrubs closely set or crowded with trees, implying a *thick* wood or, in a larger sense, a *thick* forest.

Thick Stuff.—Converted timber $4\frac{1}{2}$ in. and upwards in thickness. *See* "Stuff, Thick and Thin," *and* "Thin Stuff."

Thin Stuff.—Converted wood not exceeding 4 in. in thickness. *See* "Thick Stuff" *and* "Stuff, Thick and Thin."

Thorn.—A tree or shrub armed with sharp ligneous shoots, as the black-thorn, white-thorn, sallow-thorn, buck-thorn, etc. Some districts—Lincolnshire, for instance—have place-names beginning or ending with "wood," and well endowed with those of "thorn." It is presumed they register a time, now forgotten, when "wood" and "thorn" were interchangeable terms.

Three-ply.—Three scale-boards, peeling-boards, veneers or thin boards glued together, the grain of the centre board being at right angles to that of the other two. In instances of more than "three" the stock is termed "multi-ply." *See* "Plywood or Built-up Boards" *and* "Multi-ply Boards."

Throat.—On a saw, the rounded cavity in which sawdust accumulates and is carried from the cut.

Throwing.—(1) The operation of felling timber. (2) Throwing, connected with wood is an old term for "turning of balusters, spindles and parts of turned chairs," still properly termed "throwan chairs," as distinct from "throne chair." The term is still popular in the textile trade, where it inclines to "twisting," as in "thrown silk." *See* "Thrown or Throwan-chair."

Thrown or Throwan-chair.—A chair made by a wood-turner, of turned legs, rails, spindles, etc., "thrown" being the old trade- or craft-term for a wood-turner. *See* "Throwing."

Thunder Shake.—A crude term for a rupture of the fibres of the tree across the grain, which in some woods does not always break through the new or latest layers of wood

Tideland Spruce.—*See* "Sitka Spruce."

Tie Beam.—The beam which connects the feet of a pair of principal rafters and prevents them from thrusting out the wall, otherwise "principal beam," as distinct from "hammerbeam" (*which see, also* "Tension").

Ties.—An American and Canadian term for railway sleepers.

Tight Cooperage.—Packages, consisting of two round heads and a body composed of numerous staves held together with hoops, which are used as containers for liquids.

Tight Cooperage Stock.—Staves for making barrels intended to hold liquids.

Tile (*the old or obsolete name for* "*brick*").—A plate or form of baked or burnt clay, otherwise "earthenware," used in various forms for roof-covering, "roofing-tiles," paving or "floor-tiles," and for drainage or sewage purposes—"drain-tiles," etc. *See* "Pantile," "Floor-tile," "Drain-tile," "Wall-tile," "Encaustic-tile," "Roof-tile," *and* "Pavers."

Tile-lath or **Rock-lath.**—Wood strips or laths, nailed on the spars or common rafters of a roof after the manner of "slate laths." They take their names, not from their own ligneous substance, but from the class of material they are converted for, or destined to carry, as roof-covering.

Tilting Fillet.　*See* " Eaves Board."

Timber.　The word timber has various meanings, and must be interpreted by reference to the intention of the parties, the purpose in question, the context and the circumstances; and it must always be remembered that by local custom the precise meaning varies not only in different countries but frequently in the various localities of each separate country, and in many states the word has a statutory meaning, and even in the same state the word has often several statutory meanings different and varying from each other according to the object and purpose of the statute.　The legal meaning in England in particular is possibly coloured by historical circumstances no longer existing, and many of the legal decisions in England concern the meaning as regards settled land and are frequently not applicable to commercial transactions.　Subject to this warning

(1) The general meaning is standing trees suitable for building or structural purposes or the portions of severed trees that have been actually sawn or hewn into structural material or are capable of being adapted to such use.　This partly explains the varying meaning in different localities as different woods are often used in different places for constructional purposes, just as such varying use itself may possibly arise from differences in the soil, etc., producing differences of adaptability in the trees growing therefrom.

(a) Concerning standing trees, the word timber by the English law usually means Oak, Ash and Elm of twenty years of age and upwards of not less than 6 in. quarter girth, but the precise meaning in each district should generally be ascertained by inquiry of a good Land Agent there. Beech has been considered timber in certain parts of Berkshire and Yorkshire, Willow in parts of Hampshire, Beech in parts of Gloucestershire, Bedfordshire, Surrey and Buckinghamshire (but not in Oxfordshire). Whether these meanings hold to-day must be ascertained by local inquiry.　Apart from local custom, such valuable broad leaved trees as Walnut, Chestnut, Cherry, Sycamore, Beech, Poplar, Willow, Alder, Lime, Hornbeam, Plane and Acacia are not usually timber in England.　In Ireland the timber trees by statute include Oak, Beech, Ash, Lime, Larch, Sycamore, Walnut, Chestnut, Cherry, Poplar, Elder, Mountain Ash, Holly, Sallow, Apple, Birch, Cedar, Pine and Fir.　In the different States of America the local meaning varies

the head note.   For railway purposes in England, reference
should be made to the Railway Classification of goods.

(2) Used as part of a compound word, the word has a much
wider and varying meaning, e.g., Timber-trade, Timber-
merchant, Timber-yard, etc.   *See also notes with this prefix.*

Timber (*used as a compound word*).—Besides the instances
given in these notes, the following may, in passing, be mentioned : "Timber-brick," a variant of "wood-brick" (*which
see*) ; "Timber-head," on a ship ; "Timber-trade," a trade
or occupation ; "Timber-tree," "Timber-work," a construction in timber ; "Timber-yard" or store ; "Timber-
toe," a facetious term for a "wooden leg" ; "Timber-saw,"
etc., etc.

Timber Broker.—*See* "Broker."

Timber Clips or **Dogs.**—Clips for gripping logs when hauled along
a track or lifted by a crane, generally so arranged that the
more power exerted the tighter they grip the wood.

Timber Dryers (*Automatic*).—In which moist air is circulated in a
specially constructed building to dry and season timber.
Steam is generally used in the process to keep the air moist.
The air is circulated either by natural draught or by a fan.

Timber Measure or **Measurer.**—The "standard measure" between shipper and importer, importer and merchant or consumer in England, is the "Customs measuring department"
at the ports.   Those of Scotland vary in detail in more
minute parts of inches, being worked upon and recorded in
the "timber measure" or "blue books." *See* "Scribe or
Screeve Marks" *and reference there to* "The Standard
Timber Measurer."

Timber Merchant.—One who deals in or "handles" wood or
timber (English or foreign).   The latter was, until a century ago, known as a "Raff merchant." *See* "Monger,"
"Woodmonger" *and* "Raff Merchant."

Timber, Preservation of.—Wood is usually prevented from decay
through damp, atmospheric action or the destructive operations of animals or parasitic plants by injecting into the
vessels of the wood some mineral material, which, by com-
bining with the woody tissue, prevents its decomposition.
Creosoting (injecting creosote or dead oil of tar under pressure)
is the usual method adopted for treating railway sleepers,
telegraph poles and wood paving blocks.   In the Rüping
process compressed air is forced into the cells and pores of
the wood, which has previously been air-seasoned or steamed
in a retort, and at a higher pressure creosote oil is also forced
in ; in the Kyanising process the wood is soaked in a solution

J

of corrosive sublimate ; in the Burnettizing process the tendency to decay is destroyed by subjecting the wood to the action of chloride of zinc ; in the Powellizing process the timber is placed in a tank, covered with a patent solution mainly of sugar, which is boiled and cooled, after which the timber is dried ; in the Boucherie process a solution of sulphate of copper in water is introduced into the tree by means of a crosscut, and expelling the sap tubes takes their place. Various preparations are also used either as a paint or for immersion, the best known being Carbolieum, Petrolineum, Solignum, Jodelite, Smearoleum, Microleum, Sideroleum, etc.

Timber Sword.—A flexible steel sword-shaped instrument, with handle and slot at the point, in which to place a tape or line in order to draw it under trees or logs of timber for measuring purposes.

Time Charter.—A form of charter party, under which a vessel is fixed for a stated length of time. Owners usually supply crew and provisions and charterers pay port charges and supply coal. Other varying special conditions are made.

Tire.—That part of a band saw blade, extending an inch or so back from the throats, which has not been stretched to conform to the segment to which the balance of the blade is tensioned. This leaves the saw lighter at the tire than it is in the middle. The width of the tire varies with the width of the saw blade and the amount of tension carried.

Ton.—A ton of shipping is 42 cubic ft.

Forty cubic ft. of square or 50 cubic ft. of round oak, ash, elm or beech timber, and 50 cubic ft. of fir, or deal, poplar or birch, not cut into scantlings, and 60 cubic ft. of light goods, is deemed and estimated as 1 ton.

Tongue (*as in "tongue and groove"*).—(1) A projection on the edge of a board which fits into a groove. (2) The name given to the ornament in the *Echinus* moulding which alternates with the egg-shaped figure ; hence the name *Egg and Tongue moulding*. *See "Groove."*

Tonguing and Grooving Machines.—Machines used for tonguing and grooving boards, staves, etc., sometimes provided with automatic feed and at others with hand-feed only.

Toothing and Toothing-plane.—(1) In architecture, bricks or stones left projecting at the end of walls, that they may be bonded into later extensions. (2) A plane, the iron of which is finely " V " fluted, fixed but slightly inclined in the woodstock, and offering a number of points projecting beyond the plane-face. Its use is to " tooth " the ground for veneering

and the " glue-side " of veneers, the better to hold glue.
(3) To prepare wood intended to be covered with cloth.
(4) To face hardwood, or work in advance of the " scraper "
(*which see*).

Top Cutting.—A term used for the operation of running out or
cutting up of the tops of trees into cordwood, stackwood or
faggots, and the top cutting of a log or tree to distinguish it
from the " bottom cutting " or " butt."

Top Rail.—Horizontal piece of the frame of a door or fence or any
framing nearest the top of same.

Top Sawyer.—One who stands above the log and aids in operating
a pit saw from the top of the sawpit.   Known also as " Top-
man."

Tornado Shake.—*See* " Thunder Shake."

Torrak.—A Swedish term to denote wood sawn from dead trees
or trees which have died at the roots.

Torrfuru.—Deadwood, synonymous with " Torrak."

" Torroba " Box.—Boxes of which each part is one piece and each
piece made of small lumber joined by double-wedge-dovetail-
glue-joints.

Torus.—A large moulding used in the bases of columns.   Its
section is semi-circular, and it differs from the astragal only
in size, the astragal being much smaller.   It gives name to
" Torus-skirting," in which it is a popular moulding on that
wrought stock.

Totara (*Podocarpus tobira*).—A native of New Zealand, producing
a valuable wood second only in importance to Kauri pine.

Touchwood.—The wood of willows and some other trees softened
by decay.

Tow.—A raft or rafts of floated wood all towed simultaneously by
the same means.

Tracery.—(1) The ornamental stone or wood-work in the upper
part of Gothic windows, screens, etc., formed by the ramifications of the mullions.   The term, drawn from the old
French *Tracer*, is not ancient.   (2) The subdivision of
groined vaults, or any ornamental design of the same character, for doors, panelling or ceilings.

Trams.—Short sleepers used in coal mines.

Transom, Transommer or Cross-beam —(1) A horizontal mullion
or cross-bar in a window, etc.   (2) In ships, transoms are
beams or timbers fixed across the stern post to strengthen the
after-part, variantly known as " Main transom," " Half-
transom " and " Transom-knee."

Transverse Strain.—Side pressure ; instance, a beam carrying a floor ; if that breaks by being overloaded the fracture has been caused by " transverse strain," which is distinct from " tension " and " compression " (*which see*). " Joists," in the timbering of floors, being deeper than they are thick is provision against " transverse strain," whereas compressive and tensive strains suggest that their sections be square or equal-sided.

Tray.—A temporary agricultural fence. *See* " Fleak."

Tread.—The horizontal surface of a step.

Treadle Plank Cross Cut.—In which a circular saw is carried on a swinging arm and brought into and out of cut by means of a foot treadle, the plank or board being stationary during the process.

Treads.—Wood in the steps of staircases.

Tree.—A plant of considerable height, growing with a single trunk. The oldest trees in the world are four in number : the *Baobab* or *Bo-tree of Senegal* ; the *Dragon-tree of Orotava*, in Teneriffe ; the deciduous *Cypress of Chapultepee* in Mexico ; the *Chestnut trees on Mount Etna*. *See* Brewer's *Phrase and Fable*.

Tree.—As a piece of converted wood, occupies a strange position in the wood and other trades. As a noun it was clearly in old times a variant of " timber " and " wood " ; instance, roof-tree, cross-tree, mantle-tree, ridge-tree, axle-tree, saddle-tree, boot-tree, stocking-tree, heel-tree, spade-tree, single-tree, whiffle-tree, etc.

Tree-felling Machines.—A machine in which a cross-cut saw is used for cutting through the trunk of a tree by power. A steam cylinder is fitted on a swivel with guide bars attached to carry a slide actuated by a piston rod attached to a piston working in the cylinder. The saws are fitted to the slide and a reciprocating motion is imparted to it by steam. The saw lies in a horizontal plane close to the ground, and is fed into the trunk by a quadrant and handwheel.

Treenail (*i.e., a nail of wood*).—(1) Used as a " nail " in the instance of securing wooden planks or sheathing to the ribs and timbers of a ship. (2) A strong wooden " pin " or " peg " used in timber-framing to secure and draw close the mortised and tenoned joints, as in " half-timber work," " roofing-timbers," " bell-frames," etc. The smaller examples in old wainscots and furniture are termed " pins." " Treenails " are used in fixing railway-chairs to wooden or stone sleepers. *See* " Dowel " *and* " Drawbore."

Trellis or **Trellice.**—Open grating or lattice-work, either of metal or wood; the name is usually confined to such as are formed of straight bars crossing each other. In architecture its use is mainly for screens, doors and windows. The usual term is "Trellis-work."

Trench.—In carpentry, a cut or channel wrought for use or ornament; a term largely applied to "wall" or "string-boards" in staircase-work or building, where they are "trenched" to receive the step-ends, i.e., the "treads," "risers" and "nosings." In other instances trenching is resorted to in producing circular work, door- and window-casings, the thickness being reduced in parts to admit of bending on the centring.

Trencher or **Platter.**—A "trencher plate" or "platter-board," usually a turned piece of maple or sycamore, which served until recent times the purpose of the earthenware plate, pewter and silver or even gold plates serving at higher tables

Trenching Plane.—One of a set of carpenter's hand-tools, retaining a place in that number diminished by the introduction or adoption of machinery. This plane is largely used for cutting trenches across the grain of the wood to weaken it for bending, as in the instance of circular casings to doors and windows. *See* "Plane."

Trimmer.—A flat brick arch for the support of a hearth in an upper floor

Trimmer Joist.—The joist against which the trimmer abuts.

Trimmer's Wood.—Consisting of a knife fitted into a frame. The knife is bevelled to give a shearing cut. It is used to trim off the end of a piece of wood by moving the knife by a hand lever or self-acting motion across the wood. By means of swivelling fences, mitres and angles may be truly cut.

Trowel and Trowelling-off.—"Trowels" are tools of varied form and size used by plasterers, masons, bricklayers, etc. "Trowelling-off" is putting a smooth face upon the last or finishing coat of plaster on walls, ceilings, etc. *See* "Skimming" *and* "Float."

Trug Basket.—A shallow trough or tray basket made of wood, used in gardening operations.

Truss, Trussed, or Tied Together.—The collection of timbers forming one of the principal supports of a roof, framed together, so as to give mutual support to each other; common terms are "Trussed beam" (*which see*), "Trussed roof," and "Trussed partition."

Trussed Beam.—A compound beam, composed of two beams, secured together side by side with a truss, generally of iron, between them.

Trying-up Machines.—Machines used for trueing up warped and twisted timbers. Consisting of an adzing block revolving at high speed, and a travelling table to which the work is securely cramped. The table is made to travel backwards and forwards under the block by self-acting gear.

Tucking and Tuck-pointing.—The sense of this is a "push-action," as in tucking up a bed. It is here plaster or fine putty "tucked" into a "raked-out" or "gaping" joint. *See* " Pointing " *and* " Hick-joint Pointing."

Tulip Tree (*Liriodendron tulipifera*).—An American tree, whose flowers resemble the tulip ; it produces the yellow poplar wood of commerce.

Tulip Wood (*Physocalymma scaberrimum*).—This high-class fancy wood obtains its name from its roe figure, red and diagonal, or yellow, which resembles the tulip in flower, displaying its striped colours. As a wood, used for banding and inlaying, it is somewhat at a discount, inasmuch as the bright colours are wont to fade.

Tult (or dozen).—A Norwegian measure consisting of 12 logs of 18 ft. in length, or 216 running ft.

Tupelo or **Tupelo Gum** (*Nyssa aquatica*).—This tree is a member of the dogwood family. It grows in the Southern States of U.S.A. The wood resembles yellow poplar in colour and general appearance, and often passes for that wood. In the American market it is known as " Bay poplar."

Turkey Oak or Adriatic Oak (*Q. cerris*).—A tree common in south-east Europe as well as in Asia, but not one whose wood figures generally in commerce. Its bark and fruit are rich in tanning qualities.

Turner (*of wood, iron, etc.*).—One who turns substances in a lathe. It is fairly clear that these operatives worked with "reciprocating-lathes " till about the middle of the eighteenth century, when they were practically replaced by the rotary foot-lathe, which held the field for fully a century ; the "treadle" in both cases was mainly a long pole, one end resting on the floor, the other in a rising and falling state from the pressure of one foot of the operator. *See* " Lathe."

Tushing.—*See* " Snigging."

Twisted Fibre.—A defect in timber caused by the fibre or thread-like portion of the tissue being deposited in a twisted form.

U

Unassorted or Unsorted.—All the merchantable pieces together without selection; the opposite is "assorted" (*which see*).

Under.—As in "underclerk," "underpin," "underprop," "underpate," "undergrowth," "undershrub," "undersign," "undersold," "undertaker," "undervaluation," "underwood," "underwrite," "undersized," are understood tradeterms in daily use, the meaning of which is suggested by their names. *See "Over" for their opposites.*

Undercut.—The notch cut in a tree to determine the direction in which the tree is to fall, and to prevent splitting.

Underwood.—Generally small trees and bushes that grow under large trees; coppice, underbrush. Legally in England underwood has been called a species of wood which grows quickly and sends many shoots on one stool, the root remaining and producing a succession of new shoots from time to time.

Underwriter.—*An Underwriter at Lloyd's*, one who insures to a stated amount, so called because he writes his name under the policy. *See "Policy of Insurance."*

Universal Moulding Machine.—A moulding machine having a top and bottom revolving spindle, the top spindle being fitted into a vertical slide for forming irregular shaped and ornamental recesses.

Universal Saw Benches.—Saw benches fitted with two spindles with a rip saw on one spindle and a cross-cut on the other. Sometimes called "a combined rip and cross-cut bench." Those known as Universal Benches have canting tables.

Unmerchantable.—Not saleable; below the commercial standard of quality. *See "Merchantable Quality."*

Upsets.—Fibres crippled by compression. This is a variant for "Thunder Shakes" (*which see*).

Usage.—A practice for the time being, as opposed to Custom (*which see*).

V

Valley Rafter.—The rafter in the re-entrant angle of a roof.

Variety, or Varieties.—In Botany, "variety" differs from "species" in points of structure, which are developed only under certain circumstances, arising from climate, cultivation and other influences, and which are not essential to the species. "Varieties" are liable to return to the original form or species or to deviate into others, so that a variety cannot be preserved without much care. "Variety" in a tree, if not apparent in its progeny, may be viewed as an arborical "freak" or "sport," figuratively a truant that has returned home. *See* "Species," "Genera," *and* "Natural Order."

Vaulted Ceiling or Ground Ceiling.—A ceiling arched or domed in character, a form distinct from the ordinary flat or horizontal "ceiling" (*which see*).

Vegetable Substances are subject to three fundamental laws : (1) If they contain *more* hydrogen than water, they are acid ; (2) If *less*, they are resinous, oily or spirituous; (3) If an *equal* quantity, they are saccharine, mucilaginous or analogous to woody fibre or starch. These laws were discovered by O. Thenard and Gay-Lussac, French chemists.

Veined Wood, or Marble.—Full of veins or veined, streaked, or variegated in pattern or colour ; as a descriptive term, especially in association with wood, it is another or variant term for "figured."

Veneer.—A thin leaf or layer of choice or expensive wood to overlay an inferior or cheaper kind ; a veneer may be of sawn wood from a "veneer saw" or a knife-cut production from a "rotary" or a moveable bed machine. *See* "Toothing-plane" *and* "Knife." Circular saws are used for cutting veneers of sawn wood, and rotary (peeling) scale boards for knife-cut veneers.

Ventilators.—Boards or planks of teak or other indigenous woods, used for making air passages in rice and other grain cargoes exported from Burmah.

Vertical Band Saw.—In which the band-wheels are placed over each other so that the saw travels in a vertical direction.

Viewly.—A term occasionally used by importers of wood goods which are well manufactured and in good, bright condition ; one such "is a viewly stock." Dr. Ogilvie in his *Imperial Dictionary* says it means "lightly, striking to the view, handsome (*obsolete or local*)."

Voltmeter.—A meter for indicating the strength of an electric current, which is known as the voltage of the current.

Volts.—Represents the pressure or intensity of electric current ; thus the same quantity of current of 400-volt strength is equal to double the same quantity of 200-volt strength.

W

Wagon Scantling.—A set of the large and small scantling necessary for framing the whole of the woodwork of which a wagon is built.

Wainscot.—A Dutch or Low Country term which has been in use in England for many centuries, but now imperfectly understood. Its original form was *Wandschote* (from *wand*, a wall, and *schotte*, to defend or preserve). The preserving agent was here wood in the form of boards (literally *wall-boards*).

Wainscot Oak.—Oak suitable for being wrought into wainscoting, the panels being procured from riven slabs sawn into pairs, the saw exposing the radial figure which, before the eighteenth century (or " the painted age ") was rated as a point of beauty in the wood, as it is now for first-class fittings in this hardwood.

Wainscot Oak, Varieties of.—At the opening of this century Austrian wainscot oak held the field in England, " Russian oak " from Riga having declined or receded from its old leading position. In the last century Odessa and American white-oak wainscots were put on the English market, but are not seen now. The still older-fashioned " Dutch wainscot " is a thing of the past, and " English wainscot " nearly so. The term " wainscot " is not yet (1921) extended to Japanese oak.

Wainscot Oak, English.—It is fairly well understood that all wainscot oak is foreign or imported, but occasionally we see English-grown wood sawn up into planks and boards from the half tree or log. It is generally believed that as late as the close of Elizabeth's reign (1603) wainscot panelling and oak-work was wrought in English-grown oak.

Wainscot Oak " Billet."—This is an old term for the wainscot oak log, now in large measure *sawn* on the sole and sides, an innovation in the trade during the last half century ; when *riven* and *hewn* it fell into the category of the billet of wood so produced from a larger body ; 18 cubic ft. was the standard contents and were marketed by the billet or piece. *See* " English," " Dutch " *and* " Wrack Wainscot."

Wainscot Oak Boards.—Correctly speaking, are boards cut on the quarter and figured on the face. Centuries ago this was a large branch of business in Holland, the wood coming down the Rhine to be sawn at the windmills about Amsterdam and Rotterdam. Sir Christopher Wren and William III, our Dutch king, largely extended its use in England. During the last century wainscot oak boards became a special branch of trade in London and, to a less degree, in other ports.

Wainscot Oak Logs.—As understood in the trade, are half logs from the boles or stems of large grown trees, riven or sawn on the soles, and chopped or sawn at the sides, as imported from Riga in the Baltic, and, of recent years, from Trieste, the latter being called "Austrian wainscot." One of the four sides (the crown or top) is a segment of the outer face or circumference of the original tree that yielded two logs.

Wainscot Oak "Stick."—Is another and variant term for *wainscot oak "log"* or *"billet" (which see)*. "Stick" is often applied to a tree of timber size, e.g., "a clean bole or stick," and is quite in order with a wainscot oak log or billet, but not with a "plank" or "board."

Wainscot Wood.—Any species of wood suitable for wall boarding or framed and panelled lining or covering work. In England in the fifteenth and sixteenth centuries the wood was oak; in the seventeenth and eighteenth centuries, oak, fir or deal. In America a favourite wainscot-wood is that of the "Tulip tree" (*Liriodendron tulipifera*), otherwise "Yellow poplar," or "Canary whitewood," etc.

Wainscoted.—As in the instance of a "wainscoted hall or room" lined with plain wall-boards or sheets of panelled-framing, which served the purpose of covering or finishing the rough or bare walls, after the manner of drapery, curtains, upholstery, tapestry of Arras, etc., another and possibly an older form of wall-covering suspended, or hanging.

Wainscoting.—Literally "lining with boards," extended to "lining with boards and panels," later "lining with framed panels." In the eighteenth century, when the panels became large in size, some of them were composed of silvered glass, hence "wainscoted with looking-glass"—*Addison*. "Wainscoting" is now understood to refer to "wall-panelling."

Walings.—Small perpendicular pilings, chiefly 10 in. × 5 in.

Wall (Latin *vallum*).—A work or structure of stone, brick, wood or other material raised to some height, serving to enclose a space and afford defence, shelter or security. "Dry-walls," used for fences or boundaries, are of stone, etc., built without being bedded in mortar. "Half-timber walls" derive their names from being built of posts at intervals of about their own widths, the spaces or panels being made of other partly plastic material. *See* " Half-timbering " *and* " Post and Pan."

Wallboard.—*See* " Beaver Board " and " S.X. Board."

Wall Boards.—Wrought boards, usually narrow and tongued and grooved, used for covering or giving a finished face to walls inside or out ; in the former they are akin to " wainscots " or " wainscoting," plain or panelled, the one being English, the other Dutch or Flemish.

Wall Handrails (*of stone or brick*).—Occur on or in the walls of " winding " or " corkscrew " staircases ; instance, Tattersall castle (stone) and Wainfleet school towers (brick), Lincolnshire. They consist of large mouldings with small upper beads or rolls, designed for hand-grasp. " Wall handrails of wood " occur commonly attached by " bearers " or " brackets." *See* " Handrail."

Wall Plate.—A general term applied to nearly all horizontal timbers placed in walls as bonds, pads, etc., to receive other timber work.

Wall-tile or **Tiles.**—A modern form of wall-lining or sanitary facing for bath-rooms, dairies, closets, sculleries, passages, station or refreshment rooms, etc. They are thinner and finer earthenware than floor-tiles, if indeed they do not extend to porcelain. Their quality runs high in flat or raised ornament, colour and glaze, which extends to panels in house-furniture. The higher-class are termed " Faience-ware," from Faenza, in Romágna, where it is said to have been invented in 1299. *See* " Tile."

Walnut, Black American (*Juglans nigra*).—A favourite but rapidly diminishing wood, used for fittings and furniture As its name implies, it is, in the heartwood only, black, or nearly so. In the first half of the nineteenth century it played a subordinate part in making-up European walnut furniture ; later, as the fashion of figure or ornament in the wood itself declined, the black walnut came to the front, being suitable for a lighter class of furniture with ornament centred in form, outline, mouldings, etc. Its use in the twentieth century is declining in face of diminishing supply. *See* " Fashion in Wood."

Walnut Burrs.—The produce of European and Asian grown walnut-trees. " Burr " in this instance may not be a protuberance, as the name implies, but a body of wood contorted in its fibrous grain in and around the root of a tree, hence the trade-term " root-burr," or " figured-wood " from the root, as distinguished from the plain or straight grained wood in blocks, planks or flitches. "Burrs" are invariably cut into veneers by the knife process, in which form they occasionally realize high prices. *See* "Burr-woods" *and* "Burr."

Walnut Tree (*Juglans regia*).—One of the most beautiful fancy woods in the world. In great request among cabinet-makers and also used by manufacturers of gunstocks. The wood is not corrodible when in contact with iron.

Wandering Heart.—A tree in which the pith runs irregularly through the stem, causing boards cut from it to be "short" in the grain and weak for bearing purposes. Usual in wood where the trees are not plantation growth.

Wane.—The natural rounded edge of the log ; the defective angles of timber ; lack of wood on the corners from any cause. *See* "Wane, Scant, or Cant-corner."

Wane, Scant, or Cant-corner.—Timber wanting in substance, or not die-square at the corners. This is usually a mark of inferiority, but in first-class log timber, as in "waney yellow or white pine," mast-pieces, etc., it is not ; they are only prevented from being shipped in the round by the loss of stowage space in a ship which would view them as being their full squares, hence they are shipped "partly squared," and come under the category of "waney timber." Small Baltic fir timbers, known as "Egyptian balks or squares," are waney more or less in their upper parts, hence their tops may be round.

Waney-board Pine Logs.—Selected clean butts of Canadian white or yellow pine partially square. An old form of shipment, used a century ago for riving into plasterer's laths, etc., but now rare and costly. *See* "Waney Timber."

Waney-edged Goods.—Goods not sawn or shipped "die-square" on the edges, or "not free from wane." It is a term that fits common boards wrought into flooring, and common battens.

Waney Timber.—Timbers not hewn or sawn die-square, implying a mark of inferiority in Baltic goods, but of superiority in "Canadian white or yellow pine," where "waney-board pine" logs are the highest quality. *See* "Waney-board Pine Logs."

Washboards.—(1) Boards with a ribbed surface used for washing clothes. (2) The boards or skirting in a structure level with the floor. (3) A kind of board used by a ship or boat.

Washer.—A piece of iron, leather, etc., in the form of a flattened ring interposed as in "handrail-screws" (*which see*), and the head or nut of a bolt. They are common as "beds" for nuts to work upon.

Water-logged.—A ship is waterlogged when rendered immovable by too much water in the hold. When a ship is water-logged it implies that it is afloat with a cargo of wood, hence the saying that the cargo often brings the ship instead of the ship bringing the cargo.

Water Streak.—A dark streak in oak lumber due to injury to the standing timber.

Wattle.—A hurdle formed by twigs interlaced.

Watts and Kilowatts.—Watts are the number of volts of an electric current multiplied by the number of ampères used. One watt equals 1 ampère × 1 volt. 1,000 watts equal 1 kilowatt and 740 watts are equal to 1 HP.

Wavy Grain.—An undulating grain. In maple, caused by denser or darker wood cut across in sawing.

Wayleave.—An understood obligation resting on a proprietor who sells standing timber to a merchant to grant wayleave or arrange for a road by which the timber can be removed. The time allowed for removal is a matter of mutual arrangement.

Weatherboard.—A feather-edged board used for fencing and covering of wooden houses. *See* " Clapboard."

Wedge.—A piece of wood or metal, thick at one end and sloping to a thin edge at the other, used in splitting wood, etc. ; as an instrument, allied with a hammer swung by manual force, it exerts immense power in cleaving and lifting objects of great size or weight. The use of " wood-wedges " in oil-presses has declined in the presence of hydraulic presses, but in the riving of billets or breaking up of timber, lathwood, etc., it holds a prominent position.

Weights of Timber.—*See* Appendices III and IV.

Well-hole.—That part of a staircase that is left open in floors for the descent of light. It is guarded or protected by handrails (*which see*), newels and balusters (*which see*) on the floors, landings and steps. A stair of this kind is termed " open sided " in one or double degree.

Welsh Slates, Covering Power with 3-in. lap, per mille of 1,200 slates :—

in.	in.	sq. yds.	in.	in.	sq. yds.	in.	in.	sq. yds.
21 × 12		116	20 × 10		78	16 × 8		48
22 × 12		105	18 × 10		69	14 × 8		40
20 × 12		95	16 × 10		60	12 × 8		32
18 × 12		80	14 × 10		50	10 × 8		26
16 × 12		72	13 × 10		46	14 × 7		36
14 × 12		60	12 × 10		40	13 × 7		32

Other sizes in proportion. *See* " Welsh Slates, Computed Weight of."

Welsh Slates, Computed Weight of a Mille of 1,200 Slates of the following sizes :—

in.	in.	T.	C.	Q.	in.	in.	T.	C.	Q.	in.	in.	T.	C.	Q.
24	× 12	3	10	0	20	× 10	2	7	2	16	× 8	1	10	0
22	× 12	3	5	0	18	× 10	2	2	2	14	× 8	1	5	0
20	× 12	3	0	0	16	× 10	1	17	2	12	× 8	1	0	0
18	× 12	2	10	0	14	× 10	1	15	0	10	× 8	0	17	2
16	× 12	2	2	2	13	× 10	1	7	2	14	× 7	1	2	2
14	× 12	1	17	2	12	× 10	1	5	0	13	× 7	1	0	0

other sizes in proportion. *See* " Welsh Slates, Covering Power of, etc."

West India Quality.—A quality or classification in pitchpine calling for all heart.

Westmorland Slates.—An old, strong, heavy class of slates not graded in sizes, but used on the principle that the eave portion of a roof has to deal with the greater part of the rainwater, hence the largest are there fixed, and the smallest are allocated to the ridge. It is a durable but somewhat costly covering, though still used, especially on estate-work. *See* " Welsh Slates."

Wet or Tight Cooperage.—Casks made to hold liquids. *See* " Tight Cooperage."

Wheelwright.—(1) A mechanic who makes wheels. (2) A machine capable of performing a number of operations necessary in the construction of wheels, such as planing, jointing and shaping the felloes, mortising the hubs, boring the felloes, and tanging the ends of the spokes.

Whiffle-tree.—A swinging bar, to which the single-trees are attached, used in a pair-horse wagon.

Whin or Whim.—A pole suspended on two wheels, used for hauling timber, known by various names locally, some of which are : " Timber gin," " Long-shaft bob," " Timber tug," " Timber janker " (in Scotland), " Timber nib," " Pole timber carriage," " Big wheels," " Timber gill," " Timber drug," " Timber gig," " Timber cutts," " Timber jim," etc.

Whip Saw.—A strong gauge two-handed saw. A saw used by hand in pit-sawing of timber. It has no frame, and consequently is not stretched or tightened. It is used for breaking down logs, i.e., in making the " falling-cut " (*which see*).

White Cooperage.—Includes such articles as churns, pails, etc., which for the most part have straight sides, and are mostly wrought in sycamore.

White Mahogany.—*See* " Prima Vera."

White Oak, West India.—A description of hogshead staves, expressed as " W.O.W.I."

White Pine.—The American name for the *Pinus strobus*, known in Great Britain as yellow pine.

White Willow (*Salix alba*).—*See* " Willow."

Whitebeam (*Pyrus aria*).—A very slow-growing tree, and is (with the hawthorn) the toughest and hardest of native woods, and has extreme closeness of grain. Used by musical instrument makers, millwrights and engineers. Known also as " White-leaf Tree."

Whitewood.—A soft, durable, very fine-grained wood used in England for joinery work. This term is very loosely used with regard to various kinds of coniferous woods. It is applied to Baltic whitewood (*Picea excelsa*) or white deal, and to Canadian white spruce (*Picea alba*). A whitewood is also imported from New Zealand, and is known as New Zealand whitewood (*P. dacrydioides*) or white pine. Mexican whitewood has been imported. American yellow poplar or Canary wood (*Liriodendron tulipifera*) is known as Canary whitewood.

Whittle.—Now understood to mean a small pocket-knife, but formerly as a " sheath-knife," worn by the common people who were not entitled to wear swords. Chaucer alludes to such knives being worn in the time of Edward III ·—

> " A Shefeld thwytel bore he in his hose "

" Whittle " is a common term for aimlessly cutting wood. The Americans " whittled down the forest trees."

Wicken Tree.—The *Sorbus aucuparia* of the arboriculturist ; a well-known tree when bearing its load of red fruit or berries. It is otherwise known as the " Roan " or ' Rowan tree " and the " Mountain Ash."

Wicket.—(1) A small door formed in a larger one to admit of ingress and egress without opening the whole. (2) A hole in a door through which to communicate without opening the door. (3) A sluice-gate in a canal, etc., lock.

Willow (*Salix*).—A very rapidly growing tree, many varieties of which grow in England. A very durable (unless exposed to alternate wet and dry), non-combustible wood, and not liable to split. The wood is used by shipbuilders, clog-makers, turners, toymakers, and wheelwrights, and the species *Salix cerulea* is the best wood for making cricket bats.

Willow Oak.—The willow oak (*Quercus Phellos*) is a native of the States and Canada, and draws its name from the willow-like form or shape of its leaves.

Wind Break.—(1) To prevent breaking of trees by wind. (2) Portion of a forest maintained as a protection against wind, a wind screen.

Wind Shake.—*See* "Thunder Shake," popular terms only.

Winder.—Steps or treads, broad at one end and narrow at the other, occupying what would otherwise be "quarter" or "half-landings." In some cases they form the whole stair, winding round a pillar or a well-hole, hence "corkscrew stair."

Window or Window Frame.—The frame of a window which receives and holds the sashes or casements.

Window Nosings.—A piece of planed torus board fixed on the sill of a window to receive the bottom of architrave moulding.

Wintered.—Kept or stored during the winter months.

Wintering.—*See* "Wintered."

Witch Hazel.—A shrub supposed to be efficacious in discovering witches. A forked twig made into a divining rod for the purpose. *See* "Divining Rod."

Wood.—(1) A collection of trees; a forest. (2) The hard fibrous substance which composes the body of a tree and its branches. *See* "Timber."

Wood Bricks.—Blocks of wood of the shape and size of bricks, inserted in the interior walls of a building as groundwork on which to fix joinery, etc. Blocks of less thickness or of other sizes than bricks are usually called "wood-pads" (*which see*).

Wood Cogs.—Occur in cog-wheels of iron fitted with teeth of wood in one of a pair of wheels transmitting power. The object of their use, always costly in labour, is to deaden sound. The most favoured woods for the purpose are "Hornbeam" and "Greenheart." Cogs of this kind will wear for a length of time in powerful machinery. They represent practically the last detail in the lost trade of the wood "millwright."

Wood Column.—Wood columns were much in use until about a century ago. Instance, the houses forming the celebrated "Rows" of Chester, the "Long row," etc., at Nottingham, and the roof columns of the City, or Guildhall, at York.

Wood Fibre.—Narrow shavings cut from a round block of wood by a special machine.

Wood Flour is made from dry sawdust or small wood waste ground to powder in a mill similar to that in which corn is ground. It is used for making explosives and linoleum.

Wood Pulp.—Usually made by either one or two general processes, mechanical or chemical. In the mechanical process, the wood, after being cut into suitable sizes and barked, is held against revolving grindstones in a stream of water and thus reduced to pulp. In the chemical process the barked wood is reduced to chips and cooked in large digesters with chemicals which destroy the cementing material of the fibres and leave practically pure cellulose. This is then washed and screened to render it suitable for paper-making. The chemicals ordinarily used are either bisulphite of lime or caustic soda.

Wood Screw.—Applied to screws in iron or brass used for wood work. In wood, as "joiner's-bench screw" and sundry tools.

Wood Vinegar.—Another name for pyroligneous acid.

Wood Wool.—Fine shavings made from wood; used as a substitute for hair in plaster; largely used for packing purposes; when made from pine and specially prepared, used for surgical dressings.

Wood-boring Marine Animals.—These are numerous, especially in tropical waters. The *Teredo navalis*, or "ship-worm," the terror of wooden ships and overlying stocks in saline waters, is too well known, from actually boring and burying itself in the wood; another destructive insect is the "sea-shrimp," which eats floating timber or that at the water-line of wood piling, not by boring in, but eating away the outer layers or skins.

Woodman's Measure.—In some localities it is customary to measure the length of a tree with a 5 ft. or a 3 ft. rod, and an allowance is made of a handbreadth between each 3 ft., to make up for irregularities and defects.

Woodmonger.—The old name of a timber merchant or dealer. *See* "Monger." "The Company of Woodmongers" was formerly one of the trade-guilds of the city of London. *See* "Timber Merchant" *and* "Raff Merchant."

Wood-pads.—Blocks of wood varied in size according to their purpose—"large" in the instance of roof-principals placed as their beds and built in the walls; "small" when their thickness is only half or a fourth of that of "wood bricks" (*which see*).

Woodware.—A branch of the wood-trade allied to that of the "cooper"; woodware largely curtailed by the development

M

of pottery or earthenware, consisting of domestic kitchen requisites mostly turned or throwan (thrown) in sycamore or maple, as "bowls," "dishes," "platters," "trenchers," "ladles," "spoons," "mugs," "cups," "boxes," "noggins," and items too numerous to here chronicle. A survival is the "wooden-spoon" awarded for incompetence at certain colleges.

Wood-wool Machines.—A machine for manufacturing wood wool, in which a very thin shaving is removed from a piece of wood by a fixed knife, the shaving being divided into very narrow strips by means of lances.

Woods Scale.—The scale of the logs made in the woods.

Worm Holed, Wormy or Wormed.—Holes made in wood by worms burrowing. This is the work of numerous insects in the larva or grub state. In England the most destructive is the furniture-beetle, which leaves the wood a sponge-like dusty substance, rightly termed "dry-rot" (*which see*, and "Wood-Boring Marine Animals").

Wot.—A contraction meaning that the wood is planed or wrought.

Wrack.—Wood sorted out for defects. *See* "Wrack-wainscot." This term and that of "brack" are allied, possibly derived from "wreck," implying damaged from some cause.

Wrack-wainscot.—Logs or billets sorted out of the ordinary merchantable wood. *See* "Wrack." Wainscot billets often fall into this grade from being shallow, or below 12 in. in depth from sole to crown.

Wrest Plank.—Beech planks cut on the quarter from the butt of the tree to form the part of a piano in which the wrest pins that hold the wires are inserted.

Wringing-machine Rollers.—*See* "Roller Blocks for Wringing Machines."

Wrought.—Planed wood is said to be wrought. Sometimes written "Wrot" or "Wot."

Y

Yang (*Dipterocarpus tuberculatus*).—A valuable hardwood exported from Siam, closely allied to the Eng or In tree. Sometimes used as a substitute for teak.

Yard of Flooring.—A trade term defining 9 sq. ft. of flooring boards, computed in the width of the boards before being reduced by planing or working in the machine. *See* " Square."

Yard Keeper.—The keeper of a yard, usually for storage, or goods on rent.

Yard Stocks.—Stocks of wood goods stored in a yard or on a storage ground.

Yard Trade.—A business in wood goods from yarded stocks.

Yardman.—The foreman of a yard, timber or otherwise.

Yellow Deal.—A term used in the London trade for sawn deals made from Scandinavian redwood or Scots fir.

Yellow-pine Flooring.—An American term for what is known as " pitchpine flooring " in England. From this wood being very marked in its annual growths or layers of wood, the floors wear into shreds or " shivers " unless the wood is cut on the true quarter, the same as wainscot oak, i.e., with the edges of the grain presented as the wearing face. *See* " Edge-grain " *and* " Shive and Slivering."

Yew (*Taxus baccato*).—An extremely fine and even-grained wood, and very durable. Found in Europe, India and Canada. Used for turnery, sticks, etc. The leaves are poisonous to live stock.

Z

Zebra Code.—A cable code specially designed for the wood trade.

Zebra Wood.—A term applied to striped woods of pleasing colour and imported from various tropical sources.

BIBLIOGRAPHY OF TIMBER

THE MAHOGANY TREE (Chaloner and Fleming). 1850.

THE TREES OF COMMERCE. By Wm. Stevenson. 1894.

TIMBER AND TIMBER TREES, NATIVE AND FOREIGN. By T. Laslett. 1894.

WOOD : ITS USE AS A CONSTRUCTIVE MATERIAL. By Wm. Stevenson. 1894.

WOOD : A MANUAL OF THE NATURAL HISTORY AND INDUSTRIAL APPLICATIONS OF THE TIMBERS OF COMMERCE. By Prof. G. S. Boulger. 1902.

TIMBERS OF COMMERCE AND THEIR IDENTIFICATION. By Herbert Stone. 1918.

TEXT-BOOK OF WOOD. By Herbert Stone. 1921.

BRITISH FOREST TREES. By John Nisbet. 1893.

MANUAL OF INDIAN TIMBERS. By J. S. Gamble. 1902.

TIMBER. By J. H. Baterden. 1918.

TIMBER. By W. Bullock. 1918.

THE TREES OF GREAT BRITAIN AND IRELAND. By H. J. Elwes and Dr. A. Henry.

TIMBER MERCHANTS' HANDBOOK. By Frank Tiffany. 1919.

FORESTRY HANDBOOK. By Angus D. Webster. 1920.

THE FORESTS OF WEST AFRICA. By Prof. Unwin. 1920.

BRITISH-GROWN TIMBER TREES. By Angus D. Webster. 1916.

ENGLISH TIMBER AND ITS ECONOMICAL CONVERSION. By Acorn. 1916.

SHIPPING MARKS ON TIMBER. 1920.

STANDARD TIMBER MEASURER. By E. A. P. Burt. 1888.

STANDARD STAVE MEASURER. By E. A. P. Burt. 1912.

THE PRESERVATION OF WOOD. By A. J. Wallis-Tayler. 1917.

WEBSTER'S PRACTICAL FORESTRY. By Angus D. Webster. 1919.

Appendix I

CONTRACTIONS AND ABBREVIATIONS IN USE IN THE TIMBER TRADE

@	from, or at
a.a.r. . . .	against all risks (insurance)
A/C . . .	account current
A/c . . .	account
act. std. . .	actual standard
a.f.b. . . .	allowance for bark
a/d. . . .	after date
amt. . . .	amount
a/o . . .	account of
a/s . . .	account sales
bdls. . . .	bundles
B/E . . .	Bill of Entry
B/L . . .	Bill of Lading
B.M. . . .	Board Measure
B/P . . .	Bills payable (applied to Bills of Exchange)
B/R . . .	Bills receivable (applied to Bills of Exchange)
Ç or std. . .	standard
c. ft. or cft. .	cubic foot
cal. . . .	calliper measure
c. & f. . . .	cost and freight
carr. pd. . .	carriage paid
carr. for^d. .	carriage forward
c i.f. . . .	cost, insurance, freight
c.i.f.e. . .	cost, insurance, freight, exchange
Cr. carr. . .	credit carriage
C.M. . .	calliper measure
C.O.D.. . .	cash on delivery
c/p . . .	charter party
Cr.	credit or creditor
c/s	cases
cub. met. or m³	cubic metre
D. & H. . .	Dressed and Headed
D. & M. .	Dressed and Matched
dia.. . . .	diameter
d/d. . . .	days after date
dft.. . . .	draft (Bill of Exchange)

dld. . . .	delivered
dly. . . .	delivery
Dr. . . .	Debtor or Debit
d/r . . .	dock return
d/s . . .	days after sight
E.E. . . .	Errors excepted
E. & O.E. . .	Errors and omissions excepted
Entd. . . .	Entered
ex. . . .	out of
Exd. . . .	Examined
f.a.c. . . .	feet average cube
f.a.q. . . .	fair average quality
f.a.s. . . .	first and second
f.e. . . .	feather edge
fm. . . .	fathom
f.o.b. . . .	free on board
f.o.c. . . .	free on car (American)
f.o.q. . . .	free on quay
f.o.r. . . .	free on rail
f.o.t. . . .	free on truck
f.o.w. . . .	first open water (Baltic trade)
ft. . . .	feet
ft. sup. or sup. ft.	superficial foot
G.F.A. . .	Good fair average
G.S.M. . .	Good sound merchantable
in. . . .	inch
inv. . . .	invoice
J/A . . .	Joint Account
K.D. . . .	knocked down, or taken apart for shipment
lds. . . .	loads
l.ft. . . .	lineal foot
Md. . . .	Moulded
M.ft. . . .	1,000 ft.
M. or Mille .	1,000 (pieces)
M.s.ft. . .	1,000 superficial feet
m/d . . .	months after date
m/s . . .	months after sight
mldgs. . .	mouldings
no. . . .	number
nom. std. . .	nominal standard
n/s . . .	new style
N.S. . . .	Not sufficient (to meet cheques, etc.)
O/a . . .	On account
O/d . . .	On demand
O.G. or ogee .	A moulding of two members, one concave, the other convex
O.G. Mouldings	Old Greek mouldings
o.s. . . .	old style

p an. . . .	panel
pcs. . . .	pieces
Pd. . . .	Paid
Pet. std. .	Petersburg standard
P/N .	Promissory Note
p.p., per pro, or per proc.	per procuration
P.S.H. . . .	Petersburg or Petrograd Standard Hundred
R.	Red
R.D. . . .	Refer to drawer of a cheque
Recd. . . .	Received
S.P. . . .	Supra protest
sq. ft. . . .	square feet
s.u.b. . . .	string under bark
sup. ft. or s.ft.	superficial ft.
sup. yds. .	superficial yards
t.o.b. . . .	tape over bark
u/a . . .	unassorted
u/s . . .	unsorted
W.	White
W.I. puncheon	West Indian puncheon staves
W.O.W.I. . .	White Oak West India
Y. or Yeo .	Yellow
yd. . . .	yard or square yard
′ or ft. . . .	feet
″ or in.. . .	inches

CHARTERING

a.a.. . . .	always afloat
A.R. . . .	Antwerp, Rotterdam
a/s . . .	Alongside
B.C. . . .	Bristol Channel
b.d. . . .	bar draft
B/H . . .	(A port between) Bordeaux and Hamburg
B/L . . .	Bill of Lading
b.t. . . .	berth terms
c.i.f. . . .	Cost of cargo, insurance and freight
c.f.o. . . .	Calling for orders
C.N.S. . .	Cardiff, Newport, Swansea
c.p.d. . . .	Charterers paying dues
d.b. . . .	deals and battens
d.b.b. . . .	deals, battens and boards
Ex.. . . .	excluding
E.C.G.B. . .	East Coast of Great Britain
E.C.I. . . .	East Coast of Ireland
E.C.U.K. . .	East Coast of United Kingdom
E.E. . . .	Errors excepted

E. & O.E.	Errors and omissions excepted
f.a.	free address
f.a.a.	free of all average (insurance)
f.a.s.	free alongside
f.d.	free dispatch
f.f.a.	free from alongside
f.g.a.	free of general average (insurance)
f.i.b.	free into barge
f.o.b.	free on board
f.o.r.	free on rail
f.o.t.	free on truck
f.o.w.	first open water
f.p.a.	free from particular average
f.s.	free shorts
f.t.	full terms
fth.	fathom
G.A.	General average
H to H or H/H	Any direct port between Havre and Hamburg
K.C.M.	King's calliper measure
L.C.	London clause
L/H	(A port between) Lisbon and Hamburg
L.H.A.R.	London, Hull, Antwerp, Rotterdam
L.H.B.	Liverpool, Havre, Bremen
M.D.	Millwall Docks
Merblanc	White Sea charterparty
n.a.a.	not always afloat
n.c.	new charter
n.r.	net register
o.c.	open charter ; overcharge
Pix pinus	Pitch pine charterparty
p.p.	Picked ports
P.P.	Pitch Pine
pt. or ppt.	prompt
R.M.S.	Royal Mail Steamer
Russpruss	Petrograd, Danzig, Memel, etc., charterparty
Scanfin	Scandinavian charterparty
S.C.D.	Surrey Commercial Docks
S.N.	Shipping Note
s.p.d.	Shipowners paying dues
s.s.	steamship
std.	standard
T.L.O.	Total Loss only (insurance)
U.K.	United Kingdom.
U-w.	Underwriter
W.C.E.	West Coast of England
W.C.G.B.	West Coast Great Britain
W.I.D.	West India Docks
Y.A.	York Antwerp rules

FLOORING AND PLANED WOOD

d.s.. . . .	double sunk (mouldings)
C.B. . . .	centre beaded
C.V. . . .	centre V-jointed.
D. 1 S.. . .	dressed one side
D. 2 S.. . .	dressed two sides
Ex. 1st . .	Extra firsts
f. & g.. . .	feathered and grooved
f.g. & v. .	feathered, grooved and V-jointed
inf. . . .	inferior
p. & chd.. .	planed and chamfered
p.e.. . . .	plain edges
p.s.e. . . .	planed and square edges
p.t.g. & bd. .	planed, tongued, grooved and beaded
p.t.g.v.v. . .	planed, tongued, grooved and V-jointed two sides
p.t.g.v.c.v. .	planed, tongued, grooved and V-jointed with centre V point
p.t.g.v.2s. . .	planed, tongued, grooved and V-jointed two sides
p.t.g.b.2s. . .	planed, tongued, grooved and beaded two sides
p.t.g.b.c.b. .	planed, tongued, grooved, beaded and centre beaded
p.t.g. & v.j. .	planed, tongued, grooved and V-jointed
p.t.g. & b. .	planed, tongued, grooved and beaded
p.t.g. & r.. .	planed, tongued, grooved and rabbeted
p.t.g. . .	planed, tongued and grooved
rbtd. . . .	rabbeted
r. & b. . .	rebated and beaded
r. & v.. . .	rebated and V-jointed.
s.e. .	square edges
S. 1 S.. . .	dressed one side
S. 2 S.. . .	dressed two sides
S. 1 S. 1 E. .	dressed one side and one edge
S. 4 S.. . .	dressed four sides
sq. yds. .	square yards
t.g. & b. .	tongued, grooved and beaded
t.g. & v-jtd. .	tongued, grooved and V-jointed
t.g.v-j.c.v.. .	tongued, grooved, V-jointed and centre V-jointed
t. & g.. . .	tongued and grooved
w.b. . . .	weatherboard
Wot . . .	planed or wrought wood.

DOORS

B. & B. . .	bead and butt
B. & F.P. . .	beaded and flush panels
b. & f.. . .	bead and flush

Bol. & flush . bolection one side
D.M. . . . double moulded
F.M. 2 sides . flush moulded two sides
Mar. Light or
  M.L.. . . marginal lights
M. 1 S.. . . moulded one side
M. 2 S.. . . moulded two sides
M.O.S. . . moulded on solid
S.M. . . . single moulded
S. 2 S.. . . square two sides

SKIRTINGS

S. & M. . . sunk and moulded

Appendix II

COMPARATIVE TABLE OF ACTUAL AND NOMINAL MEASUREMENT OF PLANED GOODS, SHOWING THE GAIN FOR FREIGHT

Sizes.	Nominal Standard.	Real Standard for Freight.	If actual Freight is 1, then on nominal it is only	Squares in Pet. Std. nominal.	Gain %
	Run. ft.	Run. ft.			
1¼ × 7″	2716	3129	·869	15·088	13·20
1¼ × 6½″	2924	3379	·866	15·389	13·47
1¼ × 6″	3168	3673	·863	15·840	13·75
1¼ × 5½″	3456	4023	·859	15·709	14·10
1¼ × 5″	3802	4446	·855	15·841	14·48
1 × 7″	3394	4023	·844	18·855	15·64
1 × 6½″	3655	4345	·841	19·237	15·88
1 × 6″	3960	4723	·838	19·800	16·14
1 × 5½″	4320	5171	·835	19·636	16·46
1 × 5″	4752	5717	·831	19·800	16·88
⅞ × 7″	3879	4693	·827	21·550	17·35
⅞ × 6½″	4178	5069	·824	21·989	17·58
⅞ × 6″	4526	5510	·821	22·630	17·86
⅞ × 5½″	4937	6035	·818	22·440	18·19
⅞ × 5″	5431	6669	·814	22·629	18·56
¾ × 7″	4526	5632	·804	25·144	19·64
¾ × 6½″	4874	6083	·801	25·653	19·88
¾ × 6″	5280	6611	·799	26·400	20·13
¾ × 5½″	5760	7241	·795	26·182	20·45
¾ × 5″	6336	8003	·792	26·400	20·83
⅝ × 7″	5431	7040	·771	30·172	22·86
⅝ × 6½″	5848	7603	·769	30·779	23·08
⅝ × 6″	6336	8264	·767	31·680	23·33
⅝ × 5½″	6912	9051	·764	31·418	23·63
⅝ × 5″	7603	10004	·760	31·679	24·00
½ × 7″	6788	9387	·723	37·711	27·68
½ × 6½″	7311	10138	·721	38·478	27·89
½ × 6″	7920	11019	·719	39·600	28·12
½ × 5½″	8640	12069	·716	39·273	28·41
½ × 5″	9504	13338	·713	39·600	28·75

Appendix IV

OFFICIAL STANDARD WEIGHTS OF HARDWOOD LUMBER as Adopted by the American Hardwood Manufacturers' Association

					Rough Dry.
Ash				3/8"	1500
				1/2"	2000
				5/8"	2500
				3/4"	3000
				4/4"	3800
			5/4"	6/4"	3900
				8/4"	4000
Basswood				4/4"	2600
Beech				4/4"	4000
Birch				4/4"	4000
Black Gum				4/4"	3400
Butternut				4/4"	2800
Buckeye				4/4"	2600
Cherry				4/4"	4000
Chestnut				4/4"	2800
Cottonwood				1/4"	1050
				3/8"	1050
				1/2"	1400
				5/8"	1750
				3/4"	2000
				4/4"	2800
			5/4"	6/4"	2900
				8/4"	3000
Cypress				1/4"	1200
				3/8"	1200
				1/2"	1500
				5/8"	1900
	4/4"	5/4"		6/4"	3000
				8/4"	3200
	10/4"	12/4"		16/4"	3500
Elm (Soft)				4/4"	3200
			5/4"	6/4"	3300
				8/4"	3500
		10/4"		12/4"	3600
Elm (Rock)				4/4"	3800

			Rough Dry
Gum (Red)		1/4″	850
		3/8″	1300
		1/2″	1750
		5/8″	2200
		3/4″	2700
		4/4″	3500
	5/4″	6/4″	3600
		8/4″	3800
Gum Sap		1/4″	800
		3/8″	1250
		1/2″	1700
		5/8″	2100
		3/4″	2500
		4/4″	3300
	5/4″	6/4″	3400
		8/4″	3600
Hickory		4/4″	5000
Axles and Reaches			5000
Rim Strips			5000
Holly		4/4″	3500
Locust		4/4″	4200
Magnolia		4/4″	3500
Maple (Soft)		4/4″	3250
	5/4″	6/4″	3350
		8/4″	3500
Maple (Hard)		4/4″	4000
Oak (Eastern)		3/8″	2000
		1/2″	2200
		5/8″	2700
		3/4″	3200
		4/4″	3900
	5/4″	6/4″	4000
		8/4″	4200
Chair and Furniture Stock			4200
Squares			4200
Wagon Stock and Felloes			4500
Plough Handle Strips			4250
Oak (Memphis Ter.)		1/4″	1100
		3/8″	1700
		1/2″	2150
		5/8″	2700
		3/4″	3250
		4/4″	4200
	5/4″	6/4″	4300
		8/4″	4500
Chair and Furniture Stock			4200

			Rough Dry
Oak (Memphis Ter.)—*continued*			
Squares			4200
Wagon Stock and Felloes			4500
Plough Handle Strips . . .			4250
Oak (La. and Tex.)		3/8"	1750
		1/2"	2200
		5/8"	2750
		3/4"	3400
		4/4"	4400
	5/4"	6/4"	4500
		8/4"	4800
Pecan		4/4"	4800
Poplar		3/8"	1050
		1/2"	1400
		5/8"	1600
		3/4"	2100
		4/4"	2800
Sycamore		4/4"	3200
Tupelo		4/4"	3000
	5/4"	6/4"	3100
		8/4"	3200
Walnut		4/4"	4000
Willow		4/4"	2800

Appendix V

GLOSSARY OF TIMBER TRADE TECHNICAL TERMS

English.	French.	German.	Spanish.	Swedish.
Acacia	Acacia	Acacia	Acacia	Acacia
Account current	Le compte-courant	Contocurant	Cuentacorriente	Kontokurant
Adzes	Erminettes	Deisseln	Azuelas	Skarfyxor ; Däxlar
Agalloch (see Eagle wood)				
Alder (wood)	Aune	Eller ; Erle	Aliso	Al ; Ahl
Amboyna wood	Bois d'Amboine	Amboinische Planken	Tablas d'Amboine	Amboina plankar
American Maple (see Plane wood)				
Architraves	Architraves	Bindebalken ; Unterbalken	Arquitrabes	Tvär bjelker
Ash tree	Frêne	Esche	Fresno	Ask
Aspen	Tremble	Espe	Alamo	Asp
Aspen pulp	Pâte de tremble	Espenmasse	—	Aspmassa
Augers	Tarières	Strangenbohrer	Barrenas	Nafvarar Borr
Axes	Cognées	Aexte	Segures	Yxor
Balks	Poutres	Balken	Quartones	Balkar
Barrels (casks)	Futailles	Fässer	Botas	Fastager
Battens	Bastins	Battens	Tablillas	Battens
Beams (see Balks)				
Beechwood	Hêtre	Buche	Haya	Bok ; Bök
Bill of Exchange	Lettre de change	Wechsel	Letra de Cambio	Vexel
Bill of Lading	Le connaissement	Connossement	Conoscimunto	Konnossement

English.	French.	German.	Spanish.	Swedish.
Billet wood (see Firewood)				
Birch	Bouleau	Birke ; Birkenholz	Abedul	Björk
Black Alder	Bourgène; Bourdaine	Faulbaum	Arraclan	Brakved
Blood wood (see Nicaragua wood)				
Blue	De coloré bleu	Geblaut	Azul	Blånad
Boards	Planches	Bretter	Tablas	Bräder
Boathook	Gaffes	Bootshaken	Bicheros	Båtshakar
Bobbins (lace)	Fuseaux	Spitzenklöppel	Majaderillos	Knyppelpinne
Bowsprits	Beauprés	Bugspriete	Beaupres	Bogspröt
Boxes	Boîtes	Büchsen ; Dosen	Cajas	Bössor ; Burkar
Boxwood	Buis	Buxbaumholz	Box Leña	Buxbom
Brack (see Inferior than Fifths)				
Brack timber	Bois de rebut	Wrackholz	Madera de desecho	Vraktimmer
Brazil wood	Bois de Brésil	Brasilienholz	Palo Brasil	Breslia
Braziletto wood	Brösillet	Brasilettholz	Brasillito	Bresletta
Brokerage	Le courtage ; La provision	Mäklergebuhr	Corretage	Provision
Broomhandles	Manches à balai	Besenstiele	Cabos de Cepillas	Kvastküppar
Building materials	Matériaux de construction	Baumaterialien	Materiales	Byggningsämnen
Building timber	Bois de construction ; Bois de charpenté	Bau-holz	Madera da Fabricare	Byggnings-timmer
Button wood (see Plane wood)				
Cabinet maker's ware	Ebénustérie	Kunsttischler-Arbeit	Ensambladura	Konstsnickare arbete
Cam wood	Bois de cam ; Bois de cham	Kammholz	Palo de Cam	---

English.	French.	German.	Spanish.	Swedish.
Campeachy wood (logwood)	Bois de Campêche	Campescheholz; Blauholz	Palo de Campeche	Campaschetrá; Kampescheträd
Candle wood	Bois citron; Bois de chandelle; Bois à flambeau	Citronenholz	Madera de Limon	Citronträ
Captain	Capitaine de navire	Seekapitän	Capitan	Skeppskapten
Cardboard or Carton	Carton	Papp or Carton	Carton	Papp or Kartong
Carton manufactory	Fabrique de carton	Holzpappfabrik	Fabricca de papel	Kartongfabrik
Cases (boxes)	Étuis; Fourreaux	Futtrale	Estuches	Foder
Cash	Comptant	Baar	Contado	Kontant
Cask-bottoms (heading staves)	Fonçailles	Bodenholz	Tempanos	Bottnar; Bottenstäfver
Casks	Futailles	Fässer	Botas	Fatverk; Fastager
Cedar wood	Bois de cèdre	Zedernholz	Cedro	Cederträd
Charcoal	Charbon de bois	Holzkohle	Carbones de Lena	Träkol
Charterparty	Le chartepartie	Certepartie	Contrato de Fletamiento	Certeparti
Chemical	Chimique	Chemisch	Chimico	Kemisk
Chisels	Ciseaux; Cisoirs	Meissel	Escoplos	Mejslar; Huggjern
Clapboards	Bordillons; Douvains	Klapholz	Madera para Cubas	Klappholts
Clogs (wooden shoes)	Sabots	Holzüberschuhe	Almadreñas	Träskor
Commission	La commission	Commission	Commission	Kommission
Consignment	La consignation	Consignation	Consignacion	Konsignation
Contract	Un contrat	Contract	Contrato	Kontrakt
Cordwood (stackwood)	Bois de corde; Bois de stère	Klafterholz	Leña de Cuerda	Kast ved

English.	French.	German.	Spanish.	Swedish.
Cork wood	Liége	Korkholz	Corcho	Kork ved
Cracked	Craqué; Fendu	—	Roto	Sprucket
Crook timber (compass or knee timber)	Bois tortu	Krummholz	Palos de Vuelta	Krumtimner
Cross shakes	Gelfs	Querrisse	Roto cuadrato	Tvärspricker
Curled Maple (see Speckled Wood)				
Custom inward (see Import Duty)				
Custom outward (see Export Duty)			—	
Cutter-planed	Rabote anex le porte outils	Mit Rundmesser gehobelt		Kutterhyfiadt
Deals	Madriers	Planken	Tablas ; Tablonos	Plank
Deck planks	Bordages de pont	Deckplanken	Tablas para Cubiertas	Däcks plankor
Defect	Le manque ; défaut	Manco	Daño	Mänko
Del Credere	Ducroire	Delcredore	Ducroire	Del credere
Discharging (see Unloading)				
Discoloured (see Blue)				
Dogwood (cornel tree)	Cornouiller	Hartriegel (Wilder Kornelbaum)	Sanguiñol	Benved
Dozen	Douzaine	Zwölfter	Docena	Tolfter
Draft	La traite	Tratte	Letra de Cambio	Tratta
Drawers (chests of)	Commodos ; Layettes ; Tiroirs	Schiebladen	Gavetas	Skuflådor or dragkistor
Dry	Sec ; Sèche	Trocken	Seco	Torr
Dutch timber	Poutres hollandaises	Holländische Balken	Madera de Hollanda	Holländska bjälkar
Dyewoods	Bois de teinture	Farbehölzer	Maderas de Tintas	Färgträ

English	French	German
	Quatrelle, bois	
	Planche de debout	
d wood (see Young timber)	Lofret; Cargaison	
	Affretement	
	Fustel; Bois jaune de Brezil	Gelbholz
uttocks (see Knee timber)		

English.	French.	German.		
Gimlets	Vrilles	Fritt-bohrer	Barrenas Pequeñas	Handborrar ; Nafvarer
Gouges (carp.)	Gouges	Hohlmeissel	Gubias	Gyts
Grenadilla (red ebony wood)	Grenadille ; Ebène rouge	Grenadill-holz	Ebano-rojo	Grenadille-hout
Guarantee (see Del Credere)				
Gunstocks	Bois de fusl ; Fûts de fusil ; Montures	Flintenschäfte	Cajas de Escopetas	Böss stockar ; Böss kolf
Hafts (see Handles)				
Half-cellulose	Pâte de bois demi-chimique	Halb-Cellulose	—	Halfcellulosa
Hammers	Marteaux	Hammer	Martillos	Hamrar
Handles	Manches	Griffe	Cabos	Grepe
Hand saws	Scies à main	Handsägen	Sierras de Mano	Hand sågar
Handspikes	Anspects ; Hanspacs	Handspaken	Espeques	Handspakar
Harbour (see Port)				
Harbour Dues	Droits de mouillage ; Charge de port ; Taxe de port ; Péage	Hafengeld	Derechos de Puerto	Hamnafgifter
Headings (heading staves) (see Cask-bottoms)				
Heart	Cœur	Kern	Corazon	Kärna
Heartshakes	Fentes de cœur	Kernrisse	Daño al Corazon	Karnsprickor
Helves (see Handles)				
Hewn wood	Bois haché	Gehauenes Holz	Leña	Tillyxadt virke
Holly tree	Houx	Stech-palme	Acebo	Jernek ; Christ törne

English.	French.	German.	Spanish.	Swedish.
Eagle wood (agalloch)	Bois d'aigle ; Agalloche	Adlerholz	Agaloco	Aloeträd
Ebony	Bois d'Ebène	Ebenholz	Ebano	Ebenholts
Elm	Orme ; Ormeau	Ulme	Olmo	Alm
Export	Exportation	Ausfuhr	Exportacion	Export
Export Duty	Droit de sortie ; Droit d'exportation	Ausfuhrzoll	Derechos	Utförseltull
Felloes, fellies	Jantes	Felgen	Pinas de Rueda	Lötar
Fifths, 5ths	Cinquième, 5ième	Fünfte	Quinta	Kvinta
Fir (spruce)	Pesse ; Sapin blanc	Fichtenholz	Pinabete	Gran
Firewood	Bois de chauffage ; Bois en buches ; Bois à bruler	Brennholz	Leña	Bränsle ; Vedbrand ; Splitved
Firsts, 1sts	Premier, lier	Prima	Prima	Prima
Fiset wood (see Young Fustic)				
Fixing (see Freighting)				
Floorings	Frises à parquet	Gehobelte Bretter	——	Hyflade bräder
Folding doors	Portes brisées ; Portes à deux battants	Flügelthüren	Puertas de dos Hojas	Falldörrar ; Flygeldörrar
Fourths, 4ths	Quatrième, 4ième	Vierte	Cuartos	Kvarta
Frame timber	Planches de dehors	Ausserriss	Tablas de Fuere	Ubritning
Freight	Le fret ; Cargaison	Fracht ; Ladung	Carga	Frakt
Freighting	Affrètement	Befrachtung	Flete	Befraktning
Fustic	Fustel ; Bois jaune de Brézil	Gelbholz	Fustoc	Gul holts ; Gul bresilja
Futtocks (see Knee timber)				

English.	French.	German.	Spanish.	Swedish.
Gimlets	Vrilles	Fritt-bohrer	Barrenas Pequeñas	Handborrar ; Nafvarer
Gouges (carp.)	Gouges	Hohlmeissel	Gubias	Gyts
Grenadilla (red ebony wood)	Grenadille ; Ebène rouge	Grenadill-holz	Ebano-rojo	Grenadille-hout
Guarantee (see Del Credere)	(see Del Credere)			
Gunstocks	Bois de fusil ; Fûts de fusl ; Montures	Flintenschäfte	Cajas de Escopetas	Böss stockar ; Böss kolf
Hafts (see Handles)				
Half-cellulose	Pâte de bois demi-chimique	Halb-Cellulose	—	Halfcellulosa
Hammers	Marteaux	Hammer	Martillos	Hamrar
Handles	Manches	Griffe	Cabos	Grepe
Hand saws	Scios à main	Handsägen	Sierras de Mano	Hand sågar
Handspikes	Anspects ; Hanspacs	Handspaken	Espeques	Handspakar
Harbour (see Port)				
Harbour Dues	Droits de mouillage , Charge de port ; Taxe de port ; Péage	Hafengeld	Derechos de Puerto	Hamnafgifter
Headings (heading staves) (see Cask-bottoms)				
Heart	Cœur	Kern	Corazon	Kärna
Heartshakes	Fentes de cœur	Kernrisse	Daño al Corazon	Kärnsprickor
Helves (see Handles)				
Hewn wood	Bois haché	Gehauenes Holz	Leña	Tillyxadt virke
Holly tree	Houx	Stech-palme	Acebo	Jernek ; Christ törne

English.	French.	German.	Spanish.	Swedish.
Hop-poles	Perches de houblon	Hopfstangen	Palos para Lupulos	Humle stänger ; Humle stör
Horn-beams (small beech trees)	Charmes	Hagebuchen	Charmillas	Afven bökar ; Hag bökar
Ilex (evergreen oak)	Chêne vert ; Yeuse	Steineiche	Encina Verde	Grenek
Import	Importation	Einfuhr	Impuestos	Import
Import Duty	Droit d'entrée	Eingangszoll	Derechos	Införselstull
Inferior than Fifths	Rebut	Ausschuss	Madera Muy Ordi-nario	Utskott
Inlaid work (mar-quetry)	Marqueterie	Eingelegte arbeit	Embutido	Inlagdt arbete
Interest	Intérêt	Zinsen	Interés	Ränta
Invoice	La facture	Factura	Factura	Faktura
Jack-planes	Guillaumes à ébau-cher ; Riflards	Schrupphobel	Guillames	Skrubbhoflar ; Grofhöflar
Joinery	Menuiserie	Tischlereien	Carpinteria	Snickeriarbeten
Knees, timber (futtocks)	Courbes : Genoux	Kniehölzer ; Sitzer	Curvas	Sitror ; Knäu ; Knä timmer
Ladders	Escaliers ; Echelles	Leiter ; Treppen	Escaleras	Stegar ; Trappor
Landing-place	Destination ; Dé-barcadère	Löschplatz	Puerto de des embarco	Lossningsplats
Larch tree	Mélèze	Lärchenbaum	Alerce	Lärkträd
Lathes (turners')	Tours	Drehbänke	Tornos	Svarf-bänk
Laths	Lattes	Latten	Ripias	Läkt
Lathwood	Bois à lattes	Lattenholz	Leña de Lattas	Lathwood
Lath-work	Lattis	Lattenwerk	Obra de Lattas	Lektverk
Lattice-work (see Trellis-work)				
Leaves	Feuilles	Blätter	Hojas	Bladar

English.	French.	German.	Spanish.	Swedish.
Lignum Vitæ (pock wood)	Bois de gaiac	Pock-holz	Guaiaco	Pocken holts
Lime tree	Tilleul	Lindenholz	Tilo	Lindträ
Loading	Charger un navire	Laden	Embarco	Lastning
Loading-place	Place d'embarquement	Verschiffungsplatz	Puerto d'embarco	Lastningsplats
Logs (of wood)	Souches; Blocs; Bûches	Klötze	Leños	Kubbar
Logwood (see Campeachy wood)				
Lumber (see Timber)				
Madriers (thick planks)	Madriers; Blanches épaisses	Dicke Breter; Bohlen	Tablones	Tjock plankor
Mahogany	Acajou	Mahagony	Caoba	Mahogony or Mohogniträ
Mallets	Maillets	Schlägel	Mazos	Trahammare
Manager	Directeur gérant	Director	Encargado	Disponent
Maple wood	Bois d'érable	Ahornholz	Arce	Lönn
Marine Insurance	Assurance maritime	Seeversicherung	Seguros; Aseguracion	Sjoassurans
Market price	Le cours du marché	Marktpreis	Precio del Mercado	Marknadspris
Marks	Marques	Marken	Marcos	Märken
Marquetry (see Inlaid work)				
Master (see Captain)				
Masts	Mâts	Mastbaume	Palos	Master
Mechanical	Mécanique	Mechanisch	Mecanico	Mekanisk
Merchandise	Marchandise	Waaren	Mercaderia	Varor
Mixed	Mêlé	Gemischt	—	Mixed
Moist	Humide	Nass	—	Vât

English.	French.	German.	Spanish.	Swedish.
Moulding planes (ogee planes)	Doucines; Guillaumes	Karniesshobel; Gesimshobel	Molduras	Ploghyflar; Kelhyflar
Mouldings	Moulures	Leistenwerk		Lister or listverk
Mulberry (tree)	Mûrier	Maulbeerbaum	Morera	Mulbärsträd
Naves (wheels)	Moyeux	Naben	Lorigas	Nafringar
Nephritic wood	Bois néphrétique	Griesholz	Palo Nefretico	Blatt sandelträd
Nicaragua (wood)	Nicaragua	Nicaragua	Palo Nicaragua	Nicaragua
Notching planes (carpen.)	Coulisseurs; Feuillerets	Falz-hobel	Junteras	Fals-höflar
Nut-wood	Bois de noyer	Nuss-holz	Nogal	Nöt-trä
Oak (timber)	Bois de chêne	Eichen-holz	Roble	Ek
Oak bark	Écorce à tan; Écorce du chêne	Bork; Eichenrinde	———	Bark; Ekbark
Oars	Rames; Avirons	Riemen; Ruder-stangen	Remos	Åror
Option	L'option	Option; Wahl		Option
Osier twigs	Gaules; Osiers	Weidengerten	Mimbres	Vidjor
Palisander wood (violet wood)	Bois de palisandre	Veilchen-holz	Palisandra	Palisander-holt
Palm-wood (see Boxwood)				
Paper manufactory	Papeterie	Papirfabrik	Fabricca de Papel	Pappersfabrik
Pasteboard (see Cardboard)				
Pernambuco wood (see Brazil wood)				
Pick-axes	Pics; Pioches	Spitz-hacken	Picos	Hackar; Raotyr
Picture frames	Cadres pour tableaux	Gemälderahmen	Marcos para Cuadros	Skilderieramar; Tafvelramar
Pieces	Pièces	Stück	———	Styeken
Piles (see Stakes)				

English.	French.	German.	Spanish.	Swedish.
Pine (wood)	Bois de pin	Föhre	Pino	Furu
Pine pulp	Pâte de sapin	Weisse Holzmasse	—	Granmassa
Pipe-staves	Douves (à pipes); Pipailles	Pipen-stäbe	Duelas para Pipas	Pip kimmar
Pit-props	Poteaux de mine	Grubenstollen; Grubenstützen	—	Props or Pitprops
Planed boards	Planches rabotées	Gehobelte Bretter	—	Hyflade bräder
Planed wood	Bois raboté	Gehobelte Waaren	—	Hyfvellast; Hyfladt virke
Planes	Rabots	Hobel	Planas	Höflar
Plane wood (button wood) (American maple)	Platanes	Platanen	Platanos	Amerikansk lönn
Planing mill	Raboterie	Hobelfabrik	—	Hyfleri
Plank timber (saw-ing timber)	Bois de sciage	Sägeblöcke	Leña de Serrar	Sågstockar
Planks (see Boards)				
Pock wood (see Lignum Vitæ)				
Poles (stakes)	Pieux; Echalas	Pfähle	Estacas	Pålar
Poplar	Peupliers	Pappel-baum	Alamo	Poppel-träd
Port	Le port	Hafen	Puerto	Hamn
Port Charges (see Harbour Dues)				
Port Duties (see Harbour Dues)				
Posts	Poteaux	Pfosten	Postes	Stolpar
Prickle wood (see Spindle tree)				
Pruning knives	Serpettes; Croissants	Gartenmesser	Hocinos	Trädgårdsknifvar
Pulp wood	Rondins	Cellulose Holz; Rundhölzer	—	Slipved; Pappers-ved;Trämasseved

English.	French.	German.	Spanish.	Swedish.
Quite square edged	À vive arrête	Scharfkantig Völlständig	—	Skarpkantig (utan vankant)
Rafters (Roof)	Chevrons	Dach-sparren	Cabrios	Tak-sparrar
Railings (trellis, lattice work)	Treillage	Gitterwerk	Enrejados ,	Gallerverk
Rate of Exchange	Le cours	Cours	Cambio	Kurs
Red (Yellow)	Rouge	Röth	Pino Rosso	Furu
Roof laths	Lattes à toit	Dachlatter	—	Takstickor
Rosewood	Bois de rose ; Bois de rhôdo ; Bois de Chypre	Rosen-holz	Palo de Rose ; Pulixander	Roser-träd
Round timber	Bois rond	Rundholz	Palos	Rund-holts
Sailer	Bâteau à voile (voilier)	Segelschiff	Bugne ; Veliero	Segelskepp
Sailing ship (see Sailer)				
Sample of no value	Echantillon sans valeur	Muster ohne Werth	Muestras de nin-gun Valor	Prof utan värde
Sandal wood	Santal	Sändel-holz	Sandalo	Söndel
Sap	Aubier ; Sève	Weichholz	Vejija	Ytved
Sapan (wood)	Sapan	Sapan	Palo de Sapan	Sapan
Sash windows	Fenêtres à coulisse ; Fenêtres à guil-lotine	Schiebfenster	Ventanas-Corredizas	Skuffönster
Saw-dust	Sciure ; Brande scie	Säge-spähne ; Säge-mehl	Asserradara	Sågspån
Saw logs (sawing timber) (see Plank timber)				
Sawmill	Scierie	Sägemühle	—	Sågverk
Sawn wood	Bois sciés	Gesägtes Holz	—	Sågadt virke

English.	French.	German.	Spanish.	Swedish.
Saws	Scies	Sägen	Sierras	Sågar
Scaleboards	Éclisses de hêtre	Buchen-spahne; Slowen	Astillas de Madera	Bok-spän; Spjälar
Screws	Vis	Schrauben	Tornillos	Skrufvar
Seconds, 2nds	Deuxième, 2ième	Seconda	Segundas	Sekunda
Service tree	Cormier; Sorbier	Sperber-baum	Serbal	Rönn
Shafts (of a vehicle) (thills)	Brancards	Gabel-deichseln	Limones	Gaffel-stänger
Shavings	Copeaux; Planures	Hobel-spähne	Acepilladuras	Höfvel spån
Shingles (*see* Roof laths)				
Shipbroker	Courtier maritime	Schiffsmäkler	Corredor de Navios	Skeppsmäklare
Shipment	Expédition	Verschiffung	Encargamiente; Envio	Skeppning
Shipping (*see* Shipment)				
Shipping Charges	Frais d'embarquement	Ladenkosten	Granos y cargos	Lastningsutgifter
Ship's cargo	Chargement d'un navire	Ladung	Cargo	Skeppsladdnng
Shutters (windows)	Volets	Fenster-laden	Contraventanas	Luckor
Shuttles (weaver's)	Navettes	Weber-schiffchen	Lanzaderas	Väf spolar
Sixths, 6ths	Sixième, 6ième	Sechste	Sextas	Sexta
Skirtings	Plinthe	Fussleisten	—	Fotpanel or Fot-list
Sleepers (railway)	Traverses	Langschienen; Bodelbalken	Carlingas	Bundbalkar; Fondationbalkar; Sliprar
Small square timber	Poutrelles	Sparren Kantholz		Sparrar
Spars (timber)	Espars; Sparres	Spieren	Perchas	Spiror

English	French	German	Spanish	Swedish
Speckled wood (curled maple)	Bois madré	Maser-holz	Madera Vetada	Masur
Spigots (vent pegs)	Douzils ; Faussets ; Broches	Zwicken	Espitas	Svickor ; svikke Luft
Spills (Spiles)	Goupilles ; Broches	Spiker-pinnen	Espiches	Spik-pinnar
Spindle tree (prickle wood)	Fusain	Spindelbaum	Bonereo	Alster
Splitwood (see Firewood)				
Spokes (of a wheel)	Rais	Speichen	Rajos	Hjulekrar
Square edged	Bois carré	Scharfkantig (Gewöhnlich)	—	Skarpkantig (van-lig vankant)
Square timber	Poutres	Balken		Bjälkar
Stack wood (see Cordwood)				
Stakes (piles)	Pieux ; Echalas	Pfähle	Estacas	Pålar
Staves	Douves	Stabholz ; Dauben	Duelas	Stafor ; Stäfver
Steam sawmill	Scierie à vapeur	Dampfsägemühle	Molino de Scierro	Ångsåg
Steamer (see Steamship)				
Steamship	Bâteau à vapeur ; Bâtiment à vapeur	Dampfer	Bugne de Vapor	Ångbåt
Sulphate mill	Fabrique de pâte de bois au sulfate	Sulfat-Cellulosen Fabrik		Sulfatfabrik
Sulphate pulp	Pâte au sulfate	Natron-Cellulose	—	Sulfatcellulosa
Sulphite mill	Fabrique de pâte de bois au bisulfite	Sulfit-Cellulosen Fabrik	—	Sulfitfabrik
Sulphite pulp	Pâte au bisulfite	Sulfit-Cellulose	—	Sulfitcellulosa
Sun shakes	Fentes	Trocken Risse		Solsprickor ; Torrsprickor

English.	French.	German.	Spanish.	Swedish.
Teak wood (India oak)	Bois de teck	Teek-holz	Teca	Tekträ
Thick planks (thick stuff) (between 4 and 12 in. thick)	Planches épaisses ; Madriers	Bohlen	Tablones	Tjock plankor
Thills (see Shafts)				
Thirds, 3rds	Troisième, 3ième	Tertia	Terceras	Tertia
Timber	Bois	Holz	Leña ; Madera	Bjälkar
Timber agent	Agent de bois	Holzagent	Agente da Madera	Trävaruagent
Timber-slabs	Dosses ; Croûtes	Schell-holz	Cagas	Bakar
Turner's work	Ouvrages en tour	Drechslerarbeit	Torneria	Svarfvare-arbete
Turning lathes (see Lathes)				
Unloading	Décharger	Unladen ; Löschen	Descarga	Lossning
Unsorted, unas-sorted	Non-classé, non-assortis	Nicht assortirt	—	Osorterad
Veneers	Placages	Furnier	Taraceas	Faner spånor
Venetian blinds	Jalousies	Jalousie-gitter	Trasparentes	Jalusier ; Fönster galler
Vessel (see Sailer)				
Wainscot	Lambris ; Boiserie	Tafelwerk	Enmaderamienta	Panel-verk
Wane	Flache	Baumkante ; Wahnkante	—	Vankant
Waney	Flacheux	Wahnkantig	—	Vankantig
Weed-ashes	Guedasses	Waid asche	Vedasa	Veid-aska
Wheelbarrows	Brouettes (à une roue)	Schiebkarren	Carretones	Skott-kärror
Wheels	Roues	Räder	Ruedas	Hjul
Wheel-spokes (see Spokes)				

Lightning Source UK Ltd.
Milton Keynes UK
10 December 2010